Cinematic Shakespeare

D1563508

Genre and Beyond

A Film Studies Series

Series Editor: Leonard Leff, Oklahoma State University

Genre and Beyond offers fresh perspectives on conceptions of film as well as cinema's role in a changing world. Books in the series explore often overlooked or unconventional genres as well as more traditional themes. These engaging texts have the rigor that scholars demand and the creativity and accessibility that students and interested readers expect.

Titles in the Series
Cinematic Shakespeare
Michael Anderegg

Forthcoming in the Series
African American Film Now
Mark A. Reid

High Comedy in America Cinema
Steve Vineberg

Queer Images: Homosexuality in American Film
Harry M. Benshoff and Sean Griffin

Killing in Style: Artistic Murder in the Movies
Steven Schneider

Cinematic Shakespeare

Michael Anderegg

ROWMAN & LITTLEFIELD PUBLISHERS, INC.
Lanham • Boulder • New York • Toronto • Oxford

ROWMAN & LITTLEFIELD PUBLISHERS, INC.

Published in the United States of America
by Rowman & Littlefield Publishers, Inc.
A wholly owned subsidiary of The Rowman & Littlefield Publishing Group, Inc.
4501 Forbes Boulevard, Suite 200, Lanham, MD 20706
www.rowmanlittlefield.com

P.O. Box 317, Oxford OX2 9RU, UK

British Library Cataloguing in Publication Information Available

Library of Congress Cataloging-in-Publication Data

Anderegg, Michael A.
    Cinematic Shakespeare / Michael Anderegg.
        p.   cm. — (Genre and beyond)
    Includes bibliographical references and index.
    ISBN 0-7425-1091-3 (cloth : alk. paper)—ISBN 0-7425-1092-1 (pbk. : alk. paper)
    1. Shakespeare, William, 1564–1616—Film and video adaptations.   2. English
drama—Film and video adaptations.   3. Film adaptations.   I. Title.   II. Series.
PR3093.A525   2004
791.43'75—dc21   2003010830

Printed in the United States of America

⊗ ™ The paper used in this publication meets the minimum requirements of American
National Standard for Information Sciences—Permanence of Paper for Printed Library
Materials, ANSI/NISO Z39.48-1992.

To Jim & Patti
and
Sharon & Lucy,
for being there

Contents

Genre and Beyond: A Film Studies Series

Genre, meaning *kind* or *type*, describes an exercise that sorts movies according to their content, form, or style. Hollywood turned to genre for economic reasons: conforming to genre conventions helped rationalize the industry and maintain a consistent product flow that satisfied audience expectations. In the process, according to the first wave of genre criticism, the movies got more than they bargained for. Lying at the nexus of history, narrative, and reception, genre embodies cultural myths and social conflicts that resonate with American audiences and beyond.

Genre analysis has been (and remains) fraught with challenges, in part because both film producers and film critics have laid claim to it, in part because definitions and classifications tend to blur. Consider film noir. Its roots were in, among other phenomena, German expressionism, police procedurals, and early-twentieth-century American hard-boiled fiction. Its visual and thematic markers included (among others) chiaroscuro lighting, *femmes fatales* and anomic *hommes*, and a frayed moral landscape sometimes littered with a corpse or two. Noir shared certain characteristics with other genres, namely, the thriller and the family melodrama; most genres, like noir, are not "pure."

Almost since the inception of the movie industry, filmmakers (and commentators on film) have viewed genres as more fluid than fixed. Makers of the first westerns, silent and early sound, bent or broke the "rules" of the genre in order to keep their pictures vital. From the 1940s through the 1960s, writers and directors went even further. *High Noon* was transparently more social problem film than western, whereas *Giant* and *Hud* moved Texas ranchers (and their psychological burdens) well into the twentieth century. *Cat Ballou* and especially *Blazing Saddles*—a descent into parody, and not always affectionate—seemed to stamp "paid" to the genre.

As shown by a more recent and conservative specimen of the western, *Unforgiven*, one should not discount the power of the rules. It may be, as French theorist Christian Metz noted, that genres advance through cycles of change; it's also true that they do not always end in critiquing themselves. *Chicago*, another of the more conservative films of the last fifty years, could be considered a reaction to the last half century's "liberties" with the musical genre. *Chicago* has more in common with, say, a 1930s Warner Bros. melodrama than with *Hedwig and the Angry Inch*, even though both *Chicago* and *Hedwig*, as so-called numbers musicals, adhere to many conventions of the form. Movies like *Hedwig* challenge more than the dominant ideology. They also resist easy classification, which, as a cornerstone of genre analysis has, like the monster in most horror films, refused to die. Is *Hedwig*, then, a rock musical? a gay film? an adaptation from theater? Some would call the last named not genres at all. Others might hedge.

Genre analysis sails between Scylla and Charybdis. On one side lies the temptation to be inclusive, to construct or stipulate genres that hark back to the classical period and accommodate a broad range of works—"comedy," "tragedy," "epic." On the other lies the temptation to be very, *very* specific. Whatever the merits of James Cameron's blockbuster, its 1950s predecessors, and the bouncy *Unsinkable Molly Brown*, a study of the *Titanic* genre (a subgenre of the disaster film, itself a subgenre of the action film) seems too exclusive. So does a study of the transgendered rock musical genre, into which *Hedwig* (and little else) might fit. Nonetheless, the study of "subgenres" (or "niche genres," "crossed genres," "overlain genres") can help us understand genre as well as important patterns of production and reception. In the "Genre and Beyond" series we hope to sail a steady course while not excluding the possibility of discovering and exploring new territory.

Genre study in cinema has advanced through at least three generations. The work of pioneers Robert Warshow and André Bazin remains instructive. Their heirs, building on their work in the 1960s and after, were the auteurists—for whom the director was the prime mover in moviemaking—and the structuralists. Some among the latter took experimental films as their laboratory samples, but nonnarrative works never became the dominant focus. By the 1980s analysts had again embraced classical, nonexperimental narratives.

Even analysts who read movies against the grain (deconstructionists and others) took Hollywood genre movies as their preferred reading.

Launched at the beginning of the twenty-first century, the "Genre and Beyond" series appears at a time when genre films have reasserted their supremacy over cinema, especially American cinema. Accordingly, genre analysis and genre theory have reassumed a prominent place in cinema studies.

The authors in this series come from varied disciplines and employ a range of methodologies. Their work sometimes traverses international borders and almost always references history, gender, culture, audience expectations, or the role of the studio, the performer, and the press in the constitution of genre. Their work centers on familiar genres as well as those that defy straightforward classification, description, or analysis.

The hallmarks of genre and genre analysis—flexibility and catholicity— also characterize our authors and their work. As genre study continues to evolve, we look forward to engaging you, the reader, in an ongoing dialogue about kinds and types of movies and the critical approaches and theories that shape our perceptions of them.

—Leonard Leff, Series Editor

Preface

On a Sunday afternoon in 1955, Laurence Olivier's *Richard III* received its American premiere, broadcast by NBC on the same day it began its New York theatrical run. This was an extraordinary event, which, to my knowledge, was never repeated. Broadcasting and film exhibition, constantly in tension since television's advent, were here wedded in a forecast of the synergy to come. For me, a twelve-year-old, this telecast was remarkable in a number of ways. *Richard III* brought together four worlds that would continue to form an important nexus in my imaginative life: Shakespeare, English history, larger than life acting, and movies. (Television, on the other hand, though its appeal was certainly central to my childhood and early adolescence, would never become an object of affection in itself.) The most compelling aspect of this *Richard III* broadcast was Olivier's performance in the title role—a bravura turn that almost seemed aimed, in its intimate moments, for the first-person mode that was central to television, the talking head and direct address of everything from news and variety programs, kiddie shows ("Hi, kids, I'm Buffalo Bob"), and even some sitcoms (George Burns to the camera, "Let's see what Gracie's up to"). Maybe this is one of the reasons this first viewing was not matched by subsequent ones, even though I later saw *Richard III* in color on the big screen in its original VistaVision splendor. Although I remain quite fond of Olivier's film, or at least of parts of it, it would never again seem quite as magical as it did on this memorable Sunday afternoon.

Richard III was more than Laurence Olivier, of course, even if, in Olivier's adaptation, Richard is almost constantly on screen. I enjoyed John Gielgud's moving rendition of Clarence's dream and Ralph Richardson's sardonic, dryly witty Buckingham. All three were actors whose performances I would search out and enjoy in years to come, actors who provided a counterweight of sorts to my love of Hollywood movies and American stars. There was an element of snobbism here, an Anglophilia that drew me to British actors who came out of a theatrical tradition. Hollywood I took for granted. Its products were simply part of my daily life, part of the air I breathed. But British actors, even when they appeared in Hollywood films, were an alternate reality, a glimpse into the world of Shakespeare and theatrical tradition, which was, I then thought, far more worthwhile, far more compelling than mere movies. Eventually I came to value Hollywood movies as much as, if not more than, foreign imports. But my continuing fascination with Shakespeare on film, born of that *Richard III* broadcast, has remained with me and is reflected in the pages that follow.

Cinematic Shakespeare does not pretend to be a comprehensive overview of Shakespeare on film and television. It is, rather, a highly selective consideration of some of the ways Shakespeare's plays have been reproduced, photographically and electronically, in the century of cinema that just ended. I write "cinema" here advisedly. Some Shakespeare "films" are not cinema at all, just as some "Shakespeare" films have little to do with Shakespeare. Although I include a chapter on television, my emphasis throughout is on film productions. Film as film has an identity that differentiates it from videotape and digital modes of reproduction, however much the boundaries can be and have been blurred. Rather than collapse the distinction between film and other, closely related media, I prefer, in the face of current critical practice, to highlight and emphasize that difference. Precisely because of the proliferation of new technologies, the uniqueness of film needs to be recognized as having cultural, social, aesthetic, and material significance. That the medieval fresco gave way to easel painting in oil does not make frescoes and oil paintings identical to the art historian and art critic. On the contrary, the qualities that make the fresco a particular medium can more easily be isolated when it is differentiated from, rather than collapsed with, oil painting, watercolors, charcoal drawings, etchings, and so forth. *Omne simile non est idem*, or, in the words of Shakespeare's Brutus, "every like is not the same." As Russell Jackson remarks, "The images and sounds—the visions—that Shakespeare has provoked in film-makers will remain potent in the context of any medium."[1] There is value in reminding ourselves of what an older technology/art accomplished in its (in the instance of film, anyway) brief life.

With considerable regret I also exclude, apart from a passing mention from time to time, silent films and foreign-language films as well as English-language films that, though they may closely adhere to Shakespeare's plot and themes, dispense with his words (an example would be the Andrew Davis *Othello* [2001] for the BBC). I make a perhaps more controversial assumption, namely, that a Shakespeare film should include Shakespeare's words spoken in English. However reactionary this may sound, it is, nevertheless, a reasonable expectation. Brilliant films in languages other than English have been inspired by Shakespeare. I yield to no one in my admiration for Akira Kurosawa's Japanese-language adaptation of *Macbeth*, entitled *Throne of Blood* (1957). Kurosawa, however, necessarily avoids the principal challenge a filmmaker faces in adapting Shakespeare to the screen: how to give cinematic life to the verse and prose out of which "Shakespeare" as text and as cultural object is fundamentally constituted. I have, furthermore, limited myself insofar as possible to films readily available on videotape and DVD (I make exceptions when discussing early television). In order to keep this study within reasonable bounds, I have paid scant attention to Shakespeare "offshoots," films only loosely based on the plays, such as *Forbidden Planet* (*The Tempest*, 1956), *Joe Macbeth* (1955), *Jubal* (1956), and *O* (2001)—the last two inspired by *Othello*—and films that, like George Cukor's *A Double Life* (1947) or Kenneth Branagh's *In the Bleak Midwinter* (1995; U.S. title, *A Midwinter's Tale*), incorporate the performance of scenes from Shakespeare's plays. (I do, however, discuss *Shakespeare in Love* [1998], which is ostensibly all about Shakespeare.) More largely, and quite arbitrarily, I have chosen to write about films that interest me, and I have avoided saying much about films that don't.

I received help from archivists and librarians as well as friends and acquaintances. I particularly want to thank the staffs of the Margaret Herrick Library, the UCLA Film and Television Library, the USC Special Collections (especially Ned Comstock), the Library of Congress, and the Folger Shakespeare Library. Richard Burt commissioned an essay from me, parts of which find their way into chapters 2–3. José Ramón Díaz Fernández and Paula Willoquet-Maricondi invited me to read conference papers on *Prospero's Books* in West Palm Beach, Florida, and Benalmedena, Spain, respectively. An earlier version of chapter 7 was published in Peter Greenaway, *Prospero's Books: Critical Essays*, edited by Christel Stalpaert. The transformation of my initial proposal into a book was aided by the expertise of series editor Leonard Leff and, at Rowman & Littlefield, Dean Birkenkamp, Alison Sullenberger, Janice Braunstein, and Chrisona Schmidt.

I have learned much about both film and Shakespeare from Richard Burt, Samuel Crowl, Alvin Kernan, Bernice Kliman, Richard Lanham, Courtney Lehmann, and Kenneth Rothwell. Jim McKenzie, good friend and true, gave frequent encouragement and help. My son Tim, a college freshman when I began to work on this book, helped me with such youth culture questions as how to find lyrics to a Radiohead song, while my son Niles, a ninth grader at the time, shared with me his insights into *Romeo and Juliet* and Baz Luhrmann. Jeanne, my wife, partner, and dearest friend, helped in all sorts of ways, not the least of which involved reading my drafts and keeping me honest.

Note

1. Russell Jackson, "Shakespeare and the Cinema," in *The Cambridge Companion to Shakespeare*, ed. Margreta de Grazia and Stanley Wells (Cambridge: Cambridge University Press, 2001), 217–33; 231.

CHAPTER ONE

Introduction:
The Shakespeare Film and Genre

Linking the term *genre* to a discussion of Shakespeare on film raises as many questions, perhaps, as it answers. What are the implications of treating films based on Shakespeare's plays in terms of genre? What do Shakespeare films have in common apart from being based on Shakespeare's plays? What are the "markers" or signs by which the genre can be recognized? One might even want to ask precisely what the words "Shakespeare," "film," and "genre" mean in this particular context. These are all questions with no simple answers. Discussions of film genre have traditionally focused on easily recognizable categories familiar to all fans of the Hollywood cinema—westerns, horror films, musicals, science fiction, gangster films, and so on. Genre in the Hollywood context identifies common story elements, sets of characters, and iconic imagery that remain more or less constant from film to film even as they are configured and arranged in a seemingly infinite number of variations. More adventurous attempts to define the role of genre have added less clear-cut examples, such as the women's film, the biopic, the spectacle, and film noir. At this point, it becomes difficult to differentiate genre from mode, cycle, or style. Genres, furthermore, are often divided into subgenres or are seen as constituting hybrid forms, so we can have the noir western or the science fiction thriller. Even films categorized with such broad and general labels as "melodrama" and "art cinema" can share a sufficient number of characteristics to constitute recognizable generic identities.[1]

The Shakespeare film, though not self-evidently a genre in the same way that westerns, musicals, and gangster films are genres, exhibits common traits that go beyond its source in the Shakespeare text even as the text helps determine the presence of those traits. Kathy Howlett, citing Leo Braudy, notes that Shakespeare films share with other genre films the quality of speaking "to the audience's desire for repetition and formula."[2] Howlett further remarks that commercially successful Shakespeare films, like Baz Luhrmann's *Romeo + Juliet* (1996), illustrate "how Shakespeare films can exploit generic and recognitional abilities in viewers, so that the untrained spectator is able to master visual conventions with little or no reference to linguistic ones ('the original Shakespeare')."[3] Shakespeare films, furthermore, tend to include traces of more traditional film genres. For example, critics identify Franco Zeffirelli's *Hamlet* (1990) as a western or Roman Polanski's *Macbeth* (1971) as a horror film.[4] In this chapter, I will explore some of the ways Shakespeare films can be thought of in generic terms by concentrating on several distinct categories. Starting with the assumption that their relationship to language and to what we may term "the literary" may be the most notable characteristic of films derived from Shakespeare's plays, I will consider these films as constituting a subgenre of the "literary adaptation" film. Second, I will look at the Shakespeare film as a special instance of the "star vehicle," a type of film that foregrounds, or centers on, the performance of a particular actor. Third, I will discuss the Shakespeare film in terms of what it borrows or incorporates from other genres. I will then briefly suggest how the Shakespeare film might be considered in terms of mode of production, thereby complicating the very term "Shakespeare film" by emphasizing the distinctions that can be made between film, video, and television.

Language and the Literary Adaptation

Shakespeare films do not merely derive from Shakespeare's plays; they often include the words Shakespeare employed in the plays. No matter how deeply the text is cut, no matter how updated the setting, no matter how avant-garde the production, Shakespeare films (excepting silent or foreign-language films and films that do not foreground their Shakespearean origins) exhibit an almost mystical devotion to Shakespeare's words—the language and diction of Elizabethan English, a language and diction at once poetic and theatrical. This may seem like a point too obvious to deserve comment, but a moment's reflection will reveal that probably no other writer has had his or her words treated with a similar fidelity. The temptation to simply paraphrase Shakespeare's language is almost always resisted. We identify a Shakespeare film as such to the extent that its language, however much or little of it there may be, is recognizably Shakespeare's language. Filmmakers are taking a tremendous risk, given that large segments of their audience will inevitably be puzzled, at least initially, by the unfamiliar syntax and diction the actors recite, no matter how clearly and carefully this is done. This in part explains why, in both Kenneth Branagh's *Much Ado about Nothing* (1993) and Baz Luhrmann's *Romeo + Juliet* (1996), we are presented with the initial words of the film in both written and spoken form (in *Romeo + Juliet*, we are actually given the words of the opening Chorus three times). Branagh even provides a graphic bouncing ball effect for his interpolation of the song "Sigh No More" (this is particularly interesting, given that *Much Ado* is one of Shakespeare's most prosaic plays and features an opening dialogue, all in prose, that is quite modern sounding). Olivier's *Hamlet* too, though for different reasons, opens with a voice-over by Olivier that is simultaneously presented with a scrolling version of the spoken text on screen.

The centrality of language points to the way the Shakespeare film can be considered a significant and distinctive subgenre of a type of film that has an uncertain relationship to genre—the literary adaptation. Shakespeare films, not surprisingly, are more likely to be mounted and publicized for their literary status than any other film version of literary works, apart, perhaps, from Dickens and Hemingway. At times, the emphasis on the name Shakespeare is oddly comic—do people need to be told that it was *William Shakespeare's Romeo + Juliet* or *William Shakespeare's A Midsummer Night's Dream* that they have been encouraged to see? One suspects that on Baz Luhrmann's part at least, the object was to counteract the impression that the film would not retain Shakespeare's language or that it would in general stray too far from the original. (The 1962 film *Hemingway's Adventures of a Young Man* at least had the rationale that Hemingway had written no work with "Adventures of a Young Man" in the title.) The literary adaptation, in any case, can be considered as a film that foregrounds its status as adaptation, that wants to be seen as an adaptation or, even better, as the literary text itself.

Which suggests a related area of generic identification. Shakespeare films frequently provide an introduction, prologue, or other marked-off section to lead us in various ways into the play, taking us from present to past (Taymor's *Titus* and, in its own way, Olivier's *Henry V*), from speaker to what is spoken (a process considerably aided by Shakespeare himself, who at times does a very similar thing—so *Romeo and Juliet* films happily retain the artificial, theatrical device of the opening Chorus), from still to animated images (Cukor's *Romeo and Juliet*), from production to performance (Branagh's *Henry V*), from writing to staging.[5] Much of this flows from established Hollywood conventions for the adaptation of literary works—books that open, pages of text, a voice reading, ornamental borders, credits presented as literary text (Gothic letters, for example), and so on—all iconic clues that speak to us of "Literature." In a Shakespeare film, "Shakespeare" is generally contextualized in some way, prepared for, introduced, and even held off. Far from the theatrical, in media res openings of so many Shakespeare plays, Shakespeare films look for prologue-like opportunities. The 1995 *Richard III* gives us blood-red lettering on screen ("Civil War divides the nation") that introduces, nondiegetically, the political context, followed by a close-up of a teletype machine spitting out a strip of tape on which we see the (now diegetic) writing "Richard of Gloucester is at hand . . ." What follows is a rough equivalent to Colley Cibber's eighteenth-century version of *Richard III*: a nearly wordless distillation of the action from *Henry VI, Part III*, 5.5 and 5.6. In some films, the prologue may be matched with an epilogue, the two together becoming a framing device, closing off the Shakespeare world at both ends.

In a curious way, Shakespeare's films are often not thought of as "adaptations" primarily, at least not in the same way that films derived from Jane Austen or Charles Dickens or Ernest Hemingway (or Margaret Mitchell, for that matter) might be. A novel needs to be "transformed" in order to become a film, but the same is not self-evidently true of a play. A play, one might

Shakespeare in Disguise

The name Shakespeare may have considerable marquee value, but some Shakespeare films seem to go out of their way to downplay or disguise their Shakespearean origins. The DVD of Julie Taymor's *Titus* (1999), for example, omits Shakespeare altogether from the front of the packaging, where we read "A Julie Taymor Film." On the back, one has to search the small print of the credit display at the bottom to find "Adapted from 'Titus Andronicus' by William Shakespeare." The inset brochure reveals the conflicted impulses of the marketing department. On the cover of the paper inset we read "A Julie Taymor Film: Titus." On the inside, however, we have a brief *New York Times* essay entitled "A Shakespeare Tale Whose Time Has Come" by Jonathan Bate. Likewise, with Branagh's *Henry V*, "the name 'Shakespeare' [was] entirely omitted from promotional advertisements for the film." "Thus disguised," Donald Hedrick writes, "Branagh's film is a little touch of Shakespeare in the night, concealing its class and status to gain advantages on some presumably well defined but indispensable target market from which it might build allegiance, presumably 'gentling their [the audience's] condition.'"[6]

think, can be simply transposed to the screen intact. If few films include all of the dialogue from a play, the theoretical possibility is sufficient, it would seem, to make the question of theatrical adaptation more or less problematic. But a more significant question arises here: would a word-for-word transcription of the play's dialogue to the screen result in a duplication of the "original"? Kenneth Branagh included "all" of *Hamlet* (indeed, perhaps more than all) in his 1996 film, but does that make his film equivalent to Shakespeare's play? Few would think so. Neither did the Academy of Motion Picture Arts and Sciences, which nominated Branagh for an Oscar in the category Best Screenplay Adapted from Another Medium. The assumption here, presumably, is that a screenplay is much more than dialogue, just as a film has to be something other than a play or novel. A film is more than an enactment or a production of a play; it is, also and at the same time, less than the original. When we read a play, even when we see it in the theater, the language, the words, are paramount—everything else is secondary. In a film, however, the words no longer have pride of place, as the "opsis," or spectacle, tends to take over. If a stage production of a play is in a sense an adaptation of it, a specific realization, so too must a film version be.

Some Shakespeare films, of course, are much more "adapted" than others. When is a Shakespeare film no longer a Shakespeare film? The determinants are not at all clear-cut. Critics treat Akira Kurosawa's Japanese samurai film, *Throne of Blood* (1957), as among the best Shakespeare films, even though it uses none of Shakespeare's language. On the other hand, Peter Greenaway's *Prospero's Books* (1991) has been described as a derivation of or variation on Shakespeare's *Tempest*, even though it uses much of the original text and adds little or nothing verbally to it. With *Throne of Blood*, the argument seems to be that Kurosawa captures the thematic essence of Shakespeare's *Macbeth* and finds visual equivalences for his figurative language. The film is therefore "faithful," in some essential way, to Shakespeare's poetic and dramaturgical imagination, whatever freedom it exhibits from the plot, characters, setting, and cultural markers of the original. (Much of this praise of *Throne*, it should be pointed out, was expressed at a time when "art cinema" was at its height and admiration for "foreign films" in the Anglo-Saxon film community went hand in hand with a devaluation of, in particular, the Hollywood cinema.) *Prospero's Books*, on the other hand, is so exceedingly "visual," so flamboyant and eccentric in its style, that the Shakespeare text appears to sink under the weight of Greenaway's imagery to such an extent that a completely new text superimposes itself in the viewer's consciousness.

A film that has been adapted from a literary work nearly always contains "fossils" or remnants of characters and situations that only make full sense in the context provided by the original text. An adaptation may be recognized simply by the structural looseness—or even incoherence—of the film's narrative. The phenomenon is most obvious in films adapted from novels, where the process of compressing the original leaves motivations incomplete or entirely missing, cause and effect vague, plot lines unfinished, and characters floating free of the narrative. Anomalous material is less likely to make its presence felt in films adapted from plays, where the original shaping is generally much tighter, the scope narrower, and the characters fewer. A number of Shakespeare's plays have something like the breadth and narrative complexity of a novel, particularly the histories, but the principle holds true for the most part. What most often creates anomalies and dissonances in a Shakespeare film is a failure on the part of the filmmaker to recognize the extent to which theme, character, and tone, as well as specific narrative elements, are all woven into the tapestry of Shakespeare's text. The greatest danger in adapting a Shakespeare play to the screen is that the linguistic structure collapses. The problem is not simply that too much has been cut but that what is left has not been provided with a structure or form of its own to compensate for what has been lost. The words that remain are literally incomprehensible because they lack context. It is bad enough that listeners have to struggle with the inherent difficulty of comprehending sixteenth-century English arranged as blank verse, with all of the syntactic complexity this implies, but they frequently have to do so without the clues, markers, and signs that Shakespeare provided. The words float in the air, unattached to what comes before and after, unassimilated to concrete acts of characterization.

For example, in Laurence Olivier's *Hamlet* (1948), Claudius, after a dozen lines confirming his marriage to Gertrude, says, "And now, Laertes, what's the news with you?" In Shakespeare's play, this line follows twenty-five lines wherein Claudius deals with Fortinbras, sends a letter to Norway, and gives instructions to his ambassadors, Cornelius and Voltimand. Having moved from establishing his and his new queen's authority to the dispatching of pressing state business, he can relax and turn to the purely domestic question of whether Laertes should continue his year abroad. "And now" clearly means "finally," "at last," as well as "there's nothing around here I can't handle." This point is completely lost in Olivier's adaptation, where one might think that Claudius seemingly has nothing better to do than make travel arrangements for the son of his prime minister. This is a minor problem that may go unnoticed by most filmgoers; on the other hand, we may be seeing and hearing a moment where context would have helped the viewer follow more clearly what goes on in this scene—the fact that Claudius sees the question of coming and going from his court as a state matter, not to mention the foregrounding of his deliberate, ostentatious granting of a requested leave of absence for Laertes that he will deny to his "son" Hamlet, something that may go by unnoticed in the absence of the build-up Shakespeare has provided.

More often, eliminating much of Shakespeare's verbal texture also eliminates characters and entire scenes. In contrast to films that employ prologues and framing devices, some films begin without the explanatory opening scenes or expository speeches Shakespeare employed as a means of getting his audience into the text. For example, Shakespeare begins *King Lear* with a brief scene of quiet conversation, in prose, among important but nevertheless secondary characters. Even as we learn something of Gloucester, Kent, and Edmund, we are introduced to the central action of the play, the dynamics of Lear's family, and the thematic issues of parent and child, father and son, friendship and loyalty, virtue and vice. And all in less than fifty lines. Because the scene is cut entirely in Peter Brook's film (1971), we are positioned immediately in Lear's mind and are made to engage with Lear's rhetorical style. Brook would no doubt argue that the opening is dispensable and that information it contains can be presented in other ways and that he can more clearly stress his nihilistic interpretation of *Lear* by having the first word spoken by Lear be "no," followed by a pause (only as Lear continues do we understand that the word was "know"). All of this is true enough, but there is a trade-off: Brook's *Lear* is in danger of becoming less accessible than Shakespeare's play.

The impulse to cut Shakespearean openings works against not only comprehension but often important structural and thematic points as well. Zeffirelli begins *Hamlet* with act 1, scene 2, as if eager to get the star actor on. That Shakespeare clearly wanted us to see the ghost before Hamlet saw it, and before we saw Hamlet, must have seemed unimportant to Zeffirelli. But in cutting that opening scene, Zeffirelli sacrifices an opportunity to create a tone, mood, and atmosphere that cannot be subsequently regained (not to mention the loss of Fortinbras). I am not arguing that nothing should be cut. Shakespeare's plays have almost from the beginning been adapted, altered, bowdlerized, rewritten, combined, or incorporated into other texts. The idea that Shakespeare is in some sense a "sacred" author is relatively recent: it was unknown throughout all of the eighteenth and most of the nineteenth centuries. My point is that cutting a particular scene, character, speech, or line may have multiple effects. Rightly or wrongly and whether intended or not, the elimination of 1.1 contributes to a *Hamlet* incongruously picturesque, bright, and airy; Zeffirelli has eliminated the dark side.

Cuts and alterations to Shakespeare's text can be considered from the point of view of not only the play text but also the film audience. Here we are not so much concerned with what has been "done to" the text of Shakespeare's play as we are with how coherent the film is as film and, more largely, how the cuts and alterations affect the film's meaning. Filmmakers seldom have the courage of their convictions. If they really believed their frequent claims that film is a visual medium, so that images can substitute for words, they would cut much more of Shakespeare's text than they generally do, or, indeed, create an entirely new verbal structure. Again, Kurosawa's *Throne of Blood* provides an exemplary instance even as it is inimitable. Both *Macbeth* and not *Macbeth*, Shakespeare and not Shakespeare, a "pure" film that is highly theatrical, *Throne of Blood* draws as much on Shakespeare's sources as on Shakespeare. Kurosawa's triumph was to create a completely coherent, self-contained text that in no way depends on familiarity with the original even as it enriches our appreciation of Shakespeare's play.

Insisting that a production of Shakespeare, on film or in the theater, ought to be allowed to "speak for itself" is especially pointless when an abridged version of a play is presented. The play is no longer "there" to speak. The act of abridgment involves multiple interpretive choices. The central question is whether these interpretations are intentional or accidental. Clearly, editing that has been performed with some end in mind other than—or at least in addition to—time constraints will result in a more coherent final script. If, once again, *Hamlet* 1.1 is cut (as, oddly enough, it often is), and if, in addition, allusions to Fortinbras in 1.2, together with his appearance in 4.4, are also eliminated, what is the point of bringing the Norwegian prince in at the play's conclusion, as Peter Wood does in the 1970 Hallmark Hall of Fame television production? Better to give some of his lines to Horatio, as is sometimes done. When deep cuts are made in a complex text, we need a through line of interpretation to make sense of the more or less skeletal structure that remains. And "interpretation" does not necessarily refer to a revelation of the play's meaning: the through line may be stylistic as well as thematic. For example, the commedia dell'arte style sometimes employed for productions of *Taming of the Shrew* provides a stylistic backbone that makes an interpretive point as well, one that emphasizes the stylized, theatrical nature of the characters while encouraging viewers to accept the

Shylock Transformed: *Der Kaufmann von Venedig*

A Shakespeare film can deviate so far from its original as to hardly justify the term "adaptation" and yet can provide a fresh view of the play from which it derives. The German silent *Der Kaufmann von Venedig* (1923; English title, *The Jew of Mestri*) provides a particularly revealing insight into *The Merchant of Venice* even as it strays far from its source. The filmmakers—remarkably enough, given the time and place—construct a more sympathetic Shylock for their film than Shakespeare did. Shylock's hatred of Antonio and his friends is motivated through the introduction of a *Romeo and Juliet* plot grafted onto the Jessica/Lorenzo subplot. The sudden death of his wife, "Lea," partly as a result of abuse by Christian gallants, together with Jessica's desertion (she was supposed to marry a rabbinical student), crushes Shylock. As the Tubal character tells him, "They killed your wife and they will steal your child—now is the chance for your revenge." Most remarkable, however, is the Shylock (here called Mordecai) of Werner Kraus, the famous German actor who played Dr. Caligari in 1919 and Iago in 1922. He went on to star in the Nazi production *Jud Süss*, one of the most vicious anti-Semitic films ever made. Kraus's moneylender is no theatrical caricature, however (as he was in a 1913 French adaptation, *Shylock*, which starred the Jewish actor Harry Bauer); he is a dignified businessman, and the film places him respectfully in the context of his private life and religious activities. A particularly moving moment has Shylock lighting a candle for his lost daughter and beating his chest with his fist. We are left, in the end, not with the "Belmont" lovers, but with Mordecai/Shylock, alone, contemplating his own death. Is this a Shakespeare film? It would be easy to dismiss *Der Kaufmann von Venedig* as a travesty of *The Merchant of Venice*, but in any consideration of Shakespeare on film, or even of the theatrical history of Shakespeare's plays, one can acknowledge the value of adaptation as interpretation, and one can be grateful for a 1920s German film that presented Shakespeare's Shylock as an essentially tragic figure.

action on stage as self-conscious and exaggerated. "Director's theater" may have had its excesses, but that does not make directionlessness a virtue; as a general principle, editing is interpretation.

There is little point in pretending that a Shakespeare film should be judged entirely apart from Shakespeare's original; in practice, Shakespeare films are not simply adaptations of a Shakespeare play but are allusions to and commentaries on the play they adapt. So the question of how the adaptation has been carried out has interest in and of itself. The form and manner of adapting the Shakespeare text tell us something about how the filmmaker interprets the text he or she is adapting. Why something is cut and something else retained may have a complex of causes. Cuts, at the practical level, are made because of time constraints, but even this is not a simple matter. Were the cuts planned in advance (as with Olivier's elimination of Rosencrantz and Guildenstern) or in the course of production? Or were they a last-minute decision (Olivier's elimination of "How all occasions do inform against me")? To simplify matters, there are two primary ways of shortening a play: one is to eliminate entire scenes, characters, and blocks of text (again, Olivier's choice for *Hamlet*); the other is to trim throughout, shortening nearly every scene or speech but keeping in the film at least the outline of everything in the play (Kosintsev's *Hamlet*, even though it uses a Russian translation of Shakespeare, follows that route). In practice, the Shakespeare film falls somewhere on a continuum. Zeffirelli's *Hamlet* keeps most of the characters—Rosencrantz and Guildenstern but not Fortinbras—and trims pretty thoroughly. Cuts for time may be arbitrary, or may be advertised as arbitrary, but one cannot cut without at least considering the effect on the final film. Olivier's text editor for *Hamlet*, Alan Dent, in detailing the decision to eliminate Rosencrantz and Guildenstern ("there had to be a whacking great cut at the very outset—one preliminary, tremendous sacrifice, if the film were not to run to the impractical length of three hours or more") laments the sacrifice involved: "no Hamlet who ever existed would willingly choose to deprive himself of the magnificent opportunities for mockery that these two false friends give him, of the famous scene with the recorders, and of many other characteristic moments."[7] In other words, *Hamlet* is not as funny without these scenes, given that much of the play's humor comes at the expense of those otherwise nondescript characters, Rosencrantz and Guildenstern.

Recent textual scholarship, in emphasizing that we cannot expect ever to recover the "original" versions of Shakespeare's plays, has provided a new context for justifying modifications to the texts we have. So Ian McKellen rationalizes his method of editing *Richard III* on historical grounds: "Modern editions are an amalgam from a variety of sources—the original manuscript, before and after it was amended for performance; what his cast may have remembered having acted, when consulted months or years later by the publishers; plus the imaginative accretions of subsequent editors."[8] McKellen, like many adapters before and since, almost imagines himself "channeling" Shakespeare, adapting the play as Shakespeare would have done for, say, a touring production. "The least I could do," McKellen writes, "was change by change, cut by cut, ask myself whether he would approve."[9] Baz Luhrmann makes the point directly: "We're trying to make this movie rambunctious, sexy, violent, and entertaining the way Shakespeare might have if he had been a filmmaker."[10] It is something of a stretch to move from the assumption that Shakespeare may have produced different versions of his plays for different purposes to a claim that we can know what his intentions might have been in so doing or that we can somehow reconstruct the process today. Nevertheless, we should remember that the Shakespeare text as such probably never existed in some ideal form; even if it once did, it is unrecoverable today. Whether this knowledge gives the adapter license to do as he or she wishes is another matter.

Unlike most adaptations, Shakespeare films are made with full awareness that some viewers, many of them reviewers, will have a passing familiarity with the work being adapted and that, additionally, profits from the secondary markets and special audiences (e.g., school groups) depend in part on the extent to which the film can be sold not just as a movie but as Shakespeare. A Shakespeare film always alludes to the original, no matter how close or loose an adaptation it may be, and those allusions also refer to the three to four hundred years of theatrical history that have become part of our understanding of that play. Shakespeare films are not made for scholars or aficionados, but they are a part of the audience, and not a negligible part. The tie-in book for MGM's *Romeo and Juliet* (1936) includes, up front, an essay by William Strunk Jr., "Professor of English, Cornell University," putting his imprimatur on Cukor's film, and, as mentioned above, the DVD package of *Titus* (1999) reprints an essay by Jonathan Bate, the King Alfred Professor of English, University of Liverpool. Branagh's Shakespeare films enlist Russell Jackson (reader in Shakespeare studies and deputy director of the Shakespeare Institute, University of Birmingham) as technical adviser. Although this scholarly presence, in some instances, may be little more than window dressing, the point is that the studios and filmmakers think this window dressing necessary or, at the least, desirable.

The tendency of some critics to consider Shakespeare films only in terms of cinema, as films pure and simple, is a futile and ultimately counterintuitive approach. These films nearly always demand to be received as invocations of the Shakespeare text, and in practice they are so received. It is thus important to consider precisely what the relationship is and how it manifests itself. In practice, some Shakespeare adaptations reveal more anxiety than others. An adapter of *Hamlet*, for instance, will be more sensitive to audience expectations than an adapter of *Much Ado about Nothing* or *Titus Andronicus*. Most viewers can be assumed to know something about the ghost and to expect to hear "to be or not to be." The filmmaker may feel somewhat intimidated and boxed in when working on *Hamlet,* more free and inventive when the play is *A Midsummer Night's Dream.* In adapting the text, the filmmaker considers a variety of issues. To what extent must the structural architecture of the original be retained? How do cuts, transpositions, new sequences, added nondialogue scenes, and so on, affect the structure? How will characterization be modified? In particular, how will the relative weight of each character be altered in the adaptation process? (One revelation of Branagh's "full text" *Hamlet* is how large a role Claudius plays, something not necessarily self-evident in the reading. In Branagh's film, unlike Olivier's or Zeffirelli's film, the extent to which the play's action is a struggle between "mighty opposites" is evident.) How will the verbal structure, with its linguistic clusters and repetitive patterns, sustain itself on film, and will the alterations significantly harm the poetic integrity of the original? Additionally, what will happen to the language itself in terms of comprehension and resonance?

Again, I am not suggesting that a Shakespeare play cannot or should not be cut, that the text is in some sense sacred. But a Shakespeare film is most alive, most compelling, when the filmmaker finds in the text a "grounding," a tonal architecture, that the film can ride on. Actors trained by Sanford Meisner speak of a play text as a boat, and the river on which it sits as the emotion. The actor has his or her own personality that nevertheless needs to come to terms with the text on which he or she depends. Similarly, a filmmaker, though he or she need not be slavishly attached to the Shakespearean text, must nevertheless be constantly aware of, and at times accommodate, its presence. A full text is no guarantee that the alchemy will take place, as Branagh's *Hamlet* testifies. For all of its virtues, Branagh's film too often allows the tension between the "boat" and the "river" to dissipate, and the film slips away from the energies it should grasp. And by "text," I don't necessarily mean the words of the play: I mean, rather, the force field Shakespeare's words have created, the theatrical energies he has marshaled. These energies can be present in films where Shakespeare's words are completely absent, as with Kurosawa's *Throne of Blood* (and, to consider a different mode of presentation, in Verdi's opera *Otello*).

The most exciting Shakespeare films, if my premise be granted, are not necessarily the ones that retain the most of Shakespeare's text, but rather the ones that find ways to translate the energies of Shakespeare's language into an audio-video language of their own. This does not mean simply substituting images for words—showing poor Helena frightened by a bear in the

Warner Bros. production of A *Midsummer Night's Dream*, for example—but allowing the words to coexist with some kind of performative dynamic that is something other than mere illustration or enactment. The words—Shakespeare's text—ideally govern the sound and look of the film. The opening of Luhrmann's *Romeo + Juliet* can serve as illustration. The formal patterning of the Chorus's recitation is placed in partially supportive and partially ironic juxtaposition to the chaotic world it is evoking. Each word, clearly spoken and even calligraphically represented on screen, is tied to frantic activity, to an audiovisual display (rapid editing, zoom-outs, flash cuts, music, etc.) whose purpose is to both illustrate and reveal the limitations of the controlled language we hear and see. Just as in Shakespeare's play, the Chorus's attempt to contain and encapsulate the entire plot of the tragedy into the decorous parameters of a regular English sonnet is immediately called into question by the roving boys who come to occupy the stage upon his exit, so Luhrmann, employing simultaneity in place of sequentiality, gives us a similar effect.

The Shakespeare Film as Star Vehicle

From its beginnings at the turn of the twentieth century, the Shakespeare film has served as a showcase for performers. The actor and the star, always a factor in the commercial cinema, became foregrounded in an intensified way in the Shakespeare film. Shakespeare films have at times been little more than an excuse for capturing moments of an actor's performance on film (Sarah Bernhardt in the duel scene from *Hamlet*). The filmed performance becomes a re-creation of a theatrical original, however removed in time and space from its former manifestation. The 1913 *Hamlet*, clearly, is meant to provide a memento of Johnston Forbes-Robertson's rendering (at least in terms of physical performance) of the role, although the actor was some sixty years old. What would otherwise be an incongruous piece of casting is acceptable as a memorial to a famous star. In terms of nineteenth-century British theater, the *Hamlet* film is equivalent to the farewell benefit performance, a fund-raiser for the retiring actor. (Seventy years later, the videotaping of Laurence Olivier in *King Lear* had a similar function, though there is no incongruity in age between the actor and the character he plays.) The Shakespeare film can be a star vehicle in another way: the casting may be completely unrelated to a theatrical original and may even appear deliberately perverse, as with Mel Gibson in *Hamlet*. Now the Shakespeare film becomes a different kind of star vehicle, a showcase for the non-Shakespearean actor, something already present in the 1929 *Taming of the Shrew* with screen idols Douglas Fairbanks and Mary Pickford. In this latter instance, film, in casting a (more or less famously) married couple as Katharine and Petruchio, is borrowing a convention of the American theater (E. H. Sothern and Julia Marlowe at the turn of the twentieth century; Alfred Lunt and Lynn Fontanne in the 1920s and 1930s). Richard Burton and Elizabeth Taylor carried on the tradition for Franco Zeffirelli, with Burton playing the role of the Shakespearean actor to Taylor's Hollywood movie star.

Casting choices can be a marker of the way a Shakespeare film exhibits its cultural credentials. Many, if not most, Shakespeare films attempt some negotiation between highbrow, middlebrow, and lowbrow (and lately "no brow"). Production elements are chosen or placed along a continuum to attract the widest possible audience to the film. Kenneth Branagh is particularly noted for his mix of high and low, British and American casting strate-

Romping through *The Shrew*

Taming of the Shrew (1966) was coproduced by Franco Zeffirelli and Richard Burton and starred Burton and his (then) wife Elizabeth Taylor. It has all the trappings of a vanity project meant to focus attention on Taylor as a "serious" actress and take advantage of popular interest in Burton and Taylor, "the world's most celebrated movie couple, in the motion picture they were made for," if we believe the trailers. Under the circumstances, it may not be surprising that instead of engaging the challenges of the play, Zeffirelli chose to turn it into a witless farce. One could argue, of course, that Shakespeare's play *is* a farce as written, but therein lies the problem—what is the point of adding farcical elements to a farce? The resulting film is almost constantly irritating, filled with extended chases and varieties of horseplay. Taylor fumes and shouts her way through the role like some vulgar fishwife, at once too much and not enough of a spitfire, and Burton plays Petruchio as if the latter really were the buffoon and vulgarian he pretends to be. Admittedly, Shakespeare is not entirely clear on the point of how much of Petruchio is an act and how much is the man himself— that is precisely the trick involved in playing the role. Only in fleeting moments does Burton suggest that underneath the excesses of Petruchio's behavior there lives a character of some subtlety and complexity; for the most part Zeffirelli and Burton take Petruchio entirely at his own valuation, even to the extent of making his home into a decrepit dungeon out of a Roger Corman Edgar Allan Poe movie: it isn't only the meat that is overdone in Petruchio's house.

Franco Zeffirelli's *Taming of the Shrew*. Richard Burton played the role of the Shakespearean actor to Elizabeth Taylor's Hollywood movie star. Copyright © 1966 Columbia Pictures.

gies, but his approach has a long history. Perhaps the most notable example of cultural mishmash is the 1935 *A Midsummer Night's Dream*. The presence of Max Reinhardt provided the cultural cachet of a famous European director, while the film's codirector, former Reinhardt assistant William Deiterle, provided the Hollywood middlebrow element. The casting ranged from the British Ian Hunter, presumably on the highbrow end, down to Joe E. Brown and Hugh Herbert somewhere near the lowbrow region. Similarly, Felix Mendelssohn's incidental music (highbrow) is arranged by Erich Wolfgang Korngold (middlebrow), while the dances staged by Bronislava Nijinska take us back in the highbrow direction. The film was given road show treatment, complete with entrance and exit music derived from Mendelssohn, and then placed into general release accompanied by a publicity campaign significantly modified "down" from its highbrow original. That the film nevertheless lost money may be a testament not so much to the actual quality of the production as to the studio's failure to find the audience or audiences that it was looking for.

Star power, nonetheless, significantly drives the Shakespeare film. When Laurence Olivier made *Henry V* in 1944, he was drawing on his authority not only as a Shakespearean actor with management experience but almost as significantly as an Anglo-American movie star who was a recognizable entity on both sides of the Atlantic. His late 1930s and early 1940s film roles—notably Heathcliff in *Wuthering Heights* (1939) and Maxim de Winter in *Rebecca* (1940)—made him a household name in the United States as well as Great Britain. He was in the enviable position of having both a respectable stage career and a glamorous Hollywood image. Star power, of course, was a quality that Shakespeare himself must have taken into consideration when he wrote roles like Henry V, Hamlet, and Othello. The presence of Richard Burbage in his acting company would have been a significant factor in how he shaped and developed those roles. Burbage was not a "star" in the same way Olivier was, but we have sufficient evidence, some of it anecdotal, of Burbage's popularity among Elizabethan and Jacobean playgoers. Shakespeare's plays, though not necessarily star vehicles, often centered on a central, charismatic figure—Coriolanus, Hamlet, Richard of Gloucester, and, of course, Henry V. It is no coincidence that three of these were the three Olivier chose for screen incarnation (and, in the process of adaptation, he pared each play down to place even more focus on the leading role). *Henry V*, even as Shakespeare wrote it, is a pageant with Henry at the center of nearly every scene. Hamlet is the longest role in Shakespeare. Olivier cut two long soliloquies and cut out various characters (Rosencrantz and Guildenstern, Fortinbras) so that, in shortening the play, he did not shorten the ratio of "star" to "other players." And *Richard III*, particularly in the Colley Cibber adaptation Olivier drew on, is an egotist's delight. But if Olivier builds up his role at the expense of others, this is not a matter of egotism primarily, but cool commercial calculation. The ticket buyer comes to see the star, not to gaze admiringly on how well the vehicle has been constructed.[11]

Another way of regarding the issue of stardom would be to say that Shakespeare often wrote plays that are in some sense "about" stardom. The theatrical impulse to create star roles nicely coincides with the thematic issues underlying particular plays. *Henry V* and *Richard III* (and, to a lesser extent, *Hamlet*) are "star-making" narratives. With *Henry V*, the question is, will the young, untested "ingenue," Hal, horribly miscast in the starring role of king, live up to the challenges the role demands? Will Richard of Gloucester, who has proven himself again and again in strong supporting roles, be given—or rather take—the star part he in his own estimation so richly deserves? Will Prince Hamlet, shunted off to play a minor part by an inadequate older actor-manager with clout (Claudius), be able to wrest back the star part for himself? Will Othello, extremely well cast as a military leader, be able to play "civil governor" as convincingly? Princes and kings are stars almost by definition, but Shakespeare seems particularly interested in the question of how the man cast in the role will prove himself. Everyone in a play is an "actor," in all senses of the word, but only a few can become stars.

Laurence Olivier's stardom is intimately tied to his status as the last of the great Shakespeare actor-managers, men for whom stardom was the capital that allowed them to lease theaters and keep together acting companies whose activities centered on, though they were seldom exclusively devoted to, Shakespeare's plays. Just as Henry Irving had *The Bells* and *The Corsican Brothers*, popular Victorian melodramas, so Olivier appeared in *The Betsy* and *Boys from Brazil*, his career as a Shakespearean actor more or less subsidized by more lowbrow activities. Even in England, it was no longer possible, if it ever had been, for any theater or theatrical company, without considerable outside subsidy, to offer a steady diet of Shakespeare. Olivier's film career, then, could be seen as an extension of those of the nineteenth-century actor-managers—Irving, Forbes-Robertson, Beerbohm Tree—who, often accompanied by spouses or spouse surrogates (Ellen Terry), held together something like a family firm of Shakespeareans.[12]

Interestingly, the three Shakespeare films Orson Welles made were not star vehicles in quite the same way. Both *Macbeth* and *Othello* are something like "two-handers," each play offering two strong central roles of nearly equal weight (who, actors and nonactors often ask, is the "star" of *Othello*: the Moor or Iago?), and the *Henry IV* plays are even more generous in parceling out attractive roles (Hal, Hotspur, Bolinbroke, Falstaff). If Welles tended to consolidate each film around himself, it was partly for the same reason that Olivier did—his name brought ticket buyers to the theater. But Welles was never a star in the same way Olivier was, or rather his stardom was of a different kind, depending on something both greater and lesser than his acting personality. Welles was a true "auteur," and interest in his films did not center on how he performed Shakespeare (both his Macbeth and his Othello disappointed many critics and viewers), so much as on how he shaped the play into something distinctly his. Welles did not need or want to play appealing or attractive characters (he often chose to play the villain; when Olivier played the villainous Richard of Gloucester, he made him appealing), his persona did not require glamour. Even with Macbeth, Welles went out of his way to make the character less appealing than he is in Shakespeare's play.

Star power, as Welles's career suggests, can be unrelated to performance. And Shakespeare films have been successful without stars. Zeffirelli, in casting *Romeo and Juliet*, for example, deliberately avoided stars, both by casting inexperienced teenagers as the young lovers and by using little-known British Shakespeareans and Italian character actors in supporting roles. Even more notable, perhaps, is the example of Kenneth Branagh's *Henry V*. Branagh was a virtual unknown to movie audiences when he financed and directed his first Shakespeare film and cast himself in the leading role (he had previously played Henry on stage for the Royal Shakespeare Company). Comparisons with Olivier's *Henry V* often gloss over this very significant difference. Branagh, in a sense, becomes a star along with Henry (though, as it turns out, he did not become a real film star outside of Shakespearean roles—his non-Shakespearean projects, with a few exceptions, have been notably unsuccessful). Instead of having a star to depend on, much of the publicity surrounding *Henry V* was focused on the scrappy lad from Belfast who, through sheer pluck, charm, and raw talent, found the support and backing that enabled him to become a star. In his subsequent Shakespeare films Branagh demonstrated his ability to marshal star power to his benefit, casting Americans Denzel Washington and Michael Keaton in *Much Ado about Nothing* and a whole panoply of international stars—Billy Crystal, Gérard Depardieu, Jack Lemmon, Robin Williams, Charlton Heston, among others—to play small parts in *Hamlet*.

Shakespeare's plays always depended, to a greater or lesser extent, on star power, especially in periods when directors played essentially subservient roles. The notable productions of Shakespeare in the eighteenth and nineteenth centuries revolved almost entirely on the central actors—Garrick's *Macbeth*, Macklin's *Shylock*, Kean's *Othello*, Irving's *Hamlet*. These names constitute theater history in that era. Only in the twentieth century do we begin to hear of directors as stars—Peter Brook's *King Lear* and *Midsummer Night's Dream*, John Barton's *Richard II*, Trevor Nunn's *Macbeth*, Zeffirelli's *Romeo and Juliet* (first on stage and then on film). Once film directors became superstars, Shakespeare films could star the director. We have Kosintsev's *Hamlet* and *King Lear*, Kurosawa's *Throne of Blood* and *Ran*, Baz Luhrmann's *Romeo + Juliet*, Julie Taymor's *Titus*. The movie stars, however, do not disappear: it may be "Zeffirelli's *Romeo and Juliet*," but it is "Mel Gibson's *Hamlet*" (even if Zeffirelli directed it) and "the Laurence Fishburne *Othello*" (even if, playing Iago, Kenneth Branagh steals the film). If the movie star is big enough, and if the star's appearance in the Shakespeare film is a clear instance of "crossover" casting—Gibson as Hamlet—the film becomes, willy-nilly, a star vehicle. *Hamlet* is an interesting test of this principle. Zeffirelli assembled an impressive supporting cast of bona fide British stage and film actors to complement his American stars, Gibson and Glenn Close—Paul Scofield, Ian Holm, Alan Bates, Helena Bonham Carter among them. But Gibson's star power is so great and he is so centered in this highly compressed version of the play that the other roles are not allowed much scope. Bates's Claudius, potentially a strong counterweight to Gibson, has little to do. In the words of Robert Hapgood, "Claudius especially suffers from the omission of his functions as a ruler and the reduction of his attempt at prayer to a series of heartfelt groans."[13] (One important exception to this is Helena Bonham Carter, who is so compelling as Ophelia that she almost runs away with the film, a rare thing indeed for poor Ophelia.)

The Shakespeare Film and Hollywood Genres

Shakespeare films, as I have already suggested, are frequently hybrids, mixing genres, modes of production, periods, and performance styles. This hybrid character may be a factor in the initial concept, a part of its aesthetic scaffolding, as with Olivier's *Henry V*, or it may be circumstantial, as with the 1960 George Schaefer television film of *Macbeth*, which for pragmatic reasons was produced for both film and television exhibition. Hybridity may be considered a strong generic aspect of the Shakespeare film. Shakespeare's plays are themselves hybrids, happily mixing high tragedy and low humor, poetry and prose, history and fiction. Plots are combined and recombined from unrelated sources (*Merchant of Venice, Taming of the Shrew, King Lear*); historical periods are folded into each other; language can be, in the same work, high-flown and down to earth (almost any play); tone can vary wildly from scene to scene. It is no surprise, therefore, that in adapting Shakespeare, filmmakers find themselves borrowing from recognized and familiar cinematic genres in order to create analogues to Shakespeare's generic borrowings. Baz Luhrmann's *Romeo + Juliet*, for example, notably draws on narrative and stylistic conventions of international cinema: critics, as well as ordinary viewers, have identified allusions to Sergio Leone westerns, Hong Kong action films, Busby Berkeley musicals, *Paris Is Burning, Priscilla, Queen of the Desert*, and *Rebel without a Cause*. All of this is so self-evident that no critic is needed to come from a screening to tell us this; Luhrmann and company are perfectly happy to make the connections for us. Luhrmann's film both reflects and takes advantage of the peculiar hybridity of contemporary filmmaking practices. *Romeo + Juliet* has American stars, an Australian director, and a largely Australian and Mexican crew; financed by a major American studio, it was filmed mainly in Mexico.

Placing a Shakespeare film within a recognizable, preexisting cinematic genre can be one way to find an audience, although this may or may not be a conscious decision. Warner Bros.' *A Midsummer Night's Dream* provides an example in the direction of backstage musical, a genre that the studio was in

Bit Parts

The French film semiotician/psychoanalytic theorist Christian Metz once wrote that it is the nature of film appreciation that every film has something of interest in it: either it is the "minor work of a major filmmaker, . . . the major work of a minor filmmaker, . . . or the first film shot with a certain type of lens, or else the last film shot in Tsarist Russia."[14] In short, there is always something to make a film worth watching. For the Shakespeare film devotee, this is especially true. No matter how mediocre or marginal, no Shakespeare film is entirely without interest to a Shakespearean. Often, for example, a minor role will be played in a memorable way that defines the role, in spite of the inadequacy of everything else in the film. Even successful films may contain a particularly memorable performance by a player in a secondary role. I am thinking here of Victor Spinetti as Hortensio in Zeffirelli's *Taming of the Shrew*, Alan Webb as Justice Shallow in Welles's *Chimes at Midnight*, Bill Travers as Snout in Peter Hall's *A Midsummer Night's Dream*, Simon Russell Beale as the Second Gravedigger in Branagh's *Hamlet*. Each actor carved out a moment or series of moments that fused the actor and the role into a single unit, and in so doing appeared to define that role once and for all—or at least until the next definitive performance comes along. Michael Maloney as Roderigo in the Oliver Parker *Othello* provides a particularly notable instance. Roderigo is one of those Shakespeare characters that can be and has been played in wildly different ways and cannot be defined by a single performance. There have been handsome Roderigos and ugly Roderigos, silly-ass gulls and smooth seducers, eloquent gallants and self-regarding fools. Maloney provides yet another possibility: a high-strung young man driven near to madness by his unrequited lust for Desdemona, fiercely determined to obtain his desire, suspicious of Iago but nevertheless in his thrall. The humor of the role comes from the sheer intensity of Maloney's performance, which threatens to transform Roderigo into a tragic figure. Rather than echo Othello's own folly in a minor, burlesque key, he does so on an almost equal basis—another man driven to madness by sexual love. Indeed, because of Laurence Fishburne's dignified, low-key performance, Roderigo seems more passionate than Othello. From one point of view, Maloney's Roderigo is perhaps a mistake; he carries matters too far, throws the film off-kilter, or reveals its flaws more clearly. But this is a Roderigo one cannot ignore or easily forget. Maloney also appears in Zeffirelli's *Hamlet* (as Guildenstern) and Branagh's *Henry V* (as the Dauphin) and *Hamlet* (as Laertes). Though his Guildenstern is pretty much cut down to nothing, he lends his resonant presence in the two Branagh films.

the process of creating with such strategies as the casting of Dick Powell, Anita Louise, Hugh Herbert, and Joe E. Brown, and the heavy reliance on music, comic buffoonery, elaborately choreographed dancing, showy costumes, and so on. Similarly, MGM's *Julius Caesar* appeared in the context of a burgeoning revival of interest in the Roman/biblical epics: MGM's *Quo Vadis* (1951), which had just rescued the studio from bankruptcy and provided some of the sets for *Caesar*; *The Robe* (1953) at Fox; De Mille's *Samson and Delilah* (1949). Elements of film noir are present in 1940s Shakespeare, from Olivier's *Hamlet* to Welles's *Macbeth* (both 1948) to, once again, *Julius Caesar*. In a somewhat different vein, Kenneth Branagh deliberately set out to turn *Love's Labour's Lost* (2000) into a 1930s Hollywood musical. The mix of genres that is evoked when any given Shakespeare film is considered becomes even more evident when the publicity department has a hand in the proceedings. Partly, one suspects, out of desperation, Republic Studios flacks hoped to sell Orson Welles's *Macbeth* as a generic mix: "In terms of modern cycles, 'Macbeth' combines the thrills of Dick Tracy, Hopalong Cassidy, Roy Rogers, Dracula, and Frankenstein."[15]

The seemingly elastic categories into which Shakespeare films can be made to fit, and the elasticity of the Shakespeare films themselves, reflect the multigeneric possibilities inherent in Shakespeare's plays, themselves a mix of literary genres and subgenres, some recently developed and some drawn from older literatures. Hollywood genres can even be mixed back into Shake-

The Warner Bros. stock company in *A Midsummer Night's Dream.*
Copyright © 1935 Warner Bros.

speare. *Twelfth Night* is at once romantic comedy, musical, romance, and humors play. *Hamlet* is a revenge tragedy, a psychodrama, a ghost story, a dark comedy, and an action/adventure epic. *Julius Caesar* is a historical drama, a biopic, a revenge tragedy, a play of ideas, and a political treatise. *Macbeth* is a horror film, a costume drama, a ghost story, a revenge play, and a crime exposé. Republic Studio head Herbert J. Yates thought of publicizing Welles's *Macbeth* as the story of "the greatest gangster the world has ever known,"[16] and several gangster films (*Joe Macbeth* [1955] and *Men of Respect* [1991]) have been inspired by Shakespeare's Scottish play. The ease with which Shakespearean drama could slip in and out of generic categories frustrated neoclassical critics who preferred a stable, single identity for the plays. Shakespeare could have been pointing to his own practice when he had Polonius speak of "tragical-comical-historical-pastoral" (a good description of, say, *A Winter's Tale*, though Shakespeare, when he gave those words to Polonius, had yet to write that play).

Shakespearean films are shaped by not only the theatrical styles and methods that often lie behind them but also the cinematic movements, styles, and aesthetic and technological norms of the period in which they are made. Which is another way of saying that Shakespearean films are something special—each film is nearly always treated as "exceptional" to some degree or other, something to be noted, notable within the larger discourse of film culture—and at the same time each film fits, particularly in retrospect, into specific generic categories. The "special" status of the Shakespeare film is both a recognition of the cultural importance of Shakespeare and something constructed by and through the special efforts of the publicity machinery marshaled by the distribution and exhibition branches of the motion picture industry. Until fairly recently, few films other than those based on Shakespeare received the kind of auxiliary attention given to them, a *parerga* consisting of spin-off books, soundtrack albums, published screenplays, and so on. Olivier's *Hamlet*, notably, was accompanied by a heavily illustrated screenplay volume, another book devoted to discussions of the film by various creative personnel, and a record album of music and speeches from the film. Along with all of this publicity and tie-in material, the film was treated as a special item by the press, *Life* magazine devoting an elegantly illustrated eleven-page essay to the film, and other attention followed.

The well-crafted publicity *Hamlet* enjoyed to some extent disguised or at least put aside the extent to which Olivier's film fit into generic and stylistic categories of interest at the time of its release. It is, as noted above, a film deeply inflected by film noir lighting and narrative emphasis; it fits into the "tradition of quality" movement, which was supposed to help British films break into the American market. It follows on significant experiments in cinematography that, in the wake of Gregg Toland's work on *Citizen Kane*, *The Little Foxes*, and *The Best Years of Our Lives*, altered the look of the black-and-white film (two of these films were directed by William Wyler, who, with Toland, also made *Wuthering Heights*, in which Olivier had starred). In the design of its mise-en-scène, it can be allied with the "fantastic realism" of Powell and Pressburger films like *The Red Shoes*, *Tales of Hoffmann*, and *A Matter of Life and Death*, all of which are, in a sense, "theatrical films"—films that take place in a highly designed space, not precisely a literal stage but a kind of "psychologized" landscape designed to illuminate and support the mental life of the characters in the narrative.

Mode of Production

Although I employ the term "film" throughout this book, and although I primarily emphasize Shakespeare adaptations photographed on celluloid and originally exhibited in movie theaters, I do not wish to ignore the extent to which Shakespeare "films" are frequently not films at all. "Moving image" would be a more useful designation, perhaps, for the variety of material texts ordinarily referred to as "film." Important aesthetic issues are brought immediately to the fore when words like film, video, television, electronic, mechanical, cinematic, stagy, theatrical, monitor, screen, and so on, are used. Some of these are, or are meant to be, descriptive; some are, or easily become, prescriptive; some are material, others metaphoric, and, at times, they are both. For the moment, however, I would like to concentrate on three terms—film, video, and television. A problem arises immediately, since "video," in casual parlance, is another word for television; at other times it is a shorthand for magnetic tape as well as, more recently, for digital formats. But a video artist may create a work digitally or on magnetic videotape that is not intended for TV broadcast. And television refers at once to an industry, a method of exhibition, and an object that sits in a home. It is also necessary to distinguish between the moment of creation and the moment of exhibition, since *film* may be transferred to videotape or digitalized and subsequently shown on broadcast or cable television or watched on a video monitor.

Film, then, is a method of mechanical reproduction of a (generally) "live" (or "prefilmic") event that employs photography: a strip of negative still images is made, a positive print is struck from it, and this print is projected—normally at a rate of twenty-four still images for every second of running time—on a luminous surface in an ideally darkened auditorium. With the advent of sound film, an audio recording was simultaneously made and syn-chronized with, as well as physically wedded to, the film image, along with music and sound effects that had been separately recorded. Videotape, or video, is an electronic process of reproduction; a strip of magnetized plastic simultaneously records the images and sounds of a "live" event. Unlike film, no visible image trace is actually recorded on the plastic strip itself, which is exhibited on a video monitor. (Digital reproduction, though clearly the wave of the future, has until very recently been generally limited to *transferring* existing film and videotaped originals to, for example, digital video discs.) Live broadcast television, unlike film and video, does not involve *recording* images and sounds but rather *transmitting* them over airwaves or via cable. In the early years of broadcast television, these images and sounds were often simultaneously recorded by a special motion picture camera trained on a monitor (the Kinescope process) for later rebroadcast. In terms of aesthetics, film recording has historically created an image with a greater range of illu-mination, color quality, and sharpness of detail than that created by any other process of reproduction. My primary interest in the following pages will be in film adaptations of Shakespeare's plays. But I will discuss broadcast television and video in chapter 6, and I will make incidental reference to television Shakespeare throughout.

Among the many ways of thinking about the interrelationships among these different technologies and the extent to which each creates its own "generic" expectation, we might consider, for instance, the influence of tele-vision on film. With Shakespeare, there are unexpected connections. Lau-rence Olivier's *Richard III* (1955), for example, was filmed in a manner strongly influenced by television style and technique, even if it was not made for television: frequent close shots, long takes, and a single, multipart "unit" set. The George Schaefer film of *Macbeth* (1960), produced in part by Hall-mark Cards, was conceived simultaneously as television and as film. "This is the story behind this new great colour film of 'Macbeth': TV helping the cinema, and the cinema helping TV. Instead of enemies, allies. Instead of war, peaceful co-operation."[17] (The Cold War rhetoric seems especially appropriate for a story of murderous thanes.) Like a television production, it was made on a tight preparation and shooting schedule, much of it on a soundstage, employing significant close and medium shots. But it was shot on film, in color, with location filming in Scotland, and it features ambitious battle sequences. Furthermore, this *Macbeth* was a retread: the stars, Evans and Anderson, had played the Scottish couple on the New York stage in

1937 and had appeared together in an earlier television broadcast, directed by Schaefer, in 1954. By 1960, it may be uncharitably suggested, Evans and Anderson were rather mature for their roles, an issue that would have been of minor concern in the theater. (The 1972 *Macbeth*, directed by Roman Polanski, quite consciously takes a very different tack, casting young, relatively inexperienced actors in the leading roles.) That the finished product fell, ultimately, between stools might have been expected. The 1960 *Macbeth* ended up not quite grand or exciting enough to be cinema, while it was not intimate enough, too "distanced" from the viewer, to be television.

In the chapters that follow, I will develop the topics mentioned above by taking a closer look at selected Shakespeare films. Chapter 2, which continues and expands on the question of how theater is incorporated into film, looks at how "Shakespeare," the person and the theatrical energies his name represents, has been constructed cinematically, with particular attention to Laurence Olivier's *Henry V* and John Madden's *Shakespeare in Love*. Chapter 3 discusses *Romeo and Juliet*, one of Shakespeare's most popular and most frequently adapted plays, in the context of the kinds of choices, including the inevitable compromises, filmmakers (including George Cukor, Renato Castellani, Franco Zeffirelli, and Baz Luhrmann) face when adapting the Shakespeare text to film. More historically oriented, chapter 4 examines Shakespeare films, including those of Orson Welles and Laurence Olivier, made in the Hollywood studio era, with particular emphasis on the MGM *Julius Caesar*, Welles's *Macbeth*, and Olivier's *Richard III*. Chapter 5 focuses on the Shakespeare films of Kenneth Branagh, the actor-director who might be seen as heir of both Welles and Olivier, in the context of a revival of interest in the Shakespeare film in the 1980s and 1990s. With chapter 6, I turn to Shakespeare on television with brief case studies of two specific broadcasting moments, the 1950s Hallmark Hall of Fame Shakespeare and the 1970s–1980s BBC/Time-Life productions. Chapter 7 looks at recent Shakespeare films that, appearing at or near the end of the twentieth century, self-consciously reconfigure Shakespeare for a new millennium.

Notes

1. Recent attempts to define (or redefine) genre include Steve Neale, *Genre and Hollywood* (London: Routledge, 2000); and Nick Browne, ed., *Refiguring American Film Genres* (Berkeley: University of California Press, 1998).

2. Kathy M. Howlett, *Framing Shakespeare on Film* (Athens: Ohio University Press, 2000), 10.

3. Howlett, *Framing*, 9.

4. For an analysis of three film *Hamlets* as exemplifying preexisting generic categories, see Harry Keyishian, "Shakespeare and Movie Genre: The Case of Hamlet," in *The Cambridge Companion to Shakespeare on Film*, ed. Russell Jackson (Cambridge: Cambridge University Press, 2000), 72–81.

5. Russell Jackson notes that Branagh's *Much Ado about Nothing* includes both a "pre-prologue" ("Sigh No More") and a "delayed prologue" (the credit sequence); see "From Playscript to Screenplay," in Jackson, *Companion*, 15–34; 28.

6. Donald Hancock, "War Is Mud: Branagh's Dirty Harry V and the Types of Political Ambiguity," in *Shakespeare, the Movie: Popularizing the Plays on Film, TV, and Video*, ed. Lynda E. Boose and Richard Burt (London: Routledge, 1997), 45–66; 57.

7. Alan Dent, "Text-editing Shakespeare," in *Hamlet: The Film and the Play*, ed. Alan Dent (London: World Film Publications, 1948).

8. Ian McKellen, *William Shakespeare's Richard III*, a screenplay written by Ian McKellen and Richard Loncraine, annotated and introduced by Ian McKellen (Woodstock, N.Y.: Overlook, 1996), 16.

9. McKellen, *Richard III*, 15.

10. *William Shakespeare's Romeo & Juliet: The Contemporary Film, the Classic Play*, screenplay by Craig Pearce and Baz Luhrmann (New York: Bantam Doubleday Dell, 1996), "A Note from Baz Luhrmann."

11. That Olivier could be selfless as an actor can be seen in his production of *The Prince and the Showgirl*, as he builds up and carefully shapes Marilyn Monroe's role at his own expense.

12. See Steven Buhler's chapter, "The Revenge of the Actor Managers," in *Shakespeare in the Cinema: Ocular Proof* (Albany: State University of New York Press, 2002), 95–123. Buhler discusses Oliver, together with Welles and Branagh, as actor-managers in the nineteenth-century sense.

13. Robert Hapgood, "Popularizing Shakespeare: The Artistry of Franco Zeffirelli," in *Shakespeare, the Movie: Popularizing the Plays on Film, TV, and Video*, ed. Lynda E. Boose and Richard Burt (London: Routledge, 1997), 80–94; 92.

14. Christian Metz, *The Imaginary Signifier: Psychoanalysis and the Cinema*, trans. Celia Britton, Annwyl Williams, Ben Brewster, and Alfred Guzzetti (Bloomington: Indiana University Press, 1982), 12–13.

15. Sam Nathanson to Richard Wilson, March 7, 1950 (Richard Wilson papers, UCLA Special Collections).

16. Richard Wilson to Orson Welles, May 7, 1949 (Richard Wilson Papers, UCLA Special Collections).

17. Clayton Hutton, *Macbeth: The Making of the Film* (London: Max Parrish, 1960), 7.

CHAPTER TWO

Finding the Playwright on Film

At the beginning of Renato Castellani's 1954 film adaptation of *Romeo and Juliet*, William Shakespeare, played by John Gielgud, makes a brief appearance.[1] In Elizabethan costume and holding a copy of the First Folio, Gielgud/ Shakespeare, at once Chorus and author, recites, with impeccable diction and rhythm, the prologue to Shakespeare's play. Castellani then cuts to an Italian location setting, where, in place of British poetry, we have Italian bustle. We are in Renaissance (but also clearly modern) Italy, which has been captured, neorealist fashion, with the noise and detailed mise-en-scène of a busy market day. England and Italy, word and image, past and present, poetry and prose, theater and film. The iconic author-narrator, single and isolated, is replaced by a crowd of Italian extras. Fittingly enough, the Romeo and Juliet story, Italian in its origins but co-opted by Shakespeare, is reintegrated into Italian culture and Italian cinema, albeit with imported British actors in most of the leading roles. The Shakespeare film here is a product of the postwar internationalization of the European film, a time of coproduction, linguistically mixed casts, cross-financing, multiple soundtracks, and so on. In this instance, the neorealist impulse fits somewhat uncomfortably with the Elizabethan poetry. The British actors dub themselves, whereas the Italian actors are dubbed by English speakers (Italian films in the postwar era were nearly all postsynchronized, a process presumably reversed for Italian audiences). Additionally, British theater-trained professionals play side by side with nonactors, Italian and British, notably Susan Shentall (Juliet), who had no acting experience prior to this film.

Shakespeare films, as Castellani's *Romeo and Juliet* suggests, can exemplify a seemingly incongruous mix of elements. Much like Shakespeare himself, they are at once highbrow and lowbrow, culture and amusement, old and

27

quaint as well as new and fresh, conservative and radical. Often produced to lend prestige to the motion picture industry, they are nearly as often sold, ironically enough, as popular entertainment. Caught up in a tension between what is perceived as "theatrical," and thus of artistic value, and what is perceived as merely "the movies," base, common, and popular, Shakespeare films may be condemned on the one hand as canned theater and on the other hand as insufficiently faithful to the plays from which they have been adapted. The fate of the Shakespeare film is always to fall short of ideal, whether it be fidelity to Shakespeare or fidelity to the cinema. In part, this reflects the many purposes these films can be asked to serve. A Shakespeare film may exist primarily to record a stage production, an honorable enough goal, perhaps, but one that is seldom met in a satisfactory manner. More often a Shakespeare film attempts to capture a performance by a particular actor, an interpretation of the leading role in, say, *Hamlet* or *King Lear*. The film, in such instances, is not necessarily a re-creation of a specific production but rather the creation of a context for performance, a context that is usually not in any simple way theatrical. Other filmmakers will aim for "pure cinema" and downplay, insofar as possible, the theatrical origins of their source.

No matter how "cinematic" a filmmaker strives to be, however, the Shakespeare film will always stand in a necessary relationship to the theater (Shakespeare wrote plays, not novels or short stories), and terminology drawn from one aesthetic medium constantly crosses over to the other. So, for example, the National Theatre film of *Othello* (1965) with Laurence Olivier is described as "stagy," while Franco Zeffirelli's 1960 Old Vic stage production of *Romeo and Juliet* is found to exhibit "cinematic" elements. A cinematic version of a play, in conventional terms, is one that has been "opened out" in a variety of ways, though in practice this has often meant little more than changing locations within scenes and filming out of doors, a process that may seem irrelevant when applied to Shakespeare. His plays are already opened out in that the spatial and temporal dimensions of Shakespearean dramaturgy are seldom limited by either the strictures of Aristotle's theory (one action, one place, twenty-four hours) or the tendency of the naturalistic theater of our own time to rely on a single setting and unfold in (more or less) "real time." The danger of opening out becomes evident with, for example, Mike Nichols's filming of Edward Albee's *Who's Afraid of Virginia Woolf?* (1966). By taking his actors out of doors or moving the action to a roadside café, Nichols, some viewers thought, violated the admittedly artificial but nevertheless crucial claustrophobia of the original theatrical

Theater into Film

Peter Hall's 1968 film of A Midsummer Night's Dream is in many ways a curious amalgam of theatrical instincts and cinematic practice. In his original 1959 stage production as well as in several later revivals (1962, 1963), Hall broke away from "balletic fairies, high-powered scenic effects and the Mendelssohn music."[2] On film, Hall took advantage of the wettest time of a wet spring to make literal Titania's weather report in act 2, scene 1—hence his famous "fairies with dirty faces." Though clearly basing his 1968 film on earlier stagings, Hall makes his film "cinematic" in ways that at times suggest he had been watching too many French new wave films: jump cuts, zip pans, and other self-conscious transitional devices abound, and scenes are often shot with a handheld camera. Hall also chose to post-record the dialogue, which has the advantage that the actors are free to move as they speak their lines. But the effect is that the words at times sound hollow and flat. Hall might have been better served had he relied more on his theatrical instincts and less on his sense of what the cinema ought to be. The very real pleasures of the film come from its down-to-earth view of both the lovers and the fairies, something that had been developing in the theater for some time, as well as the way the Mechanicals are taken at their own valuation—they speak, for the most part, no more than is set down for them and their attempt at amateur theatricals, though inept, is thoroughly sincere.

experience. Albee's play depends, to a significant extent, on an essentially theatrical gambit: its characters cannot break out of the living room in which they are trapped.

Many, perhaps most, Shakespeare films lie someplace betwixt and between the poles of "pure" theater and "pure" cinema. Here, I am thinking of films that, though stemming from a specific theatrical model, are rethought thoroughly in cinematic terms. The Peter Brook King Lear (1971) provides a clear example. The film's director staged the play with the same lead actor, Paul Scofield, in a production that ran for several years, including an extensive world tour. Brook's deeply nihilistic reading of King Lear is evident in both play and film. And yet the film Lear, photographed on location, almost entirely recast, its text newly edited, its costumes and settings redesigned, differs from the stage production in almost every detail. Even Scofield, who played Lear hundreds of times on stage, gives a notably different reading on film (and had already given yet another reading in the Shakespeare Recording Society audio version in 1965; he gave one more in the

Naxos recording in 2001). Few would characterize Brook's film, with its detailed, documentary-like mise-en-scène and new-wave style jump cuts, as canned theater, but Brook nonetheless captured in it a good part of the essence of his stage production.

One aspect of nearly all Shakespeare films that remind us of the theater is Shakespeare's language, a language seemingly alien to the cinema not only because of its difficult syntax and archaisms but also because its cadences and its descriptive power seem to exist in part to picture what cannot be pictured as such on the stage. Shakespeare's language almost immediately foregrounds itself as language, demanding attention, beyond its specific function as bearer of information, in and for itself. The blank verse signifies theatricality, revealing its stage origins even as it seeks to be absorbed into a cinematic context. This effect is particularly evident in films that employ modern settings, like Baz Luhrmann's *Romeo + Juliet* (1996) and Michael Almereyda's *Hamlet* (2000). When the performers are striving, to a greater or lesser extent, to come to terms with the language, speaking the verse as if it were prose, and in every way trying to naturalize the formality of the diction and syntax, the dissonance is even more evident. This is not a matter (necessarily) of actors in some idealized way "incapable" of speaking the verse but rather of actors who are striving mightily to resist the demands of the language, playing against the verse. Julia Stiles in Almereyda's film does this with her Ophelia, a gen Xer rebelling against not only her father and her fate but indeed against the weight of the words she has been given to speak. The effect, in this instance, is particularly poignant—poor Ophelia, one senses, wants at some level to fit in, to be part of the world for which she is destined, but she is fundamentally incapable of adopting that world's appropriate tone and style.

In practice, films of this kind tend to include actors who can command the verse more or less effectively, along with others who do not or will not. In Almereyda's *Hamlet*, the prince's primary antagonists, Claudius and Laertes, are played by actors (Kyle MacLachlan and Liev Schreiber) who manage to be at once "natural" and Shakespearean. In a sense, their seeming comfort with their own words serves to underline their roles as upholders of the status quo—it is in part because they perform the verse so easily that they are Hamlet's nemeses. In *Romeo + Juliet*, the effect is more mixed as some of the performers have little or no experience with Shakespeare (Leonardo DiCaprio, Claire Danes). Others are not primarily Shakespearean actors but have considerable theatrical background and training (Paul Sorvino, Diane Venora), and a few are British actors with Shakespearean training, notably

Pete Postlethwaite as the Friar. It is not that British actors are necessarily better at speaking Shakespeare's verse than American actors (though in practice they often are). But their accents, diction, and rhythms occupy a familiar niche that even to American ears seems to fit in some essential way with Shakespeare's verse. (Some linguists and philologists have suggested that the American southern dialect is closer to Shakespeare's English than is modern "Oxbridge" dialect.)

Just as the question of language has a variety of dimensions, so too does the whole issue of the "theatricality" of Shakespeare films, as the term "the-

How Not to Speak Shakespeare

We often hear that a particular performer cannot speak blank verse properly, but we are seldom told what this means. Let's consider Jason Robards Jr. as Brutus in the 1970 film version of *Julius Caesar*. Robards was a master of down-to-earth, naturalistic acting, and he treats Shakespeare's verse pretty much as if it were prose written by Eugene O'Neill. Apart from issues of pitch and intonation (both unvarying), Robards tends to place emphases and pauses in such a way that they work completely against the blank verse rhythm. Specifically, Robards breaks many of the lines in half, creating a caesura, or pause, where none is called for by the verse; when a true caesura comes along, it loses its effect. The result is a singsong rhythm that renders Brutus's lines colorless. Here is an example from act 5, scene 5, ll. 36–38, 41–42 (// = pause):

I shall have glory//by this losing day//
More than Octavius//and Mark Antony//
By this vile conquest shall attain unto . . .
Night hangs up mine eyes,//my bones would rest//
That have but laboured//to attend this hour.

In line 38, although he doesn't pause after "conquest," Robards delivers the first half of the line with strong emphasis (especially on "By," which word he also emphasizes, oddly enough, in the first line, above). He additionally pauses, more naturally, at the end of each line, consequently breaking the speech into four-, five-, and six-foot segments. In contrast, Richard Johnson, a classically trained and at the same time "modern" performer who plays Cassius in the same film, "naturalizes" the poetry by lightly but consistently maintaining the blank verse rhythms in the context of an easy, conversational style of delivery. Robards, in ignoring the demands of the verse, paradoxically succeeds only in making his speech sound artificial and stilted.

atrical" can carry very distinct meanings. The "simple" recording of a stage production may be theatrical, but it need not be. Here "theatrical" means precisely the experience audience members undergo in the theater: the living presence of actors, the effect of stage lighting, what they choose to pay attention to, the interaction, explicit or implicit, between the actors and the audience, each in various ways affecting the other. All of this is theatrical, and little or none of it can be duplicated or experienced in film. But "theatrical" can mean something rather different: artifice, largeness of effect, intensity, flamboyance, the nature and timing of actors' entrances and exits—these too are matters "theatrical," and a film that owes little or nothing to the stage can in this sense *be* theatrical. To simply include elements of a stage production in a film does not ipso facto create theater.

By my various definitions of what is theatrical, even the most cinematic— perhaps especially the most cinematic—of films can be the most theatrical. Baz Luhrmann's *Romeo + Juliet*, for instance, has been perceived as especially cinematic because of its rapid pace, its varied and transparent editing devices, its complex, precisely calibrated camera movements, its eclectic and richly layered soundtrack, and so forth. But the film simultaneously insists on its theatricality, reveling in flamboyant effects, *coups de théâtre*, carefully paced climaxes, and ritualized performances. Luhrmann even provides a stage in the film, a deserted (movie) theater where the melodrama of Mercutio's death is enacted. Luhrmann's background in opera is very much in evidence, and his film is virtually an operatic adaptation of Shakespeare's play. The mise-en-scène, as distinct from the way it is used in Luhrmann films, is essentially theatrical in nature.

In sum, filming a stage production of a Shakespeare play does not guarantee "theater" any more than conceiving a Shakespeare film from scratch guarantees "cinema," even if these terms were clearly defined. In practice, there is always theater of some kind in film, while all films are, by definition, cinema. What may be the most upsetting to some viewers are moments when a filmmaker goes out of his or her way to avoid the theatrical ground or base in order to somehow inject or superimpose something that appears to be "cinema"—the voice-over soliloquies in Olivier's *Hamlet* (1948), for example, or, in Branagh's *Hamlet* (1996), the frequent recourse to flashback "inserts." Branagh's attempts to give concrete realization to the words spoken by the characters are especially problematic because they introduce into the text an objective reality that the words themselves are not meant to imply. The effect is to reduce or eliminate ambiguity. The issue is not whether Hamlet slept with Ophelia; the issue is that we cannot know, we are not given sufficient information to draw that conclusion. The ambiguity is precisely what is important. Ophelia's songs are poignant and disturbing because they leave open the question of just how intimate Hamlet and Ophelia were. Of course, to remove textual ambiguity is a form of interpretation, and it is not possible, in either a film or a staging, to maintain all of the ambiguities present in the written text.

Shakespeare's plays are not only "theater," of course, but theater of a particular kind, one dependent on a whole host of nonnaturalistic devices, including soliloquies, asides, nonlocalized spaces, and supernatural characters, that are not easily made "natural" or "realistic." Shakespeare's plays stretch against the outlines of theater itself. In a number of ways, it would be easier to adapt the plays of Shakespeare's contemporaries Ben Jonson or Thomas Dekker to the screen than it is to film most of Shakespeare. Jonson's *Bartholomew Fair* or Dekker's *The Shoemaker's Holiday*, with their naturalistic detail and everyday characters, would perhaps make more successful films than *Hamlet* or *King Lear*. *Shakespeare in Love*, interestingly, owes perhaps as much to Elizabethan and Jacobean "city" comedies as it does to Shakespeare's own plays. Shakespeare's comedies are much more "realistic" than his tragedies and romances, which makes it particularly surprising that the comedies have been generally less successful on screen.

Without ascribing to the view of nineteenth-century writers like Charles Lamb and Samuel Taylor Coleridge to the effect that Shakespeare's plays should not be performed at all, that they are "too large" for the stage, one can nevertheless understand the grounds of the argument. Too much specificity can be destructive to Shakespeare, too much detail can bring the drama down to earth. It could even be argued that modern-dress productions of Shakespeare are preferable to those where setting and costume are in accord with what the director believes to be "accurate" period style. Shakespeare's imagination was fundamentally contemporary. Setting *A Midsummer Night's Dream* in some version of ancient Greece is not faithful to Shakespeare. As in the paintings of Veronese or Titian, in Shakespeare's theater all times look like the present time. With place, too, specificity can be counterproductive. Kenneth Branagh's idea of placing the action of *Much Ado about Nothing* in a country estate in Tuscany makes nonsense of the play's geography and complex social structure. We are encouraged to ask awkward questions. Where does everyone sleep? Where do the comic characters live? What does it mean to "set the watch" at a country house? What is an urban police force doing here? It's not that Shakespeare's geography is precisely imagined or worked out to every detail; on the contrary, Shakespeare was careful not to give us too much. We don't want or need to know precisely where Hero's chamber is or where Don Pedro and Don John would have to be standing to see something—but not too much—of what goes on at her window (and whatever they think they see, it should not be Barachio humping Hero on the window sill). Here tact is required, but tact is hardly what Branagh wishes to provide.

A satisfying film adaptation of Shakespeare constructs some sort of stylization and artificiality to match Shakespeare's own sense of style. This does not mean that a precisely delineated mise-en-scène won't work. One reason so many viewers have praised Kurosawa's *Throne of Blood* (1957) as a true Shakespeare adaptation is that his detailed, textured evocation of feudal Japan is itself highly stylized, from the Noh grimaces of Mifune's "Macbeth" to the geometric patterns and balanced compositions that inhabit nearly every one of the film's shots and framings. Fundamentally, *Throne* is not really an adaptation of *Macbeth* at all but rather an imaginative reconfiguration of Shakespeare's themes, motifs, and even language analogical to, but very different from, the text of the play. Much the same could be said of Orson Welles's *Macbeth*, even though Welles has his thanes speak with Scottish accents. In practice, the accents do not have the effect, as they might in another film, of positioning us in eleventh-century Scotland. The film's overall mise-en-scène is so relatively unrealistic, so unlike anybody's idea of Scotland, that the Scottish burr is little more than a residual effect, a gesture in the direction of saying "this is, or ought to be, the Scottish play you have all heard about."

"The Great Globe Itself": Filming Shakespeare's Theater in *Henry V* (1944) and *Shakespeare in Love* (1998)

One way to incorporate Shakespeare's theater into film is to go back to the moment of creation, to the Elizabethan world where Shakespeare made his plays. Both Laurence Olivier's *Henry V* and John Madden's *Shakespeare in Love* are films about Shakespeare's theater as well as Shakespeare films, and both strive at once to educate and to entertain. Much like contemporary Shakespeare projects of various kinds—the restored Globe; the Stratford, U.K.; and the Stratford, Canada, festivals—both films can be seen as instances of what Dennis Kennedy calls "cultural tourism" and "edutainment,"[3] except that instead of traveling in space, the cinema cultural tourist travels in time. *Shakespeare in Love* most obviously partakes of the tourist

The "Electronovison" *Hamlet*

Perhaps the closest approximation we have to re-creating a stage performance on film is the John Gielgud/Richard Burton "Electronovision" *Hamlet* (1964), captured on videotape and then "kinescoped" for theatrical
exhibition during actual performances at New York's Lunt-Fontanne Theater in front of a live audience. Watching this "film," we see something
very similar to what the theater audience saw (though from multiple points
of view, given that as many as seven videocameras were used). The finished
production, which involved the transfer of video to film, however, combines moments from three different performances of the play. Canned theater? Yes and no. The immediacy as well as the special artificiality of the
stage production is indicated in numerous ways throughout. At the same
time the viewer is conscious of the recording apparatus, and the different
expectation of a film versus a theater audience is also made manifest. The
1964 stage audience is "in" the film along with the actors, its presence
heard if not seen, applauding, chatting, rustling programs, and coughing,
and that audience is resolutely not us. An audience, taken for granted,
perhaps not even noticed, when we are part of it becomes another element
in the production when we are watching the film. For example, the
entrance of Richard Burton, the star actor, is the occasion of a special sus-
tained round of applause, but what was undeniably a theatrical (perhaps
more specifically a *Broadway*) moment seems merely peculiar, indeed
slightly ludicrous, on film. From a purely logical point of view, it is unac-
ceptable even in the theater: Hamlet, however the scene is staged, should
be an isolated, alienated, perhaps even invisible figure at the beginning of
1.2—not the cynosure of all eyes, and not the object of adulation of any
possible audience. The moment is particularly odd because the audience
on stage is difficult to distinguish from the audience in the theater seats,
watching the play. We are tempted to ask, Just who is applauding Hamlet?
This is especially so since the entrances of Hume Cronyn as Polonius and
of Alfred Drake and Eileen Herlie as Claudius and Gertrude have also been
greeted with somewhat less enthusiastic applause. This audience may
know who the star is, but it does not seem to know that the king should
get the biggest hand. At this moment, rather than being brought closer to
the theatrical experience we are taken further away from it.[4]

experience, serving as a good advertisement for the newly "restored" Globe Theatre that opened for business on the Bankside not long before the film went into production. Both films, like the new Globe itself, take an archeological approach to Shakespeare and the Elizabethan theatrical world. Though neither film concerns itself primarily with historical accuracy, *Henry V* and *Shakespeare in Love*, albeit in different ways, negotiate the distance between the past of Shakespeare's theater and the present that is the cinema. Both films—and this could be said of other Shakespeare films as well (in particular, the Loncraine/McKellen *Richard III* and Branagh's *Hamlet*)—can be seen as obliquely related to the so-called heritage film genre (*Henry V* retrospectively), films from the late 1980s and 1990s whose setting (sometimes in and around "stately homes of England") and style are thought to support an essentially conservative agenda. True heritage films, however, capture aspects of the British Empire at its height in the late Victorian and Edwardian eras, whereas *Henry V* and *Shakespeare in Love* allude to the more modest achievements of a late-medieval and Renaissance British past.

Even viewed more than fifty years after its initial release, *Henry V*, perhaps the most accomplished and certainly one of the most ambitious British films to that time, remains a bold, courageous experiment, one that looks back to silent films with its obvious cardboard sets, forced perspective, and expressionist performance styles, at the same time that it looks forward to the postmodern, the cinema of, for example, Baz Luhrmann's *Moulin Rouge* (2001). As a dissertation on the relationship between theater and film, however, *Henry V* cannot be said to be entirely coherent. Although a number of commentators have described the film's structure as resembling a series of Chinese boxes, in practice matters are not so neat. True, the film is bookended by scenes presented at the Globe Theatre in 1600. These "theater" scenes, interestingly, are among the most "cinematic" in the film, in the sense that they aim at a documentary-like re-creation of Shakespeare's stage in a manner that resembles the studio-bound, historic films familiar both in British cinema and in Hollywood.

From the outset, however, Olivier cheats. Rather than show us actors who are performing Shakespeare, he shows us performers who are identical to the characters they embody. The archbishop of Canterbury and the bishop of Ely are twins to the actors who play them, since their behavior onstage duplicates their behavior offstage, Canterbury fussy and judgmental, Ely at once obsequious and rebellious. (One might almost think, for a moment, that these are "method" actors who remain "in character" offstage.) Even the low comedy scenes, which are presented as part music hall turns, compete with raucous audience commentary, are already "cinematic" in a peculiar way. The continuity of the performances is not really affected by the audience reaction; the laughter is clearly extraneous, meant, as are television laugh tracks, to reassure the viewer that the material is really funny. As Olivier was clearly aware, the scenes with Pistol, Nym, and Bardolph verge on tedium even if one "gets" the jokes; unfortunately, the pretense that the scene is funny is not convincing. Only Olivier, in his first scene, appears to be playing both the actor who impersonates the king and the king himself, which is evident from the nervous, diffident offstage cough that precedes his entrance, as well as the way he "plays" to both an offstage and an onstage audience, an audience both in the play and witnessing the play that appreciates both the king and the actor.

The primary effect of Olivier's effort to bring together a variety of styles for *Henry V* is that the film has no style at all; the style is in the search. It has always seemed odd that French film critic André Bazin, a champion of cinematic realism, should have considered *Henry V* as a "realistic" film, but the surprise comes in part from the fact that Bazin's view of what constituted realism has been frequently misrepresented, as have the stylizations of Olivier's film.[5] Olivier created a narrative line far more tidy than Shakespeare's, though he could not entirely avoid the episodic, pageantlike structure of his original. To a greater extent than in Shakespeare's play, Olivier's film is completely innocent of temporal cohesion, and we can never be quite sure of where we are in space or in time. Shakespeare made the victory over the French and the subsequent wooing and wedding of Henry and Princess Katharine into a continuous action, thereby compressing a good deal of time and space. Olivier's film, however, begins to seem actually surreal by the final sequences.

Olivier does not move simply from one style, and one world, to another. Rather, the various styles intertwine throughout. So the "documentary" on Elizabethan theater segues to the medieval painting mode for Southampton. But the next scene, at the Boar's Head tavern, is no longer set at the Globe Theatre but is presented with a stylized, cinematic realism, with a three-dimensional set for the tavern and a female actor—Freda Jackson—as the hostess. The stylistic cue here comes from Dutch genre painting. The costuming, almost imperceptibly, has changed—no longer pseudo-Elizabethan, as in the Globe scenes, but now pseudomedieval. The acting is less broad, and the audience has disappeared from both the visual and the sound tracks. The "cinematic" tone is firmly established with Freda Jackson's fine, low-key description of Falstaff's death. We are hardly prepared, by this point, for the

This is a pop-up book *Henry V*—almost a child's vision of the Middle Ages. Copyright © 1945 United Artists Corp.

view of the French court that follows. As with the earlier Southampton scene, we are back to the world of medieval illustrative art, with an added element of children's toy theater: all bright, primary colors and awkward—by Renaissance standards—perspective. And so it goes throughout, as we pulse among a variety of styles and modes. When, in the Agincourt sequences, we can expect the highest degree of cinematic realism, Olivier lines up the French lords on the crest of a hill, all facing "front," in a decidedly theatrical manner. The French, in a sense, carry their stylization with them, even into battle.[6]

Henry V may be as much a film about the struggle to adapt Shakespeare to the screen as it is an adaptation of Shakespeare's play.[7] Far from presenting a solution, Olivier chose to film the problem. For all of the loving care taken to show us a rough facsimile of a sixteenth-century production of *Henry V* at the Globe, the conceit wears thin even before Olivier leaves it behind. The "second" style, involving stylized sets, medieval costumes, and a camera that interacts with the actors and the scenery, results in a kind of prettified expressionism, with sets and props partly painted in two dimensions and partly built in three dimensions. This is a pop-up book *Henry V*, almost a child's vision of the Middle Ages. Before the Battle of Agincourt, the style becomes "Hollywood realism"—movie sets, substantial and convincing, out-door scenes both "realistic" and clearly filmed on a soundstage. These scenes—the three common soldiers and the king, for example—are perfectly congruent with 1940s studio style. For the Battle of Agincourt, Olivier changes style once again, to the outdoor, Technicolor epic or western, a style that, even in Hollywood, doesn't come into its own until after the war. The "realism" of the battle sequence can be seen as the apotheosis of what began as "canned" theater, film realized and transcending the stage. Looked at from another angle, however, the Globe scenes are perhaps the most cinematically realistic. Olivier is not here recording a stage production; rather, he is making a pseudodocumentary on the Elizabethan theater. The Battle of Agincourt, on the other hand, is highly stylized, from its neo-Eisensteinian tracking shots, à la *Alexander Nevsky*, its ultrabright Technicolor tonalities, its animated flights of arrows, and its rousing musical score by William Walton. By contrast, the muted browns and yellows of the early scenes at the Globe give at least the appearance of real life, if we keep in mind that realism is a convention like any other. Olivier reserves the "middle style" for the French scenes, and the *Très Riches Heures* illuminated-manuscript look is in part what makes the French appear so silly and inconsequential. Forced as they are to sit on oddly angled stools in front of precariously positioned tables, they are creatures from a fairy-tale world, clearly unable to cope with the stern martial threats of their English opponents.

In mixing styles, periods, and levels of mimesis, *Henry V* evokes a number of distinctive genres: it is at once a faux documentary of the Elizabethan theater, a medieval pageant, and an action adventure in the Hollywood mode. Some of this eclecticism is governed by the dynamic of Shakespeare's original. *Henry V* is in some ways more a pageant than a play, a double-edged celebration of England's military past that nevertheless manages to construct a powerful critique of the costs of jingoism and war. In Norman Rabkin's useful formulation, *Henry V* is a "rabbit/duck": looked at one way, it glorifies England's heroic traditions, but, observed from a slightly different angle, it offers a scathing condemnation of militarism.[8] The various and variegated scenes flow with sufficient swiftness to prevent the dominance of a single viewpoint. Made in wartime, with moral and logistical support from the government, Olivier's *Henry V* necessarily attends to the "rabbit" of patriotism and glory and downplays the potentially defeatist "duck." The exposure of the traitors at Southampton, the savage threat Henry offers the citizens of Harfleur, Henry's order to kill the prisoners, and the hanging of Bardolph, among other incidents, have all been cut or seriously modified.

The French in this film are presented as perhaps even more foolish than Shakespeare presents them, though Leo Genn, as the constable, projects a dry, sardonic, appealing wit that to some extent blunts the force of the ridicule. Raymond Durgnat has complained that Olivier's *Henry V* presents at best a "shaky parallel to historical events,"[9] given that the French were not England's enemy. The collaborationist Vichy regime of France, however, could certainly be seen as opposing an English invasion. Although based on a stage tradition (and some historical evidence) going back to at least the mid–nineteenth century, the portrayal of the French king Charles V as senile could be read as an allusion to the eighty-year-old Marshal Pétain, head of the Vichy government, who was widely thought, outside of France, not to be in full control of his faculties. Though both France and England were victims of German aggression, the two countries were neither friends nor allies after June 1940—each blamed the other for France's defeat. As in Shakespeare's day, England and France were "friendly enemies," and a plan by England to invade France, for Henry as well as for Churchill, could be dressed up as a desire to rescue her from wrongful imprisonment.

It is a mistake, I think, to assume that Olivier was only thinking of how his film would contribute to the war effort and how analogies to the current geopolitical situation could be maintained. *Henry V* may in the end seem as much an escape from wartime concerns as a commentary on them. Its mixture of realism and whimsy associates it with the Technicolor fantasies Michael Powell (who had directed Olivier in *The 49th Parallel* [1941]) initiated with *The Thief of Baghdad* (1940) and brought to a brilliant synthesis in the postwar years with *The Red Shoes* (1948) and the *Tales of Hoffmann* (1951). The primary aesthetic strategy of the film, to take us back to the medieval world via the medium of the Elizabethan theater, at once removes us from current concerns and generalizes the film's patriotic thrust. The model of Elizabethan London with which the film begins not only introduces us to Shakespeare's England, a golden age, but also reminds its original audience of a time when the skies over London were untroubled and peaceful. In a sense, the focus of propaganda here is Shakespeare himself. The British were more adept at stressing their cultural heritage than they were at constructing a political response to fascism, as even their overt propaganda films attest. *Words for Battle* (narrated by Olivier) and *Listen to Britain*, for example, both made under government auspices, celebrate poetry and music and popular entertainments at the expense of overt attacks on the enemy.

It is when the film is most true to Shakespeare's text that it most powerfully reminds us of current history. The closest point of contact may be the scene of Henry, in disguise, talking with the common soldiers (one of whom Olivier makes a boy), a scene that explicitly delineates the horrors of war. Olivier's direction is straightforward and simple—no music, little camera movement. In a five-minute sequence consisting of only ten shots, Olivier employs close and medium-close shots, presented with basic shot-reverse shot, continuity editing. The acting, in contrast to much of the rest of the film, is fully representational. Olivier and the other actors trust the words to carry the meaning. If the king is, to an extent, "rhetorical," Olivier's delivery pitched slightly higher than that of the other performers, the rhetoric serves deliberately to isolate him from the warmth and camaraderie he cannot truly share. Far from simply making a wartime propaganda film, Olivier was doing a number of different things in *Henry V*. He was honoring Shakespeare and simultaneously promoting himself as the world's premier Shakespearean actor. He attempted to balance theater and film, realism and artifice. He was making a Shakespeare film that at the same time commented on the challenges involved in making a Shakespeare film. In producing an art film aimed at a popular audience, he was promoting both Shakespeare and the British cinema.

Shakespeare in Love too can be seen as an art film that simultaneously functions as a highly commercial crowd pleaser (as of 2001, it had grossed $250 million worldwide "and still counting").[10] John Madden's film, like the restored Globe (itself a notable commercial success)[11] takes the turn-of-the-millennium audience back five hundred years to the beginning of the modern era, a moment when art, entertainment, and commerce became inextricably intertwined into a purely secular mix. *Shakespeare in Love*, of course, does not require its audience to sit on hard benches or, even more of a challenge, to stand in the pit for three-plus hours, as modern-day tourists can and do at the Globe. In editing together moments from rehearsals and a performance of *Romeo and Juliet* with the amorous and entrepreneurial adventures of the film's own characters, the space of first the Rose and then the Curtain Theatres is energized and cut up into acceptable temporal and physical chunks. "Shakespeare" once again becomes a series of purple passages and action sequences, as he had been in nineteenth-century American culture.[12] What we see of Shakespeare on the Tudor stage is further dynamized through editing and camera movement into the more familiar cinematic space to which the spectators are accustomed. Just as the film's Shakespeare does not have to work too hard to compose *Romeo and Juliet*, so the audience does not have to work too hard to absorb it. As Courtney Lehmann remarks, "What gets truly mystified in this film . . . is not love, but labor."[13]

Indeed, another name for the film could be "Shakespeare without Tears." Whereas Shakespeare's *Romeo and Juliet* ends tragically, *Shakespeare in Love* ends sentimentally. There was never any question of a conventional "happy ending" for the film, and not just because the writers did not want to alter history. The "happiest" (or at least the most emotionally satisfying) ending for a love story, as writers, including Shakespeare, have known from time immemorial, brings love to an end even as it reaches its highest pitch. Young lovers should never become old lovers; what we want is a love that cannot die. Will and his writers are explicit about this: "You will never age for me, nor fade, nor die." Love should not require too much work. Particularly popular among male authors is the version where the woman dies and the man lives on to keep his memories of her in amber—think A Farewell to Arms or Love Story. (Less often the man dies or disappears and the woman lives on— see West Side Story, a Romeo and Juliet adaptation and, of course, Titanic, starring Leonard di Caprio; the formula works almost as well either way.) Shakespeare in Love is very much in this tradition, but with a twist: Shakespeare lives on to write his plays and to be reunited, presumably, with his faithful wife, Anne; his true love, Viola de Lesseps, is transformed into "Viola," a fictional character in one of Will's plays.

The creative process is at once painful and painless as Shakespeare in Love imagines it. The way creativity as theme is played with functions both as a source of the film's humor and as a means of at once honoring Shakespeare and cutting him down to size. Indeed, the film is in general ingeniously designed to appeal to a variety of audiences, to both flatter the susceptibilities of those for whom "art" is pretty much a bore as well as the more or less "academic" or "educated" audience, the teachers and students who can recognize the allusions to Elizabethan theater and sixteenth-century culture. Every high school graduate has read, or at least been exposed to, Romeo and Juliet. Ninth graders everywhere can expect to see both its original theatrical release and its subsidiary form on video. But even viewers unfamiliar with Shakespeare appreciate the manner in which the transformation of "Romeo and Ethel the Pirate's Daughter" ("good title," the banker, Fennyman, remarks) into Romeo and Juliet serves to define the nature of artistic "inspiration." A play like Romeo and Juliet evolves through stages in the poet's mind as the original "pitch" idea ("there's this pirate") magically ("it's a mystery") turns into art that is also profitable entertainment. The joke, of course, is that Romeo and Juliet could never have been named anything very different from what it is, since Shakespeare borrowed his plot and characters from a poem, The Tragical Historye of Romeus and Juliet (1562), that was itself based on earlier versions of the same well-known and popular story. Like many a joke in the film, this one both asserts and occludes the communal nature of early modern writing practices. It may also occlude the extent to which

Shakespeare in Love itself "borrows" significantly from other treatments of the subject, including the Caryl Brahms and S. J. Simon novel *No Bed for Bacon* and the play *William Shakespeare* by Clemence Dane.

Shakespeare in Love can be (and has been) devalued for its "lowbrow" treatment of Shakespeare and the Shakespearean text. But this ignores the extent to which the film attempts to answer the hard question any film dealing with Shakespeare's life and work must confront: How do you make the work of a writer dead for four hundred years seem relevant to present-day audiences? One answer, of course, is that you do not need to. Shakespeare remains relevant to us today; indeed, that is precisely what makes Shakespeare Shakespeare. The circular argument, needless to say, begs a lot of questions. The strategy is always to bring Shakespeare to us, not to take us back to Shakespeare. Or, as *Shakespeare in Love* demonstrates, to take us back to Shakespeare by bringing Shakespeare to us, to collapse past and present, to deny that there is such a thing as "pastness." "History," from this point of view, is always "now." The publicists knew precisely what the film was up to: "Refreshingly contemporary, *Shakespeare in Love* is ultimately the tale of a man and woman trying to make love work in the 90s—the 1590s."[14] In discussing the characters and situations they have constructed, the participants in *Shakespeare in Love* continuously look for analogies: we hear, on the DVD commentary, that Ned Allyn (the actor played by Ben Affleck) is the Tom Cruise of his day, and that Wessex (Colin Firth) is J. R. (from television's *Dallas*) "with different props."

The film's attitude toward Elizabeth too reflects a bifocal vision. She is at once the wise, beloved Virgin Queen and a funny, frumpy, overly made-up woman in fancy dress. The point is made (all too) explicit in the little speech the "villain" Wessex makes to Viola's nurse: "The Queen, Gloriana Regina, God's chosen Vessel, the Radiant One, who shines her light on us, is at Greenwich today . . . and if we're late for lunch, the old boot will not forgive." The idea that a monarch would be intimately concerned with the love affairs of his or her subjects is a partly historical and partly literary conceit. The historical Elizabeth was indeed involved, for dynastic and financial reasons, with how and when her high-born subjects married, and she was quick to punish secrecy and disobedience. But our Elizabeth goes further, into the world of Shakespearean comedy, where the ruler Theseus, in *A Midsummer Night's Dream*, appears to have no higher responsibility than to investigate the libidos of his courtiers. In the end, as a deus ex machina, Elizabeth is something of a flop—though she can save the theater from disaster, she cannot resolve the romance plot in a satisfactory manner. Viola is already married to Wessex and so cannot marry Shakespeare; even monarchy has its limits.

The opening of *Shakespeare in Love* nicely encapsulates the manner in which past and present, then and now, are continually negotiated throughout the film. We are smoothly transported from the Miramax logo (a stylized view of the Manhattan skyline) to the Universal Studios logo to the initial scene. Though set in 1594, it is introduced to us via a rapid steadicam camera movement and reflects back on those two initial corporate logos. Fennyman the moneylender is torturing Henslowe the producer. After some discussion, Henslowe promises Fennyman a new play by Shakespeare, and then Fennyman balances the costs and gains of putting on a play. "The writer and the actors," he concludes, "can be paid out of the profits." "But," Henslowe responds, "there are no profits." "Exactly," Fennyman answers with obvious satisfaction. To which Henslowe, with unconcealed admiration, can only reply, "I think you have hit on something, Mr. Fennyman." As often in the entertainment culture of advanced capitalism—which, *Shakespeare in Love* wants us to believe, is not so different from the entertainment culture of Elizabethan England—the hand that feeds is not only bitten but also relishes the pain. This is, in one sense, as much a movie about money as it is about Shakespeare.

Writing itself, in this film, is an uneasy mixture of superstition, inspiration, "living life," and simple mechanical labor. The familiar writer-at-work montage sequence for once works convincingly since for an Elizabethan writer, writing is, at a minimum, a visible, mechanical process that involves sharpening pens, dipping quills into ink, and salting paper. For the most part, however, this William Shakespeare lives out the romantic image of the writer who seeks and sometimes is given inspiration from a variety of sources. We see and hear him pick up some of his best lines from the sights and sounds of London life, a populist base for his flights of fancy. One activity Shakespeare does not appear to indulge in, oddly enough, is reading. Although we are told that Shakespeare is just another cog in the "business of show," the film does not want him to be as hardheaded as the historical Shakespeare must have been. Writer's block? The playwright had only to turn to Plutarch or Holinshed or Giraldo Cinthio. That we never see the film's Shakespeare resort to books is certainly curious, since he is perfectly happy to ransack other people's spoken words and verbally expressed ideas. The film generally privileges speech over writing, so much so that Shakespeare seems incapable of writing anything that he has not first either heard or spoken himself. Again, the filmmakers want it both ways. On the one hand, Shakespeare is a hack, stealing ideas right and left, but on the other hand he is a genius who turns the dross of everyday life into immortal poetry.

Furthermore, while the "real" Shakespeare was influenced and inspired by reading other writers, our Will gets his inspiration for the plot and characters of a heterosexual romance directly from his friend, the homosexual poet-playwright, Christopher ("Kit") Marlowe, a crucial if vaguely defined presence in the film. Neither the name of Marlowe nor the name of the avowedly homosexual actor who plays him, Rupert Everett, appears in the credits for the film, and no reference is made to Marlowe's sexual identity. Interestingly, it is almost immediately after his conversation with Marlowe that Will is captivated by a "boy," Tom of Kent. That this boy is in fact a girl, Viola de Lesseps, allows for a variety of comic moments and, perhaps, some coded messages. For those in the know (the *Sonnets* and all that), Shakespeare is allowed a soupçon of same-sex desire; for everyone else, a bit of cross-dressing confusion and farce. Shakespeare presumably is drawn to a lovely boy because he is really a lovely girl—or is the lovely girl attractive to him because she looks like a lovely boy? In any case, it is in the act of chasing a boy ("Romeo") that he finds his Juliet. In the *As You Like It*-style love scenes between Will and "Tom" one may agree, with Richard Burt, that "it is never in doubt that Shakespeare is attracted to the woman underneath the boy . . . when kissed by her/him, he does not realize her/his dual identity, and responds with shock and astonishment."[15] True enough, though I would suggest that Will is more discomfited than shocked and astonished. But what does it mean to be attracted to the woman underneath the boy? That Shakespeare cannot see through Viola's deception is, of course, perfectly in accord with the "impenetrable disguise" convention of his own plays. He is, amusingly enough, fooled by the very theatrical practice he regularly employs. The subtext, however, suggests something else: it is a boy that Shakespeare lusts after, and it is more or less incidental that "he" should turn out to be a "she." Or perhaps Will simply cannot tell the difference. Even the water-taxi driver comments that Viola's disguise "wouldn't fool a child." Most viewers would no doubt agree that "biological sex becomes manifest in this film to assert that true love is always heterosexual,"[16] as one critic has noted, but it is equally manifest that we can find traces of another reading on the margins of the text. On the DVD commentary track, John Madden claims that he would have liked Viola to perform her love scenes with her wig and mustache but had to drop the idea because of "scheduling" problems. One cannot help but wonder, however, if the decision did not have more to do with a fear that a queer reading was becoming too naturalized for all concerned.

Gwyneth Paltrow and Joseph Fiennes in *Shakespeare in Love*. Copyright © CORBIS.

What the film does do, with great skill and panache, is substitute cross-dressing for cross-gender sexual desire. For a modern audience, it is particularly striking and even "educational" to see Juliet played by a boy and Romeo played by a girl. In the *Romeo and Juliet* rehearsal scenes, the film audience is allowed to experience what, in spite of Viola's earlier comment about "pip-squeak boys in petticoats," was an undoubted truth, which is that if the play-acting was sufficiently sincere, the gender of the actor did not really matter. And the cross-dressing—or, better, "cross-speaking"—continues in the bedroom as Will and Viola act out the roles, respectively, of Juliet and Romeo, which allows for the intercutting of these scenes with the rehearsal of the balcony scene from Shakespeare's play at the Rose Theatre. At the same time, of course, the gender confusion adds a certain frisson to the sexual play of the lovers. Will himself literally cross-dresses when he disguises himself as Viola's chaperone. Here, however, the disguise is unconvincing; together with the comically droll performance of Jim Carter/Ralph Bashford as Juliet's nurse, this may be the film's way of suggesting the limits of Elizabethan stage conventions.

The discourse surrounding the film, especially the documentary and the various commentary tracks packaged with the DVD, reveals much about the contradictory (or only paradoxical?) way Shakespeare is constructed for the film. Of particular interest are the comments by screenwriters Marc Norman and Tom Stoppard. *Shakespeare in Love* is the product of serial collaboration, the Brit Stoppard revising the script written by the American Norman. Amusingly enough, Norman and Stoppard, interviewed separately, speak most of the time as if the other did not exist (though Norman tells us that adding Ned Allyn as a character was Stoppard's idea). One would not know from listening to them that Stoppard was a glorified script doctor for Norman. Students of the theater have had little difficulty in finding "obvious signs of Stoppard's hand: eclecticism; conflating a previous era with a modern one; cultural observations about both; verbal wit."[17] It is tempting, though perhaps unfair, to assign all that is best in the script to Stoppard and the rest to Norman (the popular press, much to Norman's irritation, often made that very assumption).[18] Ironically, collaboration is one aspect of Elizabethan writing practice—the simultaneous and/or successive work by two or more individuals on a play—that is most like Hollywood.

Although *Shakespeare in Love* flirts with the idea of collaboration, the screenwriters never quite let go of the Shakespeare-as-lone-genius image. In their DVD commentaries, Norman is the "lowbrow" who brings everything down to his own level. He makes some of the most obvious or most egregiously fatuous comments, indulging enthusiastically in the stale "if Shakespeare were alive today . . ." game. "If Shakespeare were alive today," Norman claims, "he'd have a three-picture deal at Warner Bros., he'd be driving a Porsche, and he'd be living in Bel Air." Just as nineteenth-century schoolmasters thought that Shakespeare must have been a schoolmaster in his youth, so the screenwriter wants to claim Shakespeare as one of his own. In 1593 (when the film is set), Shakespeare, Norman assures us, was "not a magical, mysterious, genius playwright." Rather, "he was broke, he was horny, and he was starved for an idea." On the other hand, Stoppard, commenting on the casting of Joseph Fiennes, says, "His [Fiennes's] face suggests that he wrote the plays—you feel, yes, this man could be a genius." Relishing the film's central paradox, Stoppard comments that "while demystifying Shakespeare, [the script] also revealed the opposite, the deep mystery of Shakespeare." Tom Stoppard is not afraid of the "g" word: he has been called a genius himself. Norman, on the other hand, auteur of *Zandy's Bride* and *Cutthroat Island*, among other films, is in little danger of being tagged with that particular label. Fiennes plays Shakespeare in a manner sufficiently complex to encompass both readings. He gives an intelligent, witty, and spirited performance, but it is also an oddly guarded one. John Madden remarks at one point that Fiennes "has a kind of privateness about him, a slightly hidden quality" (DVD), which may be another way of saying that his performance is narcissistic. We never quite believe that this Shakespeare loves anyone more than he loves himself—even writing is a form of autoeroticism. Fiennes to some extent works against the grain of the script and refuses any play for the audience's sympathy (though both Gwyneth Paltrow and Judi Dench won Oscars for their performance, Fiennes was not even nominated). This is a Shakespeare with a mission—to be Shakespeare. He has his eye fixed throughout on the main chance. He remains unknowable not because he is acting out some proto-Romantic notion of what genius might be, but because at heart he does not want to be known.

The development of the *Shakespeare in Love* screenplay plays itself out in the language of the film. Words spoken "spontaneously" by the characters are eventually transformed, as if by alchemy, into the language of *Romeo and Juliet*. In "real life" Will and Viola speak of the owl and the rooster; in the play, this becomes the nightingale and the lark. Frequently the Norman/Stoppard script provides pseudo-Elizabethan dialogue of astonishing flatness, something the writers are presumably aware of, although one cannot be certain. At times the dialogue verges on the nonsensical, syntactic confusion merging with sheer banality: "If I could write the beauty of her eyes," Will says to "Thomas," "I was born to look in them and know myself" (the first phrase is from Sonnet 17, the second is a non sequitur); or "love denied blights the soul we owe to God." What is the point of this, if not to flatter the audience's suspicion that Shakespeare's language itself is, at some level, nonsense, fancy words that do not really mean very much? At other moments, the writing is just silly. "For sixpence a line," Will tells his "shrink," "I could cause a riot in a nunnery." "Pay attention," Ned Allyn (Ben Affleck) tells Fennyman, "and you will see how genius creates a legend." Even for pastiche, this is all pretty bad. Assuming the badness is deliberate, the point may be to suggest how difficult it is to write like Shakespeare. Which points to a different joke: writing (and talking) like Shakespeare is something Shakespeare himself has a hard time with. In the end, the film wants to both value poetry and devalue it. Even the jokes, like Henslowe's injunction, "Speak prose," marry the philistinism of the man of business with the audience's own presumed impatience with fancy words. When push comes to shove, Viola is moved to say, "I love you, Will, beyond poetry." Sex, as Viola also reveals, is better than plays, as love is truer than poetry. And yet the emotional high point of *Shakespeare in Love* is the historical reconstruction of the first performance of *Romeo and Juliet*, which, convincingly staged as it might have been in Shakespeare's theater, becomes an unambiguous celebration of art over mere life.

Shakespeare Is in the Details

One way to think about Shakespeare films would be to ask what an "ideal" cinematic adaptation would be like, basing the construct on the cumulative weight of the critical unhappiness expressed with reference to nearly all Shakespeare films. A purist would probably argue that no film is ideal. But let me, for the sake of argument, suggest possibilities. An ideal Shakespeare adaptation, some would argue, would be "definitive." What this would mean, presumably, is that it would eschew interpretation. The text, preferably complete but in any case as full as possible, would be simply "represented"—no directorial interference, no quirks, no flourishes, no "updatings." The film would be transcendent, an illustrated, enacted fulfillment of Shakespeare's intentions. All of the roles would be ideally cast by experienced Shakespearean actors whose only allegiance is to the text. This text would be delivered with such clarity and precision as to be fully understandable; no lines would be lost, nor would any words be thrown away. The costumes and settings would be true to the time and place in which the play is set (having the actors wear Elizabethan costumes while doing *Julius Caesar* would, presumably, be the "wrong" kind of fidelity). There would be no added scenes or extraneous matter of any kind, no transpositions, no interpolations. An ideal Shakespeare film, from this viewpoint, would be just like a stage performance, but it would not be stagy—no, it would be "cinematic." The director's job would be to retain all of the values of Shakespeare's text while avoiding the imposition of his or her vision on it. The actors would, of course, be British. American actors are incapable of reciting Shakespeare's verse (or prose) properly, and American accents are jarring and intrusive. An ideal Shakespeare film would sustain and uphold the most acceptable and conventional interpretations of the play available and would show no evidence of post–World War II critical theory and scholarship.

If the above is a parody, it is not far from the mark. It does not take an awareness of postmodern critical discourse to see that difficulties abound in my scenario, however. How comforting it would be to hold on to the notion of the text thus revealed—if we had a text to be faithful to. How easy it would be to be cinematic, if we only knew what cinematic actually was! How pleased we would be with our British actors if we knew that the way they speak today was the way they spoke in 1600. How convenient it would be to know that Shakespeare wanted Caesar and Brutus and company to wear togas. Indeed, how wonderful it would be to believe that (1) it was possible to reconstruct Shakespeare's intentions and (2) we still believed in the centrality of intention. Alas, the more we know, the more we are aware of what we cannot know. Even apart from our imperfect knowledge, however, the premises I have outlined have little basis in fact or logic. Why should a film be a definitive interpretation of the text, assuming we even know what definitive could possibly mean? Why could a film not be received as simply another performance of the play? Here, of course, the assumption has much to do with the idea that celluloid is somehow permanent, a record that will always be with us, unlike a stage production that disappears forever after the closing-night performance. But if a film were to be definitive, there would be no need for another film version. And maybe this is what lies behind the wish for a definitive film—a desire to shut down the process. Which takes us back, however circuitously, to Coleridge and Lamb and the antitheatrical prejudice: better to be able to act out the play in our imagination than to give it material form, a form that must always fall short of our idealization.

Rather than search vainly for that elusive ideal Shakespeare film, we can comfort ourselves with the thought that every production of a Shakespeare play holds the promise of a revelation, even if this revelation is a highly localized effect. The interpretation of one scene, one role, the staging of a particular action, a gesture at the right or wrong moment: each of these points to new possibilities, new insights, or at least an unexpected pleasure, a "frisson." Even if a single moment, a lone performance, is all that is memorable from a given production, we can add that moment to the ideal Shakespeare production of the mind, to the "dream team" film we will never see but can at least imagine. In almost any Shakespeare film, performer and imagery will come together, if only briefly, in a particularly felicitous manner: the perfect conjunction of light and shadow, texture, framing, and decoration that, together with the spoken word, distills the entire mood and feel of a film. Laurence Olivier, as Hamlet, tells the players to "Speak the speech." Dramatically this is not a climactic or even an essential moment in Shakespeare's play, but it is made mysterious and essential by Olivier's camera. A torch, velvet darkness, silver hair, the ascending and quickly descending tones of Olivier's delivery wedding for a moment advice on acting with advice on feeling, being, living, positing moderation, balance, and decorum in the face of chaos, treachery, and violent death. An unexpected revelation, a moment of stillness and calm in the midst of otherwise restless camera movements snaking through the labyrinthine ways of Elsinore—the gift to be simple. What the reproductive technologies of film and video allow us to do, at least in the imagination, is create the idealized Shakespeare performance from the material evidence at our disposal.

A spectacularly cinematic imagination may not be essential to a Shakespeare film, as heretical as that may sound. Tony Richardson, in re-creating his Roundhouse Theatre *Hamlet* (1969) in cinematic close-up, gives us something like the experience of the stage production with little that is truly

Constructing Ophelia

Helena Bonham Carter, with her round, pale face and large black eyes, her modest sensuality, and the honesty and courage of her mad scenes, gives us the beginnings of an ideal Ophelia in the otherwise undistinguished Zeffirelli *Hamlet*. Bonham Carter's achievement is particularly impressive given that Ophelia is a difficult, unrewarding role. The mad scenes are too often annoying when they should be moving, and if the actress playing Ophelia has not made an impression and won us over in the early scenes, we cannot be expected to care very much about her when she goes mad. We might prefer that Grigori Kosintsev, who filmed *Hamlet* in 1964, rather than Zeffirelli, stage her scenes and costume her (not that there is anything wrong with Anastasia Vertinskaya, Kosintsev's own film Ophelia, but she speaks only in Russian, Boris Pasternak rather than Shakespeare). Thus Bonham Carter, wearing Vertinskaya's veil, trapped by Kosintsev's Kafka-esque castle, her madness scored by Shostakovich—that would be an Ophelia indeed. And while we are at it, we might like for her Hamlet, spoken in English, to be Maximilian Schell (who starred in a 1960 German adaptation)—intense, intellectual, harsh, genuine, cruel—rather than either Mel Gibson or Kosintsev's Innokenti Smoktounovski. And so we build our ideal context for Ophelia, moment by moment, piece by piece. And, because of film and videotape, the pieces are all there, always available for our creative rearrangement.

imaginative in the filming. The direction is functional, the framings straightforward; it is, by any measure, a genuine film. But, for better and for worse, almost everything in it depends on the players and on the fact that the dynamics of the production had already been worked out onstage. Some films are created in the process of filming and editing, some, as in this instance, are made largely in the planning. This is not to say that a successful staging of a Shakespeare play can be transferred to film with minimal effort or intelligence. The Stuart Burge–directed *Othello* (1965) indicates that this is not so. Nearly every critic who saw both the film and the stage production believed the former to be inferior to the latter. But this is not necessarily a matter of the film not being cinematic enough; it is more a matter of the filmmaker having failed to capture the theatricality of the original production.

The manner in which Olivier's *Henry V* and *Shakespeare in Love* foreground the relationship between Shakespeare's theater and the modern cinema makes concrete and explicit an effect implicit in any Shakespeare film. No matter how hard the filmmaker strives to naturalize the relationship between Shakespeare and film, what may finally be most compelling are the traces of the encounter that remain in the final text. Commenting on Orson Welles's *Macbeth*, Charles Eckart observes that Welles's film "has served as . . . a touchstone to discriminate the cineaste from the Bardolater."[19] The either/ or implied here, however, not only reflects something like reverse snobbism, whereby theater becomes devalued with relationship to film, but in no way accurately describes Welles's practice. Certainly, if a filmmaker produces something called *Macbeth*, the filmgoer, Bardolator or not, is justified in expecting a film that is, in one way or another, related to a play of that name by William Shakespeare. "Bardolatry" is not the issue here. Most people with a knowledge of or an interest in Shakespeare's plays know that any production of Shakespeare will in some way be at variance with his or her preconception of the play in question. What such a viewer looks for, or at least hopes to find, in any production is a revivification of Shakespeare's text that will in some way illuminate the issues, characters, themes, and theatrical energies of the original. The cineaste who has no concern for such things is, presumably, a blank slate, with no cultural memory or interest beyond the cinema, a poor judge of any film. The Shakespeare film in its many and varied manifestations requires its viewers to have at least as much fascination with and enthusiasm for Shakespeare and for the theater as exhibited, throughout his life, by Orson Welles himself.

Notes

1. As Kenneth Rothwell notes in his indispensable history of the Shakespeare film, the effect, which "identifies the film with the grandest Shakespearean stage traditions," unfortunately falls short of the intention. See *Shakespeare on Screen: A Century of Film and Television* (Cambridge: Cambridge University Press, 1999), 126.

2. Terence R. Griffiths, ed., *Shakespeare in Production: A Midsummer Night's Dream* (Cambridge: Cambridge University Press, 1996), 64.

3. Douglas Kennedy, "Shakespeare and Cultural Tourism," *Theatre Journal* 50 (1998): 175–88, passim.

4. For a discussion of Electronovision and how it was used for the Burton *Hamlet*, see Leonard J. Leff, "Instant Movies: The Short Unhappy Life of William Sargent's Electronovision," *Journal of Popular Film and Television* 8, no. 1 (1980): 19–29.

5. See Bazin's discussion of *Henry V* in "Theater and Cinema—Part I," in *What Is Cinema?* ed. and trans. Hugh Gray (Berkeley: University of California Press, 1967), 1: 76–94.

6. Dudley Andrew provides a subtle analysis of the film's various styles in *Film in the Aura of Art* (Princeton: Princeton University Press, 1984), 131–51.

7. For a useful account of the film's production, see Harry M. Geduld, *Filmguide to Henry V* (Bloomington: Indiana University Press, 1973). The screenplay is available in the Classic Film Script series: *Henry V* (London: Lorrimer, 1984).

8. See Norman Rabkin, "Rabbits, Ducks, and Henry V," *Shakespeare Quarterly* (Summer 1977): 279–96. See also Sara Munson Deats, "Rabbits and Ducks: Olivier, Branagh, and *Henry V*," *Literature/Film Quarterly* 20 (1992): 284–93.

9. Raymond Durgnat, *A Mirror for England: British Movies from Austerity to Affluence* (New York: Praeger, 1971), 109.

10. *Shakespeare in Love*, DVD, Miramax, 2000.

11. The Globe was voted the top tourist attraction in Europe by an organization of travel journalists (Kennedy, "Cultural Tourism," 182).

12. See Lawrence W. Levine, *Highbrow/Lowbrow: The Emergence of Cultural Hierarchy in America* (Cambridge: Harvard University Press, 1988); and William Uricchio and Roberta E. Pearson, *Reframing Culture: The Case of the Vitagraph Quality Films* (Princeton: Princeton University Press, 1993).

13. Courtney Lehmann, "*Shakespeare in Love*: Romancing the Author, Mastering the Body," in *Spectacular Shakespeare: Critical Theory and Popular Cinema*, ed. Courtney Lehmann and Lisa S. Starks (Madison, N.J.: Fairleigh Dickinson University Press, 2002), 125–45; 134.

14. *Shakespeare in Love Pressbook*, Margaret Herrick Library (n.p.; n.d.).

15. Richard Burt, "*Shakespeare in Love* and the End of the Shakespearean: Academic and Mass Culture Constructions of Literary Authorship," in *Shakespeare, Film, Fin de Siecle*, ed. Marc Thornton Burnett and Ramona Wray (New York: St. Martin's, 2000), 203–31; 214.

16. Sujata Iyengar, "Shakespeare in Heterolove," *Literature/Film Quarterly* 29, no. 2 (2001): 122–27; 123.

17. Jill Levinson, "Stoppard's Shakespeare: Textual Revisions," in *The Cambridge Companion to Tom Stoppard*, ed. Katherine E. Kelly (Cambridge: Cambridge University Press, 2001), 154–70; 168.

18. Writing in *Variety*, for example, Adam Dawtrey and Monica Roman reported that Stoppard "substantially overhauled" Norman's script ("'Love' Triangle Times 3," *Variety*, March 23, 1999, *Shakespeare in Love* clipping file, Margaret Herrick Library). Such comments led Norman to respond in *Hollywood Reporter* that "Stoppard did what we call a dialogue polish," though he acknowledges that "he added some important ideas" (Dana Harris, "Much Ado about Nothing?" *Hollywood Reporter*, February 11, 1999, *Shakespeare in Love* clipping file, Margaret Herrick Library).

19. Charles Eckert, ed., *Focus on Shakespearean Films* (Englewood Cliffs, N.J.: Prentice-Hall, 1972), 3.

CHAPTER THREE

The Challenges of *Romeo and Juliet*

On February 21, 1954, CBS Television's *You Are There* took its viewers back to "December 26, 1594: The First Command Performance of *Romeo and Juliet*." This episode, like others in this popular middlebrow series, was structured to resemble a news special, complete with reporters and on-the-scene interviews. Like the series as a whole, it claimed to be solidly founded on the historical record. An informed viewer, however, would have discovered that "all things" on this particular evening were not quite "as they were then," series anchor Walter Cronkite to the contrary. Theater historians would have been intrigued to discover that, among other interesting details, a Globe-like thrust stage had been constructed at court for the players; presumably someone involved with the production wanted television viewers to experience an "authentic" open-air Elizabethan theatrical performance even if, in this instance, it was taking place indoors. William Shakespeare very likely did not, as he does here, play Mercutio in *Romeo and Juliet*. Although scholars differ on this point, it seems reasonable to assume that Richard Burbage, the "star" of Shakespeare's company, if he had the actor's instinct and the actor's ego we can be reasonably certain he had, would (given the choice) have opted to play Mercutio, not, as he does on this occasion, the less colorful and less flamboyant Romeo. Although the work of the various *You Are There* writers continues to be praised for its "accurate portrayals of historical events,"[1] history, in this particular episode, was replaced almost entirely by speculation. At least we don't have Queen Elizabeth coming to the Globe to see a play, as she does in *Shakespeare in Love*: Shakespeare quite properly goes to her. She appears to find in Shakespeare's romantic tragedy analogies to her own emotional life, much as Judy Dench's Elizabeth discovers in the later film that love can indeed be spoken of truly in a play.

Among the more peculiar aspects of "the first command performance of *Romeo and Juliet*" is that the dramatized incident never happened. It is possible that *Romeo and Juliet* was presented at court for Elizabeth, but no trace of any such performance exists. The teleplay writer—blacklist victim Abraham Polonsky, writing under an assumed name—went out of his way to dramatize a nonevent even though history could have provided him with specific dates on which one or another Shakespeare play was presented at court. *Shakespeare in Love* engages in the analogous fiction of reconstructing the very first performance of *Romeo and Juliet* at the Rose Theatre in 1593, an event for which there is an equal absence of evidence; we have no record of any performance of the play before 1598. In both instances, the writers simply wanted to construct their narratives around Shakespeare's famous tragedy of young love, no matter how inconvenient in terms of history or even legend such a choice might be. This is hardly surprising, given that *Romeo and Juliet*, of all Shakespeare's plays, is one of the most frequently performed and most often filmed. It is the most likely to be rewritten, transformed, parodied, bowdlerized, or burlesqued. Perhaps only after *Hamlet*, it may be the play that means "Shakespeare" to most people. In popular culture in particular, *Romeo and Juliet* is a kind of shorthand for Shakespeare and for love tragedy in general. When Orson Welles appeared on *I Love Lucy*, Lucy wanted to be Juliet to his Romeo. When Andy Griffith's hick comic persona went to the theater, he told of his experience in "What It Was, Was *Romeo and Juliet*." Two of the most popular Shakespeare films of all time are Franco Zeffirelli's and Baz Luhrmann's adaptations of *Romeo and Juliet*, and *Shakespeare in Love* is built around the writing and performance of the play. And then there are the jokes ("O Romeo, Romeo, wherefore art thou, Romeo?"—"Down in the bushes, the damn ladder broke"). In addition to the twenty-plus *Romeo and Juliet* films from the silent era noted by Robert Hamilton Ball ("What would filmmakers have done without *Romeo and Juliet*?"),[2] we have such parodies and imitations as *Juliet and Her Romeo*, *Doubling for Romeo* (with satirist Will Rogers), *Romeo and Juliet* (a Mack Sennett version with cross-eyed comedian Ben Turpin), *Romeo Turns Bandit*, and so on. In some of these early films, as in later ones, *Romeo and Juliet* is the play within the film, as in Edison's *Bumptious as Romeo*. "The climax," according to Ball's source (the film is lost), "comes in a balcony scene where the entire palazzo collapses on the unfortunate actor."[3]

What is it about *Romeo and Juliet* that lays it open to such treatment? One answer might be that the story Shakespeare tells is already a comedy on which a tragic denouement has been more or less arbitrarily imposed. At some point, we are supposed to stop laughing and start crying, but where exactly is that point? There is something inherently ridiculous about adolescent passion, both to the young when they can look outside of themselves and to everyone else. Shakespeare was aware of this, which is why he created Mercutio, the cynic within the play who channels our impulse to ridicule. The play's tragic ending is on one level ridiculously avoidable. However much *Romeo and Juliet* may be seen as a highly valued cultural object, the fact remains that it has, in the words of Stanley Wells, "undergone adaptation, sometimes slight, sometimes substantial, in ways that are implicitly critical of the original."⁴ The impulse to burlesque *Romeo and Juliet*, moreover, may also stem from male anxiety about something so unmasculine as romantic love, especially when carried to a tragic conclusion. Parody and burlesque in this light become defense mechanisms against the poetic rendering of love and death that makes the play both a popular favorite and something of an embarrassment.

That *Romeo and Juliet* is so open to parody suggests that it contains elements that detract from, or fail to easily fit into, its ostensibly tragic purpose, which may explain why the play is seldom performed as written. Nearly every significant production of *Romeo and Juliet* involves a "discovery" of the play's true meaning, a fresh reinterpretation, a never-before-thought-of insight. The discovery, however, is always the same one: the play is "really" about youth and passion, something intuited the first time, evidently, by Franco Zeffirelli in 1960, when he staged his Old Vic production: "not the Victorian interpretation that still dominated the English stage . . . but something truly Mediterranean: . . . sunlight on a fountain, wine and olives and garlic. New, different, real, young."⁵ Or was it Peter Brook who discovered it in 1947? Or John Gielgud in 1935? Or perhaps it was Guthrie McClintic in 1933, who asked Jo Milzener to redesign an unsatisfactory production starring his wife, Katharine Cornell: "I told him of my newly conceived idea of decor: light, gay; hot sun, hot passions; young, swift; . . . lightning-quick changes."⁶ McClintic also discovered that Juliet's age was to be fourteen rather than eighteen, as Cornell had been playing it (not a problem, evidently, for the thirty-plus-year-old actress). And here is Kenneth Branagh, describing his approach for a 1986 staging: "I wanted as young a production as possible [and to create] the effect of fate *rushing* the lives of these young people to their tragic ends."⁷

Carrying these insights into practice and making Shakespeare's play "acceptable" to a contemporary audience, filmmakers tend to disguise, gloss over, or repress everything in the original play that that audience might find off-putting. As director Baz Lurhmann states it, the question that a Shake-speare film needs to ask of its audience is, "Do you accept the revelation of the human condition that Shakespeare achieved 400 years ago can be relevant and be freed again today?"[8] The answer is probably no. There are many ways Shakespeare is not one of us (many ways in which he was already not "one of us" by, say, 1750). In his aptly titled essay "The Challenges of *Romeo and Juliet*," Stanley Wells addresses the perceived problematics of Shakespeare's play: "The history of critical and theatrical reactions to the play demonstrates the fact that Shakespeare worked in a far more literary mode than has been fashionable in the theatre of later ages, and that its literariness has often been regarded as a theatrical handicap."[9] Wells identifies the type of material often cut—long speeches that recapitulate what the audience has already seen, "intellectualism" as expressed in complex wordplay, and passages of "false emotion." After detailing the extent to which the play has been "adapted" both in the theater and on film and television, Wells concludes that the "the script can be interpreted in all of its richness and diversity only if we abandon the idea that because it is called a tragedy it must centre on the fate of individuals, and accept its emphasis on the multifarious society in which these individuals have their being."[10]

Each major film version of *Romeo and Juliet* adopts one or more generic identities, including the Hollywood costume epic (MGM's 1936 version) on one end of a spectrum and neorealism on the other (Castellani and to a lesser extent Zeffirelli). Both Zeffirelli (1968) and Luhrmann (1996) draw on their expertise in opera (Zeffirelli has made two opera films, *La Traviata* [1982] and *Otello* [1987]) for style, emotional resonance, and tonal color. If we think of a genre as a series of texts whose interest in part lies in the similarities and differences among them, the *Romeo and Juliet* film can be considered a sub-genre of the Shakespeare film, each version commenting on an earlier one, each working against the flow of the original play to draw on Shakespeare's construction of scenes and moments that virtually demand comparative treatment: the Capulet ball, the balcony scene, Juliet drinks the potion, the death of Mercutio, at the tomb, the families reconciled, and so on. For an audience familiar with the *Romeo and Juliet* film genre—and all genre films exist in great part to reveal their affinities to a savvy viewer—these are ritual moments demanding judicious analysis. Additionally, because of the special place the play inhabits in the popular imagination, a film version of *Romeo and Juliet*—much more readily than, say, a film version of *King Lear*—invokes and helps define "the Shakespearean" itself as one of its subjects.

The Grand Style: *Romeo and Juliet* at MGM

The 1936 Hollywood adaptation of *Romeo and Juliet* is probably best remembered for the critiques, mostly valid, that have been advanced against it: that the MGM film swamps Shakespeare's play under a heavy load of production values, including enormous sets, overly elaborate costumes, and hundreds of extras; that the leading actors—Leslie Howard (42), Norma Shearer (37), John Barrymore (54)—are too old to convincingly play the passionate and impulsive youth of Verona; that the direction, by the otherwise tactful and skilled George Cukor, is far too reverent and studied: he embalms the play instead of energizing it. To sum up and expand this commentary, MGM's film looks backward to a nineteenth-century theatrical model instead of either finding a contemporary cinematic solution to the filming of Shakespeare or taking into consideration the theater history of the previous several decades. To put matters in perspective, as the film went into production, John Gielgud was staging and starring in *Romeo and Juliet* at the New Theatre in London, a production notable for effectively incorporating elements of the New Stagecraft, especially the unit set by the designing team Motley that allowed for, in Gielgud's words, "quick contrasts and quick action" and "achieved simplicity and elegance through economical means."[11]

The youth of Verona: Leslie Howard (Romeo) and John Barrymore (Mercutio) in MGM's *Romeo and Juliet*. Copyright © CORBIS.

The innovations in staging characteristic of Gielgud's *Romeo and Juliet*—stylized sets, "naturalistic" acting, minimal decor, fluid, speedy transitions—would not have appealed to MGM in the 1930s. The Thalberg era at MGM was marked by a reliance on lavish production values: an MGM film, particularly one personally supervised by Thalberg, was expected to look impressive. But the style and decor that worked for a Greta Garbo vehicle was not necessarily appropriate for Shakespeare. It may even be that the visual extravagance, the elaborate sets and properties, and the showy costumes contributed more to a film when the script was by veteran Hollywood screenwriters like Zoe Akins or Frances Marion than when it was by William Shakespeare. A Garbo vehicle benefits from elegant upholstery, lighting, decor, and camerawork providing support to the "women's magazine plot" of films like *Woman of Affairs* or *Queen Christina*. *Romeo and Juliet* had little need for these production excesses. Shakespeare's play was already highly decorative in its language, its self-conscious literariness, its rhymes and rhetorical conceits. In the circumstances, gloss and glitter may be too much of a good thing. The evidence suggests that Thalberg's production unit saw itself involved in making, among other things, a costume drama: "In working on the costumes of *Romeo and Juliet* we have tried to use as nearly as possible only the materials, embroideries, ornaments, and jewels of the fourteenth and fifteenth centuries. . . . All of Miss Shearer's costumes were taken from the paintings of that day."[12] All of this attention to detail, this concern for "historical" verisimilitude unfortunately contributes to the waxworks feel of the film. These were misguided energies, even if they were not applied nearly as conscientiously as the practitioners claim. It is unfortunate that the technical adviser, Professor William Strunk Jr., was not able to apply some of his precepts, as outlined in the classic *Elements of Style*, for clear, simple prose to the production excesses in which MGM indulged.[13]

To illustrate what is most wrong with MGM's *Romeo and Juliet*, one need only consider the opening few minutes. The credits are written on what are meant to represent unrolling sheets of parchment, and the main actors are introduced as "picture" portraits in motion; after the credits, a still image, resembling an oil painting or a tapestry, comes to life, and the Chorus reads from a scroll to an aristocratic Renaissance audience. We then see a bird's-eye view of "fair Verona" (unashamedly, a painting) and then, in three dimensions, albeit with painted backdrop, a town square. Two elaborate processions introduce the Capulet and Montague clans on their way to church. Though they are presumably doing what they do every Sunday, they are nevertheless treated as something of a show by gawking bystanders. They look more like opposing armies than feuding families, even as they engage in angry stares and a variety of silly byplay.

The "parchment" scrolls and the painting-brought-to-life elements are conventional generic markers that say "literary adaptation." The effect, presumably unintentional, is to distance us from the world of the film even as we are drawn into it. The opening processions, complete with horns, flags, and marching servants, whatever else the intention, spoil the effect Shakespeare was after. Following the formal tone and rhythm of the Chorus, Shakespeare brings two minor characters on stage, Samson and Gregory, who are met by two other servants; then Benvolio; then Tybalt; then some citizens; then "Old Capulet and his wife"; then "Old Montague and his wife"; and, finally, the Prince. Each entrance ratchets up the tension or increases the violence, and each new character or set of characters is higher up on the social ladder. The stage fills up gradually to the Prince's entrance, and, at his exit, it empties again, until only Benvolio and the newly entered Romeo remain. The dramaturgic and thematic effect (it is the young who keep the feud alive) is entirely lost in Cukor's film. In place of Shakespeare's carefully crafted, economical opening, we are given a ponderous mob scene that could just as well be placed in, say, *Marie Antoinette* (MGM filmed this story with Norma Shearer two years later). As Robert Willson Jr. noted, "Cukor misses the opportunity offered by film to lend immediacy and naturalism to the play's opening."[14] This is spectacle for its own sake, and it serves as much to obfuscate as to explicate the social world of Verona.

One criticism that I find at least partly misguided relates to the age of the actors. Here comparison with Franco Zeffirelli's 1968 film is perhaps inevitable. Zeffirelli effectively publicized the innovation of casting "real" teenagers in the leading roles (if press releases are to be believed, Olivia Hussey [Juliet] was fifteen and Leonard Whiting [Romeo] was sixteen). But to insist on casting these characters according to something close to the ages Shakespeare gives them is to forget that Romeo and Juliet are not people, they are roles to be performed. Shakespeare gave them (or at least Juliet) specific ages but did not expect either to be played by a teenage actor; Juliet may have been acted by a fifteen-year-old but, if so, he was a fifteen-year-old boy. Furthermore, a teenager in Shakespeare's time would have been socially, if not physically, far more mature than a modern equivalent. In many ways Romeo and especially Juliet do not act their age.

Insofar as other elements of the production work to engage the audience, the age of the actors, as such, is not a barrier. Leslie Howard, for one, gives us a convincing Renaissance aristocrat. He is too languid and intellectual to make an ideal Romeo—his acting personality cannot encompass impetuosity and other extremes of passion—but he is in tune with the role, elegant and slightly otherworldly, light and quick in a "modern," cinematic fashion. (Appropriately, perhaps, Howard saw the role, which he admitted was essentially unrewarding, as a rehearsal for Hamlet, which he played soon afterward in New York.) It is far more difficult to know what to say about Norma Shearer's Juliet. In the early scenes, she is close to insufferable. The fault is not entirely hers, however: she is given an impossible "entrance," feeding a doe and playing with a bow and arrow. When she forgets to simper and pose, she can be affecting: she speaks the blank verse with understanding and care. (The "poetry" is not lost in this film, although often it sounds like poetry recited rather than poetry that has been internalized as speech.) And Shearer grows into the role, movingly enacting the later Juliet, a girl who must face, in quick succession, her husband's exile, her father's rejection, and frightening preparations for her own feigned death.

With John Barrymore, it is perhaps dissipation, rather than age per se (though he was fifty-four), that undermines his hold on the role of Mercutio. The greatest Hamlet of his generation, he was now a hopeless alcoholic with an unreliable memory. Barrymore unquestionably "overacts" (as does Mercutio); he provides energy and rhetorical flourish to the Queen Mab speech, but he presents it so much like a set piece that he highlights just how artificially Shakespeare injected it into the text of his play. Evidently he was not in good enough physical shape to duel with Basil Rathbone (Tybalt): a double appears to have been employed in the energetic parts of the sword-fighting scene. Rathbone later recalled how unsure Barrymore was of himself: "It was so sad to see him in such a state—the greatest Shakespearean stage actor of his time, who had forgotten more about acting than most people around him would ever know."[15]

Perhaps the major failing of the MGM *Romeo and Juliet* is that it sentimentalizes a tale already full of sentiment. The play works in part because Shakespeare does everything in his power to contain sentimentality. Juliet playing with a doe, Romeo lying among the shepherds, Tchaikovsky's music swelling up as Romeo and Juliet touch in the balcony scene, all contribute to robbing the story of ironic counterpoint. The cuts are often precisely of those scenes and moments and lines that provide an alternative to the romantic ground tone. No longer does the Nurse tell Romeo to "stand an you be a man"; the seriocomic bathos of the discovery of the "dead" Juliet is gone; the comic musicians are eliminated. The moments of violence, furthermore, lack verve. As George Bernard Shaw observed, the duel scenes in *Romeo and Juliet* require "murderous excitement"[16] or they go for naught (one might compare Michael Curtiz's duels in Warner Bros.' *Adventures of Robin Hood*, which featured some great swordplay by Basil Rathbone). The Nurse, played with a surprising absence of sympathy by Edna May Oliver, is robbed of her most comic, bawdy moments and unconscious puns. Only Barrymore's Mercutio is allowed some scope (too much, many would argue) to undercut the seriousness of the proceedings. Unfortunately he is given a good bit of pointless "business" that detracts from his function as foil and friend to Romeo.[17]

At various points in the film, Cukor provides moments of more or less incidental pleasures, particularly in his handling of mise-en-scène, moments that point to a more modest, more controlled film that lies at the corners of this one. One such moment comes after the supposed death of Juliet when, as the screenplay indicates, "the wedding decorations are replaced by emblems of mourning"—servants shroud the furnishings of the Capulet ballroom in black, and black curtains are lowered over the windows, an effective visual equivalent of Capulet's "All things that we ordained festival, / Turn from their office to black funeral." Similarly, the apothecary and the tomb are provided expressive atmosphere, and Leslie Howard finds the right notes for these scenes. Perhaps it was the gloomier aspects of the play that most interested Cukor. Whatever the reason, Howard, like Romeo, achieves a convincing gravitas as the narrative approaches its catastrophe.

Romeo and Juliet in Italy

Italian directors Renato Castellani (1954) and Franco Zeffirelli (1968), in their versions of *Romeo and Juliet*, created a highly specific social environment for their protagonists, paying homage to the "neorealism" prevalent in postwar Italian cinema by constructing a stylized but convincing "Renaissance" world, complete with the inevitable fruit and vegetable market for the opening brawl and location filming in picturesque Italian towns. For the most part, the filmmakers, Zeffirelli especially, are more interested in creating a rich, colorful, attractive mise-en-scène than they are in providing a neorealist atmosphere (neither director can be closely allied with the neorealist movement, though Castellani's comedies have been described as *neorealismo rosa*—soft neorealism—and Zeffirelli was an assistant to Luchino Visconti during the making of the neorealist masterpiece *La terra trema* [1948]). Whereas Castellani's colors are muted pastels, Zeffirelli's Verona is a world of bright, varied, highly saturated colors, the formal austerity of the earlier film, with its calculated compositions and painterly imagery, replaced by fluid camera movement and accelerated editing patterns. In the 1968 film, post–new wave, "direct cinema" effects are frequent: handheld camera, telephoto and zoom shots, extreme close-ups, off-kilter framing, and so on. Zeffirelli takes every opportunity to give us spectacle, and to that end he pays particular attention to the scenes of fighting and brawling and makes a major set piece of the Capulet ball. Both films abandon the Italianate atmosphere by featuring British actors in the major roles. Romeo, Juliet, the Nurse, the Friar, Capulet, among others, are British in both, as are Zeffirelli's Prince Escalus and Mercutio. Castellani has John Gielgud on camera as Chorus. Zeffirelli has Laurence Olivier, in voice-over, speaking an abbreviated version of the opening sonnet over a long panning shot of "Verona."

Both Castellani and Zeffirelli, perhaps not surprisingly, find it difficult to incorporate Shakespeare's language into the visual texture of their films. In Castellani's film, the postdubbing of the entire dialogue track—perhaps the signal curse of postwar Italian cinema—becomes especially problematic. At times, there appears to be virtually no relationship between the words spoken and what we see on screen. Given the potential mismatch between a "neorealist," semidocumentary style, and the formal, poetic language, the total separation—both materially and conceptually—of the sound track from the visual track, the lack of attention to what the words actually mean, comes close to creating moments of sheer nonsense. A few examples, all from early in the film: Tybalt says to Benvolio, "what, drawn among these heartless hinds," but Benvolio has yet to draw his sword; the Prince says, "Will they not hear!" but no one is making the slightest noise; Romeo's "O brawling love, O loving hate" is spoken in a field, nowhere in sight of the brawl; Benvolio's "I aimed so near" (moved from 1.1. to 1.4) is spoken in response to no evident cue; and so forth. Again and again, words, lines, and speeches are taken out of their context, creating an almost surreal effect, especially when dubbed Italian actors are speaking. Notably, the problem is less evident when the actors have dubbed themselves (Romeo, Juliet, Friar Lawrence, Nurse, Capulet, Benvolio).

If much of the verbal poetry has been sacrificed, Castellani nonetheless skillfully creates a visually poetic physical world that combines different levels of reality. Actual Renaissance exteriors, filmed in semidocumentary style, meld with location as well as soundstage interiors that are frequently designed to imitate specific Renaissance paintings (Masachio, Piero della Francesca, and Carpaccio, especially). Some of the interior scenes are so studied (4.3, Capulet makes wedding plans with Paris) as to call attention to themselves as compositions. We have, in other words, the "real" world of

Renaissance Italy; the "painterly" world of (mostly) pre-Raphaelite art; and the language, characters, and actions of Shakespeare's play. A potential tension among these elements is evident at the outset. The first image, after the credits, is of John Gielgud dressed, somewhat incongruously, as Shakespeare: he inhabits a "sixteenth-century" interior, holding a copy of the First Folio (not published until after Shakespeare's death). Gielgud recites the prologue, and we then move to what appears to be market day in the streets of an Italian town identified as "Verona." A distinguished British Shakespearean actor, Shakespeare himself, Shakespeare's book, the language of *Romeo and Juliet*, all juxtaposed with "documentary" images of ordinary people going about their everyday activities. Castellani gives us the "literary adaptation" opening but quickly counters it with "neorealist" location photography. In a similar vein, while most of the major roles are played by actors who, like Gielgud, are the products of British theatrical training, most of the minor roles—including all of the bit parts and extras—are played by Italian actors. In the end, Castellani has made a neorealist costume film, which is not as much of a contradiction as may at first appear. Luchino Visconti's *Senso* (1954) and *I Leopardi* (1963) could be similarly described.

The film's presentation of Renaissance Italy is distinctive. Unlike Zeffirelli's rich, lush, flamboyant mise-en-scène, Castellani's Renaissance is a quiet, pre-Raphaelite world of peaceful cloisters and subdued interiors. Robert Krasker's Technicolor cinematography favors muted, pastel tones—greens and browns predominate. Krasker, who photographed Laurence Olivier's *Henry V*, animates the colors and composition of murals and easel paintings and matches interior and exterior imagery to construct a world at once convincingly "real" and highly stylized. The effect is especially evident in such settings as Juliet's bedroom, a simple, unadorned mise-en-scène—a far cry from MGM's opulence—that is almost theatrical in its quiet elegance, combining pictorialism and functional minimalism. Ace Pilkington objects that "Castellani's Verona is as much a backdrop as any nineteenth-century set, with the added disadvantage that real buildings can upstage the actors, making them seem as static as figures in the Renaissance paintings from which the film drew is visual inspiration."[18] On the other hand, an early champion of the film compared Castellani to Keats: "Both artists make one feel the warm, hurried anguish of living love contrasted with the cold, immobile beauty of art."[19] Traces of the neorealist aesthetic are most evident in interpolated scenes and moments and in the staging of action sequences. Castellani provides a sequence delineating the misfortunes of Friar John and his donkey, an unnecessary addition that nonetheless provides the opportunity for populist images and gentle humor as well as mild social commentary. One suspects a similar impulse behind the staging of fight scenes, which are either, as in the opening brawl, highly fragmented, or, as with the events leading to the deaths of Mercutio and Tybalt, awkward, almost inadvertent acts of violence. No fancy stage dueling here between Mercutio and Tybalt, and no duel at all as Romeo, with a quick stab of a dagger that seems as much an act of self-defense as anything else, kills Tybalt.

In this film version, more than is usual, the most compelling presences, apart from Juliet herself, are the Friar and the Nurse. Mervyn John's Friar Lawrence is unworldly and eccentric; he revels in his own sententiousness and does not like to be interrupted, either by church bells or by an impulsive Romeo. Like the young lovers, he is something of a naïf, quickly overtaken by events. He appears at the tomb, and, unlike Shakespeare's Friar, he does not desert Juliet—though he cannot prevent her from stabbing herself. Flora Robson's Nurse, though bereft of much of the earthy language and comic amour propre Shakespeare provides for her, exhibits warmth and common sense. Her ultimate betrayal of Juliet seems as painful to her as it is to her young charge. The Friar's scenes with Romeo and the Nurse's scenes with Juliet are staged and filmed to allow the actors full scope, with medium and medium-close shots in silent interiors. It helps that these scenes feature English-speaking actors whose voices, albeit postsynchronized, are heard on the sound track in contrast to, for example, scenes involving Mercutio, played by an Italian actor who is dubbed by an English-speaking actor. The consequent reduction of Mercutio's role—no Queen Mab, no byplay with Romeo before the Capulet ball or on the following day, no foolery with the Nurse, Benvolio, and Romeo—may be both the cause and the effect of Castellani's casting decision, and it is hard to disagree with Roy Walker's observation that "Mercutio hardly lives at all before he dies."[20] Benvolio, played by Bill Travers, makes more of an impact.

Both Susan Shentall and Laurence Harvey have been widely faulted for their interpretations of the title roles. In Shentall's case, those early and continuing judgments—"everyone was embarrassed by her inability to come within speaking distance of Juliet," according to Roger Manvel[21]—seem incomprehensible: she is without a doubt the most effective and affecting of screen Juliets. Dressed and coiffed like a Botticelli angel, youthful in appearance but mature in manner, Shentall performs her role and speaks her lines with great assurance. Unlike Zeffirelli and Luhrmann, Castellani retains the substance of the "potion speech" (4.3.20–58), thereby allowing Juliet a powerful moment of emotional and intellectual reflection, and Shentall is

entirely convincing in evoking the mix of fearful apprehension and courageous determination the scene requires. The critics, however, have been
largely correct in their judgment of Laurence Harvey, who is badly miscast:
his essentially internal, dry manner works against the passionate intensity of
which Romeo is capable. Harvey's performance is too calculated and intellectual, too lacking in variety and nuance to be truly sympathetic.

If, as Anthony Davies argues, "it is in the crowd scenes and especially the
fights rather than the intimate character relationships" that Franco Zeffirelli's *Romeo and Juliet* carries most conviction,[22] it is also true that, as in both
earlier and later films, a contradiction is built into these scenes. Zeffirelli
wants it both ways: the feud is a seriocomic expression of mostly juvenile
high spirits at the same time that it is a deadly affair with grave consequences.
So we see, in the opening melee, one brawler sink his sword into what can
be presumed to be the back of another and we see Benvolio seemingly skew-
ered in the eye by Tybalt's sword. But no one appears to die, and when we
next see Benvolio, he has a scratch on the forehead. When Mercutio and
Tybalt fight later, all appears to be in good fun: neither really wants to kill
the other (earlier, in the ball scene, Zeffirelli cut Tybalt's "fetch me my
rapier, boy"). The swordfighting is milked for laughs, and when deadly vio-

Romeo and Juliet and Realism

In one sense, realism (neo- or otherwise) contradicts the essential artifice
of Shakespeare's play, and that contradiction can neither be wished away
nor fully guarded against. Indeed, Shakespeare himself confronted a similar
challenge: what works as a prose tale or a narrative poem will not necessarily work as a play. The conventions of Elizabethan theater, which might
more properly be thought of as Shakespeare's conventions, make the transition possible; other conventions will not have the same effect. We cannot
certainly know what Shakespeare's audience thought of romantic love.
Harry Levin, for one, long ago claimed that Shakespeare's contemporaries
"would have been surprised, and possibly shocked, at seeing lovers taken
so seriously."[23] Be that as it may, Shakespeare clearly anticipated possible
objections by peopling his play with a wide range of attitudes and views of
love and marriage: to slight or altogether ignore these runs the risk of
undoing the playwright's balancing act. It is quite likely that the very elements that producers and filmmakers today find indigestible were the very
elements with which Shakespeare guaranteed a sympathetic hearing for
his luckless heroine and hero.

lence comes, everyone is shocked—Tybalt is amazed to see blood on his sword. The idea that no one believes that Mercutio, an inveterate clown, is really wounded is a useful one, but Zeffirelli sustains the idea far too long. Much the same is true of the subsequent encounter between Romeo and Tybalt. What begins as an exciting fight, part duel, part street brawl, is dragged out until it ceases to contribute to the film's overall pace and design and becomes merely another set piece, existing for its own sake.

The greatest set piece in the film, almost eclipsing the subsequent balcony scene, is the Capulet ball, which occupies some sixteen minutes of screen time and seems much longer. The sense of urgency, suddenness, and speed that lends poignancy to Shakespeare's love story is here signally defused. The Capulet ball demonstrates how much Zeffirelli is in love with spectacle. In theory, there is nothing wrong with providing the scene with richly detailed costumes, an elaborate setting, and varieties of musical accompaniment, but Zeffirelli seems unwilling to step back from the mise-en-scène and focus on the essential action. Zeffirelli's background in opera is here fully in evidence. One difference between a play and an opera, however, is that in the latter, the director is presented with the more or less enforced pace of a musical score—the settings may be lush and the supernumeraries many, but the composer's tempo carries everything along, no dawdling allowed. Particularly unfortunate is the inserted song, "What Is Youth?" a pseudo-Renaissance ballad ("a blend of Elizabethan sentiment and 1960s Europop")[24] that accompanies the meeting of Romeo and Juliet, its banal lyrics and sentimental orchestration taking away from, rather than contributing to, the coming together of the lovers.

Much more effective is the staging of the balcony scene, which draws together a number of elements, including an orchard that seems more like an arboretum, with Juliet's bedroom window first seen through trees and located at the top of a high, vine-covered wall. Juliet is at one with the world of nature and at the same time the captive princess of legend. The wide balcony—it appears to run the whole width of the Capulet mansion—allows Juliet considerable movement as she scampers from one place to another. The spaciousness of the acting area provides full physical scope for the energy and impulsiveness of both Juliet and Romeo. At the same time, the very size of the Capulet garden seems to overwhelm the lovers, who are diminished by their surroundings. Again, Zeffirelli's balcony scene owes much to Castellani's, though it is clearly a set rather than a location. In both films, there is something ominous and foreboding about the Capulet garden, a place that offers strong resistance to romantic passion.

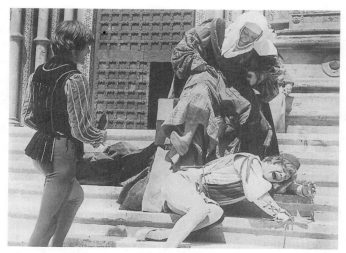

Franco Zeffirelli's *Romeo and Juliet* was inflected by stylistic quirks
borrowed from new wave and neorealist cinema. Copyright
© 1968 Paramount Pictures Corp.

Zeffirelli's film is often praised for its "cinematic" qualities, and he claims
to have sacrificed "uncinematic" elements in Shakespeare's *Romeo and Juliet*
in favor of what could be made "cinematic." But this is a circular argument,
an argument that singles out Zeffirelli's filmmaking style and methods as
"cinematic," constructs a definition of "cinema" on the basis of Zeffirelli's
films, and then demonstrates that these films are "cinematic." I would argue,
on the contrary, that nothing is essentially "cinematic" or "uncinematic." A
filmmaker can have many perfectly valid reasons for cutting and rearranging
Shakespeare's text or dispensing with it altogether, but these reasons can
have nothing to do with the question of what is cinematic. To imply, as Zeffirelli does, that, for example, Juliet's "gallop apace" and potion soliloquies
were cut because they were uncinematic is disingenuous at best.[25] They were
cut because they did not fit in with Zeffirelli's view of Juliet and his limited
understanding of what Shakespeare's play is about. An actor filmed in close-
up, reciting a soliloquy, is just as cinematic as dozens of sword fights—the
question is, Is it well or ill done? There may be value in describing Zeffirelli's
1960 Old Vic production of *Romeo and Juliet* as "cinematic"[26] if one is simply
trying to suggest that Zeffirelli has transferred a variety of techniques and
methods ordinarily found in film to the stage—in this context, cinematic
means recreating theatrically the effects of various editing patterns. But what
sense is there in claiming that Zeffirelli has transferred his cinematic

approach to film? This is not simply a question of terminology: Zeffirelli's approach, to some, appears to be the norm that all Shakespeare films should strive for because Zeffirelli is "cinematic."

In *Romeo and Juliet*, Zeffirelli gives us the young as they wish themselves to be, which may explain a good part of the film's appeal to a 1960s audience. Romeo and Juliet are not merely young (and played by young actors), they are immature—more so than Shakespeare's lovers—and in consequence they are much more the victims of an envious fate. Romeo, introduced flower in hand (as in earlier film versions, Romeo's entrance seems designed to make him appear as silly as possible), is essentially feminized by Zeffirelli's camera and Leonard Whiting's performance. However much critics may wish to relate this feminization to Zeffirelli's homosexuality, the primary effect is to further infantilize the love story. Joan Ozark Holmer puts the matter particularly well: "Zeffirelli's omissions streamline the play in order to idealize and idolize the romantic lovers and to create a relevant youth movie for the sixties by highlighting the theme of the generation gap, and by emphasizing the play's emotional, at the expense of its intellectual, power."[27] As Jack Jorgens summarizes the effect, the young lovers "never see what a corrupt and flawed world it is that they are leaving, never give any indication that they know how they contributed to their own downfall, and never understand that love of such intensity not only cannot last but is self-destructive."[28] Olivia Hussey is visually presented as essentially childlike, which means that her performance is continually in tension with her image. Though her face and, in particular, her large, expressive eyes, lend an aura of innocent sweetness, her line readings are at times artificial and coy. She points nearly every line in such a way as to suggest that she is in truth more mature than she seems.

Zeffirelli's *Romeo and Juliet*, like Zeffirelli himself, appears to have a love/hate relationship with the blank verse. As with Castellani, the postsynchronized sound track becomes a material manifestation of a conceptual problem. We may take, for example, the scene where Capulet berates his daughter, a scene involving only English-speaking actors—one of whom, Paul Hardwick (Capulet), is a seasoned Shakespearean. We have two scenes, both constructed apart from each other. On the visual track, we see movement and violent action, actors occupying different areas of the spatial configuration at different moments—a kind of visual chaos, of which Zeffirelli is quite fond. The other version of the scene, the sound track, recorded later in a completely different acoustic environment, has a hollow, distant effect, at once close up, in terms of microphone placement, and far away, in terms of emotional force. Actors are performing business that logically must interfere with the smooth delivery of their lines, but the words, coming supposedly from their onscreen representations, are spoken with the even tonalities of actors comfortably reading their lines in a soundproof booth. This is a lapse in judgment and care, not conception; postrecording is not ipso facto bad. The real villain here is Zeffirelli's lack of concern for the text, for words, a lack of concern that results in flat, tone-deaf renderings of many dialogue scenes.

As in Castellani's film—and, perhaps, as in most productions of *Romeo and Juliet*—the Friar and the Nurse are more compelling figures than are the young lovers. Milo O'Shea's Friar, for one, exhibits explicitly the contradictory way Shakespeare conceived this character. Is Friar Lawrence a well-meaning bungler or a sinister manipulator? Is he moved by considerations of religion, vanity, or mere expediency? Shakespeare gives him a long, explanatory speech, cut in all film versions in part because of its length and seemingly anticlimactic positioning, but also for its twin effect of calling attention to his machinations at the same time that he exculpates himself for their consequences ("myself condemned and myself excused," 5.3.227). Inconsistent in word and action, the Friar, in O'Shea's performance, is alternately sympathetic and sinister. By the end, the authority figure most sympathetic to the young lovers has been thoroughly discredited. And Juliet's Nurse fails her, a failure that, in Pat Heywood's vivid performance, seems especially poignant. Heywood gives us the first truly bawdy nurse on film, a woman full of energy and high spirits. She is much younger than usual in order to fit in with the all-around reduction in ages, and she is therefore a more likely confidante in affairs of the heart than Juliet's elderly nurses ordinarily are. Her betrayal of Juliet is painfully rendered: when she advises Juliet to marry Paris, she clearly does not believe what she is saying. She is giving practical, worldly wisdom, but it goes against the grain of her feelings. By the end of the scene, she knows she has lost Juliet forever.

Although much was made at the time of the film's release of the way Zeffirelli brought a buried homoerotic subtext of the play to the surface in his film, notably in his depiction of Mercutio, the effect is confusion and incoherence more than anything else. That Mercutio loves Romeo is clear enough, though Zeffirelli portrays that love as little more than homosocial affection, going a bit beyond Shakespeare without necessarily violating the construct Shakespeare presents him with: homosexual desire, as Peter Donaldson notes "hovers at the edges of the film."[29] Peter McEnery gives weight and sense to the Queen Mab speech and to the character of Mercutio in general by suggesting throughout a man not comfortable in his own skin. But Zeffirelli ultimately undercuts Mercutio, whose clowning, presented as almost pathological, becomes merely irritating absent a coherent personality that explains it. The byplay with the Nurse (totally eliminated by Castellani) is made much of—too much, some would say—presumably in order to fur- ther underline Mercutio's hostility toward women. The male aggression here displayed threatens to make nonsense of the Nurse's sympathetic interplay with Romeo that immediately follows. This Nurse would have marched right back home without delivering her message. (The authors of *West Side Story*, interestingly, turn this scene into a moment of grave consequence—their Nurse character, Anita, manhandled by the Jet boys, fatally refuses to deliver a message to Romeo/Tony.)

The importance of Zeffirelli's *Romeo and Juliet* in the history of the Shake- speare film cannot be underestimated. It was an enormous popular success; it appealed to young audiences, but not only to the young; it was a "foreign" film at a time when the foreign cinema was at the height of its popularity in the United States. At the same time it was very much "Hollywood" in style and technique, the Hollywood of *Bonnie and Clyde* and *The Graduate*, a film constructed on a solid narrative foundation but inflected by stylistic quirks borrowed from new wave and neorealist cinema. The loosening of the Pro- duction Code Administration guidelines on matters of sex meant that Zef- firelli, who was making the film for Columbia release, could play up the youthful eroticism of the lovers and at the same time explore the homoerotic subtext. Brief nudity was now possible—so Romeo's buttocks, especially, and Juliet's breast, very briefly, could be exhibited. Shakespeare was sexy. In its visual and musical styles, Zeffirelli's film found common ground among Renaissance elegance, nineteenth-century operatic romanticism, and 1960s youth culture, which included elements of preindustrial fashion—peasant blouses, tie-dyed shirts, sandals, beads, and so on. The mixture of innocence and experience, of youthful high spirits and sexual passion, all of which are present in Shakespeare's play, became the primary focus of interest in the film, which found a ready audience in the United States at a time when American culture was schizophrenically sacrificing its young to Cold War– inspired violence abroad and simultaneously creating a youth-friendly cul- ture at home.

Precisely for the reasons I just outlined, the film wore less well as the years went by. The charge of being "dated" is often made against a film when all that the observer means is that it isn't very good, but in this instance, dated seems to fit. Every film reflects the moment of its creation; with Zeffirelli's *Romeo and Juliet*, however, the problem is that it reflects very little else. In "The Artistry of Franco Zeffirelli" (1997), Robert Hapgood writes that his college students found Laurence Olivier's *Hamlet* and *Henry V* "intolerable" while embracing *Romeo and Juliet*.[30] In my experience, however, it is Zeffirelli's film that students find hard to take. Zeffirelli's adaptation of Shakespeare's play strips from it much of what does not fit comfortably into the cultural moment and the cultural attitudes he wishes to highlight. Again, viewed as an adaptation, the film is a watered-down, emaciated, overly sweetened version of Shakespeare's *Romeo and Juliet*; viewed as a work independent of Shakespeare, however, the film *as* film has little resonance. It becomes a series of interesting set pieces and a few stylistic flourishes that continually bring us back to Shakespeare's play as the only way to fill the gaps. As Ace Pilkington intuits, "Zeffirelli does not have much faith in the audience to which he caters."[31] Unlike Baz Luhrmann, as we shall see, Zeffirelli has not created a film text to stand apart from Shakespeare's play, an analogy, so to speak, for the original. Instead, he both relies on and simultaneously undercuts Shakespeare's text.

William Shakespeare's Romeo + Juliet

At first glance, Baz Luhrmann's *William Shakespeare's Romeo + Juliet* could be mistaken for yet another (mis)appropriation of Shakespeare's play for pur-

---

Domestic Violence at the Capulet House

Each major film version of *Romeo and Juliet* ratchets up the violence in the scene where Capulet berates his daughter for rejecting his plans for her marriage to County Paris. In Cukor's film, C. Aubrey Smith is dignified and distant; Sebastian Cabot, in Castellani's film, shouts and moves with great agitation; Paul Hardwick, Zeffirelli's Capulet, manhandles both Juliet and the Nurse (earlier in the film—Shakespeare's 3.3—the Friar knocks Romeo to the ground); and Paul Sorvino, in *William Shakespeare's Romeo + Juliet*, strikes the Nurse and his wife and slaps Juliet hard across the face. What is, in Shakespeare, a seriocomic *senex iratus* set piece becomes full-blown domestic violence four hundred years later. This is the recent cinematic behavior of other Shakespearean angry fathers as well: both Leonato in Kenneth Branagh's *Much Ado about Nothing* (1993) and Egeus in Adrian Noble's *A Midsummer Night's Dream* (1996) strike or push their daughters with sufficient violence to knock them to the ground. In the late twentieth and early twenty-first centuries, evidently, only physical abuse can provide film audiences the effect that Shakespeare was presumably able to achieve with words alone. (Stage Capulets can be physical too, however, as at the Royal Shakespeare Company in 1986 and 1989.)

poses of parody or even burlesque, a hip (hop?) retelling aimed at an irre-deemably lowbrow audience of clueless teenagers living in an intellectually bankrupt culture. Even Luhrmann's title is suspect. Many commentators have focused on the peculiarities of calling the film *William Shakespeare's Romeo + Juliet* from the use of the full name of the original author to the cross, or "Bazmark," used instead of the word "and" or an ampersand. Given the distinctive stylistic pyrotechnics of Luhrmann's style and the rather dras-tic cutting of the script, the intimation of irony is hard to avoid. What has been less frequently noted, however, is how truly peculiar this title is when we compare it to similar titles like, say, *Bram Stoker's Dracula* or *Mary Shel-ley's Frankenstein*. In the latter cases, the filmmakers are declaring a (more or less truthful) departure from all of the many films with the words "Dracula" and "Frankenstein" in their titles, works that have little or nothing in com-mon with the literary originals that inspired them. This, however, is simply not the case for *Romeo and Juliet*, which, no matter how often adapted to the screen, has always been, fundamentally and even mythically, William Shakespeare's *Romeo and Juliet*, and this in spite of how faithful or unfaithful the adaptation. *Romeo and Juliet means* Shakespeare, is almost identical to Shakespeare, whereas "Dracula" might mean Bela Lugosi, Christopher Lee, or Tod Browning, and "Frankenstein" might mean Boris Karloff or James Whale; most likely of all, these names simply "mean" a vampire with fangs and a cape and a zombie dressed in bandages. But if *Romeo and Juliet* is always already William Shakespeare's *Romeo and Juliet*, why assert the fact so boldly?

Romeo + Juliet (a less cumbersome title I will generally use from now on) begins with the image of a television set—a retro 1970s or 1980s model: we are in the present-day world of mass communication, but the image is of something archaic. We are vaguely in the past, a feeling reinforced by the montage of images drawn from later points in the film, as well as vaguely in the future. As the Chorus makes clear, this is a story already told, already done; its end is in its beginning. The opening sequence fragments into a cacophony of sound and image, even as the words of Shakespeare's prologue are given solidity and, by repetition (twice spoken, but also repeated as both verbal and visual language), redundancy. Barbara Hodgdon identifies a tone that "ricochets between Wall-and-Moonshine tongue-in-cheekiness and play-ing it straight, between selling Shakespeare as one-off visual in-jokes and tying its scenography, almost over-explicitly, to the word."[32] Although this initial sequence promises Shakespeare's words, the audience is somewhat deceived, as words do not play the central role we are led to suppose they will.

The following sequence of the first "brawl" continues to meld the modern and the archaic in its cinematic style: a variety of shots filmed with wide-angle and telephoto lenses, some employing rapid steadicam glides, filmed in shallow focus and deep focus, in slow motion and fast motion, in extreme close-up and in long shot, are edited together with transitional devices—horizontal and vertical wipes and irises—that go back to 1920s filmmaking. Similarly, freeze frames combined with introductory titles allude to both Sergio Leone westerns and a method of introducing characters prevalent in the silent era. This bravura sequence—and the same might be said of Shakespeare's opening scene—can be regarded as a "grabber," a powerful, dramatic, somewhat deceptive means of gaining the audience's attention. Deceptive because the stylistic flamboyance that characterizes this opening does not accurately represent the tonal ground of the film; what it succeeds in doing, most of all, is to provide a "cover" for what follows. For all of its cinematic verve, Luhrmann's Romeo + Juliet is a highly theatrical film, its style clearly drawn from Luhrmann's work in opera as much as advertising and rock videos. As James Loehlin observes, "William Shakespeare's Romeo + Juliet continually and playfully juxtaposes contemporary kitsch with the high-culture world of Shakespeare, classical music and Renaissance art and architecture."[33] The opening sequences include a strong element of parody; Luhrmann's stylistic flourishes are more retro than avant-garde.

What many critics have identified as Luhrmann's "MTV style" is primarily a mix of early experimental cinema and modernist video art. Music videos are stylistically archaic and unadventurous (Salvador Dali and Luis Buñuel set the parameters in Un chien Andalou [1929]): irrational editing patterns, impressionistic imagery, expressionist decor, surreal juxtapositions, all presented with a strong dose of épater le bourgeois (in this context "screw the parents"). Rock video, developed in the early 1980s, was cliché ridden and ossified by the early 1990s, having settled into a very few moves that were themselves already shopworn cinematic clichés. Luhrmann draws on a richer range of allusions and a wider variety of stylistic choices than can be encapsulated by the reference to MTV. In this sense, the photographic qualities of Luhrmann's film coordinate with his mise-en-scène: a future that is really a past; a "there" that is really "here"; a story that is freshly being told yet again, an effect intensified by the way Luhrmann ratchets up the sense of fate and foreknowledge already present in the play. What is most postmodern about the film is its reliance on modernism and, in general, its ransacking of the past for its subject matter and its style.

If the opening sequences—the prologue and the fight—serve to establish the filmmaker's bona fides in cinema, the sequence that follows introduces us to the world of theater. Romeo is first seen sitting on the stage of the ruins of a movie theater, and his image is constructed in a theatrical, self-conscious fashion: cigarette in hand, hair tousled, sport coat over his "Hawaiian" shirt, jotting his Petrarchan conceits in a small notebook. Later, Mercutio is introduced to the film in the most "theatrical" way imaginable, in a flamboyant "drag" costume and almost immediately on stage, the stage earlier associated with Romeo. Although this stage set is infrequently seen, it features in some of the most important moments in the film: Romeo's entrance, Mercutio's entrance, Mercutio's death. At the end of the last-mentioned sequence, a lap dissolve associates the stage as well with Juliet's bed and thus by extension with the "bed"/bier on which Romeo and Juliet die. The final setting in the film, the Capulet tomb, may be the most theatrical of all, a set illuminated by hundreds of candles and dozens of neon crosses, a wedding of sixteenth- and twentieth-century light sources, self-consciously decorated as no church or tomb has ever been.

By bringing the play up to date, Luhrmann does little more than, say, David Garrick did in the eighteenth century: he makes it into a recognizable contemporary cultural object, alert to the sensibilities of an audience whose tastes and feelings are conditioned by the culture in which they are immersed. This can be accomplished in a variety of ways, of which bringing the film "up to date" in terms of its mise-en-scène is only one. The pastiche element of the film is not, as in so much "vulgar" postmodernism, an end in itself. Luhrmann's strategy is to deprive the viewer of specific markers for pinning down time and place too precisely. Zeffirelli's 1968 film, though it recreates a Renaissance world in its mise-en-scène, does something quite similar for a late 1960s audience, something that was obvious at the time and becomes even clearer in retrospect.

The great distance between the social world of Shakespeare's play and contemporary life is perhaps most evident in the scenes that take place in the Capulet household (Shakespeare never shows us the Montagues at home). The formal, socially delineated interactions among Juliet, Lady Capulet, Capulet, and the Nurse belong to a world very foreign to our own, and one difficult to translate into contemporary equivalents. (A notable aspect of the *Romeo and Juliet*–inspired *West Side Story*, both as musical drama [1957] and as film [1961], is that the parents and parental figures virtually disappear.) Perhaps, for this reason, Luhrmann retains Shakespeare's language—or at least a reasonable percentage of it—instead of creating a verbal language of his own: the sixteenth-century syntax and vocabulary bridge past and present. Luhrmann "uses" Shakespeare's dialogue in a variety of ways, depending on the occasion. At times, the film can simply pretend that the language and "poetic" diction are not alien to the film's contemporary sensibilities. A line like "thy drugs are quick" fits easily into the psychedelic atmosphere of the Capulet ball sequence (even if the words have been transplanted from one point in the play to another). At other times, the language is allowed to remain "Shakespeare." For a critical example, the sonnet lines Romeo and Juliet recite at first meeting are spoken in their entirety in spite of the fact that the meaning of the imagery is not self-evident. Presumably Luhrmann did not want to cut one of the most famous passages in Shakespeare. Beyond that, Shakespeare's sonnet transports us momentarily back to the sixteenth century and in so doing collapses the worlds of Verona and Verona Beach. To further ensure that this scene will "work," Luhrmann—again, with the precedence of Zeffirelli—gives us the meeting of Romeo and Juliet several times over through time expansion and repetitive editing patterns and precedes the sonnet meeting with the fish tank meeting where the exchange of glances and the matching of identities have already been made.

Like much else in the film, the language is at once familiar and strange. Just as we cannot precisely tell what make of cars the characters are driving, so we cannot always tell where their language is coming from. In part, this is the consequence of how the verse is spoken; interestingly, critics differ on the overall effect. "For the most part," James Loehlin finds, "the actors speak with toneless naturalism."[34] Courtney Lehmann, however, notes that, with the exception of Claire Danes, Lurhmann's cast members "articulate the couplets in a way that draws attention to their forced, artificial, and constraining nature."[35] Much of the verse speaking is prosaic. Speaking the blank verse lines as if they were prose spoils the rhythm and music, but both of these can be sacrificed if something of equal value is put in their place. Kenneth Tynan, reviewing Franco Zeffirelli's 1960 stage production of *Romeo and Juliet* at the Old Vic, makes an important observation in this context: "It is . . . urged that Signor Zeffirelli robs Shakespeare of his poetry; but this argument is valid only if one agrees with those blinkered zealots who insist that poetry is an arrangement of sounds, instead of an arrangement of words."[36] Still, if too many of the sounds are lost, the meaning can be lost as well. Blank verse, as Shakespeare employs it, can point up what is important in a line. The trick becomes how to make the verse seem, as far as possible, like ordinary speech while retaining the necessary emphases that are clues to meaning.

This is the challenge that Claire Danes consistently fails to meet. She flattens her lines in such a way that nearly all emphases disappear. DiCaprio,

> ## Updating *Othello*
>
> In spite of compelling performances and intelligent direction, Tim Blake Nelson's ingeniously updated O (2001) falters in its attempt to be true to both Shakespeare and the teen movie genre. O reproduces *Othello* almost scene by scene and frequently provides modern paraphrases for Shakespeare's verse. Therein, however, lies at least part of the problem: the up-to-date language bends under the weight of the original, often resulting in stilted, unnatural dialogue. Iago's "Did Michael Cassio, when you wooed my lady, / Know of your love?" becomes the lame "Did Mike know that you and Desi were getting together?" (Shakespeare's own words sound more spontaneous than the paraphrase!), and one might wonder if "How we gonna kill this motherfuck" is much of an improvement over "How shall I murder him, Iago?" A larger problem is that not enough is at stake in the world of O. A high school basketball tournament cannot be equated with fighting Turks, and though issues of race and class are just as pressing and relevant today as in the past, questions of sexual honor do not quite have the "heft" they once had. (Both the 1973 rock opera film *Catch My Soul*, set in a hippie commune, and the 2001 LWT/PBS *Othello* have similar problems, though a good deal more is at stake in the latter. "John Othello," the newly appointed London police commissioner, has to confront his domestic anxieties in the context of the Brixton race riots.) Without the mediation of Shakespeare's blank verse and imagistic patterns, the plot of *Othello* can seem more preposterous than tragic.

though he sometimes falls into the same trap, finds ways—through pauses, taking deep breaths, halting his speech—to naturalize the rhythms while maintaining necessary emphases. Whereas Danes—and this is also a positive side to her performance—clings to a plain, innocent sincerity throughout, DiCaprio speaks his lines as if they were quotations—not from Shakespeare but from himself. Danes, almost perversely, never "quotes" at all, even when quotation seems to be called for. For example, she speaks the line "Too like the lightning, which does cease to be / Ere one can say 'It lightens'" (2.2.119–20) without the at least implicit quotation marks around "It lightens." And because Shakespeare's lovers speak the language of hyperbole and paradox, what they say becomes nonsensical if they are completely unaware of the exaggerations in which they indulge. Something significant is lost when Juliet says, with complete matter-of-factness, "Good night, good night! Parting is such sweet sorrow, / That I shall say good night till it be morrow"

(2.2.184–85). The rhyme alone makes clear the extent to which these words are in essence a quotation even as they are being spoken for the first time.

Leonardo DiCaprio's Romeo combines a number of cultural images: first, DiCaprio's own image (which would soon fade) as a kind of asexual love object for adolescent girls; then the sensitive, essentially white-bread teen, roughly equivalent to Richard Beymer's Tony in West Side Story; and, very consciously, the James Dean image, especially the latter's incarnation of Jim Stark in Rebel without a Cause (itself a Romeo and Juliet adaptation of sorts; interestingly, Natalie Wood, the "Juliet" of Nicholas Ray's film, later played Maria in the West Side Story film). These allusions are not necessarily aimed at the 1990s teen audience that constituted the obvious target of the film's production and marketing strategies, an audience for whom James Dean might be only slightly more familiar than Shakespeare. Luhrmann's film is cunningly designed to appeal to the parents and even the grandparents of that "natural" audience. It can be argued, however, that the various elements making up the image of Romeo in the film are available to an audience of savvy youth who have absorbed, whether at first, second, or third hand, those cultural markers. The image of Juliet, though not as complexly defined, appeals to a special kind of nostalgia for girlhood innocence not so much lost as never available in the first place. Even a jaded sixteen-year-old can be imagined yearning for the kind of protected, cocoon existence Claire Danes lives out in Luhrmann's film, a world of parental protection and direction (as well as parental control and physical violence).

Like many adapters before him, Luhrmann found it necessary to cut or significantly alter challenging aspects of Shakespeare's play. Most obviously, he virtually eliminated the scenes in which the Nurse reports Tybalt's death to Juliet and the Capulet household discovers Juliet's supposed death. Both of these incidents are based, though in different ways, on misunderstandings, and they have a strong element of the ridiculous about them, as Shakespeare undoubtedly knew. The effect is to prepare us for the actual deaths of Romeo and Juliet and, as it were, rehearse the emotional impact of the denouement. For a modern film audience, these scenes may be impossible to rid of their burlesque elements. Even the MGM version, which includes so much of the text, totally eliminates the confusion of 3.2 and greatly reduces the comic response to the seemingly lifeless Juliet. (Ironically, a twentieth-century audience may find Shakespeare to be as much lacking in decorum as did the eighteenth.) Luhrmann completely cuts the killing of Paris, the comic musicians, and Friar Lawrence's appearance at the Capulet tomb and subsequent desertion of Juliet. Other scenes are severely reduced: Juliet's forty-five-line "potion" soliloquy is pared down to two lines; the ball scene lacks most of Capulet's exchanges with Old Capulet and other characters; and the Nurse's interchanges with her servant, Peter, are gone. What a number of these cuts have in common is that they can be thought of as either rhetorical excess or violations of decorum, or both at once. These, as already noted, are pressure points in Shakespeare's play, places where his failure to adhere to classical principles and, by anticipation, neoclassical rules have in the past been regarded as close to scandalous. These are the elements of Shakespearean drama presumed to be indigestible for a contemporary audience: both *Shakespeare in Love*, which pretends to take us back to the origins of *Romeo and Juliet*, and Luhrmann's film, which projects Shakespeare's play into the twenty-first century, elide or gloss over the very same elements, the elements that run counter to the idea of Shakespeare as a screenwriter, an entertainer, "one of us."

Another strategy for translating the rhetorical essence of the play into acceptable modern terms is to make what is public in the play private on the screen. Juliet's reception of the news of Tybalt's death and Romeo's banishment, a seriocomic scene of misunderstanding—the Nurse, as usual, cannot seem to get to the point—is, as noted above, deeply cut. What remains of it is transformed into an internal meditation by Juliet alone in her bedroom. What is passionate intensity in Shakespeare's play is a passive, puzzling reflection in the film. Juliet suffers most from this avoidance of rhetoric and the tragicomic. Shakespeare created a Juliet who is quite capable of dissimulation and irony as well as anger and fierce determination: her love for Romeo quickly, if temporarily, turns to hatred when she hears the news of Tybalt's death; she engages in elaborate and deceitful wordplay, allowing her mother to think that she is mourning for Tybalt when in fact she is yearning for Romeo; she dismisses her Nurse with angry finality ("ancient damnation") when the latter encourages her to marry Paris; she fools her father with a hypocritical pretense of submission even as she is plotting her rebellion against him; and she doubts the motives of the Friar, temporarily seeing him, with mature insight, in a Machiavellian light, as she prepares to swallow the potion (and her potion soliloquy as a whole reveals her to be a young woman of vivid, if morbid, imagination). Claire Danes's Juliet, robbed of these enriching traits, emotions, motives, and inconsistencies of character, is an ideal Victorian Juliet, but she is far from the Juliet Shakespeare created. Neither a contemporary teenager nor a Shakespearean heroine, the Luhrmann Juliet has little social or cultural grounding apart from the baroque Catholicism that decorates her immediate environment.

By placing great emphasis on fate, the film robs its characters of agency, of responsibility for their own actions and choices. It is this element of the play that has caused critics to deny its tragic status: *Romeo and Juliet* is a tragicomedy, not merely because it mixes tragic and comic elements but because its tragic elements are also comic. Much of the misfortune in the play has a comic dimension, and what is the denouement but a comedy of errors? This is an aspect of the play any production has to come to terms with: how to prevent that image of Romeo and Juliet dead in the tomb from seeming bathetic. In one way, Luhrmann adds to the sense of sheer bad luck by having Juliet wake up before Romeo dies—all he had to do is glance over at Juliet before drinking the poison, and the story would have a happy ending. In the play, some kind of balance is maintained between the sense of inexorable fatality and a recognition that humans can choose to act in some other way. The coda, almost entirely cut (though not for the first time—if *Shakespeare in Love* is any indication, even Shakespeare failed to include it), exists in part to allow the surviving characters and the audience to contemplate the complex intertwining of human error and sheer bad luck. This ending also emphasizes the larger dimensions of the tragedy. As G. Blakemore Evans has emphasized, "To bring the curtain down on Juliet's death, an ending dear to the Victorians, borders on the melodramatic and sacrifices Shakespeare's finely held balance between the personal tragedy of the lovers and the larger social implications of the feud."[37] Luhrmann includes a coda, but it is highly abbreviated and fails, deliberately, to achieve any sense of social integration. The young lovers "become merely another lurid image for a media-besotted culture, body-bagged victims in a grainy news video."[38] The twice-repeated "all are punished," spoken by "Captain" Prince, words that simply recognize a tragic fact in the context Shakespeare provides, becomes a threat of retribution in the film.

The last words we hear at the end of *Romeo + Juliet* ("we hope your rules and wisdom choke you") are from Radiohead, not Shakespeare, and they affirm a generational conflict that we have not actually experienced, except intermittently, in the course of the film itself. "The moral of the story," one of the film's producers asserts, "is that if you teach hatred to your children, you lose them" (Laserdisc commentary track). This is, no doubt, what countless viewers and audiences have wanted *Romeo and Juliet* to be about. But it is not, except very superficially, what Shakespeare seems most interested in. To understand the play as primarily concerned with the "generation gap" and with teen suicide is to misrepresent its essence. Shakespeare goes out of his way to suggest that the Montague and Capulet parents may be, in today's parlance, "overprotective," overly concerned to keep their children away from the harsh world they must ultimately inhabit. "Oh where is Romeo— saw you him today?" Lady Montague inquires (in both play and film), "Right glad I am he was not at this fray" (1.1.107–9). And Capulet, even though he discovers a Montague at his party, refuses to countenance any disturbance that might spoil his daughter's coming-out festivities. He even acknowledges of Romeo that "Verona brags of him / To be a virtuous and well-governed youth" (1.5.66–67). The impulse for Romeo and Juliet to create and inhabit a world of their own is in part a consequence of parental overprotection.

Shakespeare's *Romeo and Juliet* is a double-edged sword if employed as a glorification or even validation of the young and a concomitant condemnation of grown-up values. In the social world of Shakespeare's play, it is the young—masters and servants—who maintain the deadly feud, a feud that has been inherited, it is true, from generations of parental figures, but also a feud the adults have wearied of, as Capulet's attitude toward Romeo indicates. The irrelevance of parents is made especially clear in *West Side Story:* they essentially disappear. Although *Romeo and Juliet* is inevitably remembered as a tale of young lovers whose love is forbidden by parental interdict, nothing of the kind actually takes place in Shakespeare's play. The fact is that Romeo and Juliet make no effort to discover whether or not they could marry. Juliet's eagerness to become Romeo's wife, almost as if the very act of falling in love had been a kind of self-deflowering, precludes all other avenues. Friar Lawrence's assumption that he can effect an end to the feud by marrying Romeo to Juliet actually makes sense: unfortunately, he does not have the opportunity to find out. The deadly impetuosity of the young makes such an outcome impossible.

At least as far back as Franco Zeffirelli's Old Vic production of *Romeo and Juliet* (1960), directors have tended to treat the feud as, to a greater or lesser extent, adolescent high jinks, a kind of masculine display not to be taken too seriously. Zeffirelli's film, as I have suggested, may be the best-known version of this approach, and it continues in Luhrmann's film. The advantage is that one can maintain a comic tone—and this is part of Shakespeare's strategy as well—almost uninterruptedly until the death of Mercutio; the disadvantage is that it tends to undermine the gravitas of the words spoken by the Prince, whose language ("purple fountains issuing blood," etc.) makes it quite clear that the feud has been and continues to be a matter of deadly force. Luhrmann has an added problem Zeffirelli did not have to worry about, in that the presence of guns makes it even more difficult to treat the opening segment as lighthearted good fun. In the end, Luhrmann, like Zeffirelli, has it both ways.

With the exchange of gunfire, it is unclear who, if anyone, is actually killed (the one character who appears to be shot—and in the head at that—pops up a few scenes later, apparently unhurt). Consequently, when matters turn deadly, it seems almost accidental, and the responsibility for the tragic turn of events does not so much lie in the feud as in the actions of Romeo, Tybalt, and Mercutio.

Both Luhrmann and Zeffirelli contribute to a sentimentalization of the love story by isolating and/or undercutting the role of Mercutio, effectively turning him into an outsider. But Shakespeare's Mercutio is anything but an outsider: he is a relative of Prince Escalus and at the center of the youthful aristocracy of Verona. His cynicism and satirical style are a comic expression of the sensible, if limited, view of the larger social world. In Zeffirelli's film, he is an eccentric and a hysteric, clearly infatuated with Romeo and therefore unreliable as a critic of romantic love. Luhrmann's Mercutio is played by an African American actor, in contrast to the white-bread Romeo and Juliet. Although the more or less multiracial society of Luhrmann's film allows for considerable casting latitude, Mercutio's blackness marks him as beyond the pale in more ways than one. Although he is not specifically depicted as "queer" as he is in Zeffirelli's film, he works himself into a state of hysteria with the Queen Mab speech, which suggests that the ambiguous sexuality of his "drag" get up is more than a costume—it expresses gender confusion and anxiety. Mercutio's transvestism distinguishes him further from the "straight" personae of the central young lovers. One consequence of this marginalization of Mercutio is that his role as critic is significantly modified, thus allowing Romeo and Juliet's love to flourish unchecked (*West Side Story*, interestingly, virtually eliminates the Mercutio function).

Theater directors and acting teachers talk about a "through line," a consistent intention or force that carries a play or an actor from beginning to end. Although this language can seem vague or mystical at times, the point is concrete enough: something needs to hold the work together, all parts need to be in the same magnetic field. With *Romeo and Juliet*, Shakespeare created a force field that surrounds points of tension, polarities that are based on resemblance: love/hate, ideal/real, young/old, innocence/worldliness, deliberation/haste, spontaneity/calculation, lyrical/prosaic, personal/social. All of these polarities—and more like them—are embraced by the tragicomic mode that governs Shakespeare's approach. A production of *Romeo and Juliet* will succeed to the extent that it captures and expresses these polarities. No film version of the play entirely succeeds in reproducing the essential richness of Shakespeare's text; each sacrifices some points of tension for the sake of others or, more often, slights one of the paired terms in favor of the other. Cukor's film captures the lyricism but misses the passion. Castellani's expresses the worldliness and some of the lyricism but misses the bawdy, earthy aspect. It succeeds at finding expressive means of showing the external barriers the young lovers cannot finally overcome but fails at suggesting the extent to which they are implicated in constructing barriers of their own. Zeffirelli focuses on the bawdiness, the homosocial/heterosexual divide, the *Liebestod* theme, but mostly misses the lyricism, the conflict between idealism and realism, and the worldliness. Luhrmann's film embodies these tensions most effectively of all, though it sacrifices the complexity of its young lovers in favor of drawing a powerful social picture. In this film, worldliness trumps innocence; the real overcomes the ideal; speed is all, and lyricism, though it emerges from time to time, is almost entirely transferred to the mise-en-scène and the music.

Notes

1. Robert Horowitz, "History Comes to Life and *You Are There*," in *American History/American Television*, ed. John E. O'Connor (New York: Ungar, 1983), 79–94; 93.

2. Robert Hamilton Ball, *Shakespeare on Silent Film* (London: George Allen & Unwin, 1968), 217.

3. Ball, *Silent Film*, 67.

4. Stanley Wells, "The Challenges of *Romeo and Juliet*," *Shakespeare Survey* 49 (1996): 1–14.

5. *Zeffirelli: The Autobiography of Franco Zeffirelli* (New York: Weidenfeld & Nicolson, 1986), 157.

6. Guthrie McClintic, *Me and Kit* (Boston: Little, Brown, 1955), 291. McClintic had another important insight—that the play works best with a full or nearly full text: "I had decided to play all twenty-three scenes (otherwise structurally the story falls apart), cutting only the obsolete comedy of the musicians and servants" (293).

7. Kenneth Branagh, *Beginning* (New York: St. Martin's, 1989), 173.

8. *William Shakespeare's Romeo + Juliet* (Fox Laser Disc, 1997), Baz Luhrmann audio commentary.

9. Wells, "Challenges," 4.

10. Wells, "Challenges," 14.

11. Dennis Kennedy, *Looking at Shakespeare: A Visual History of Twentieth-Century Performance* (Cambridge: Cambridge University Press, 1993), 137.

12. *Romeo and Juliet by William Shakespeare: A Motion Picture Edition* (London: Arthur Barker, 1936), 261.

13. Charles and Mirella Affron, citing a contemporary newspaper account of the lav-

ish balcony set, remark that "there is no hint that the 'enormous stage' might in fact betray Shakespeare's intimate love scene." Charles Affron and Mirella Jona Affron, *Sets in Motion: Art Direction and Narrative Film* (Rutgers, N.J.: Rutgers University Press, 1995), 8.

14. Robert F. Willson Jr., *Shakespeare in Hollywood: 1929–1956* (Madison, N.J.: Fairleigh Dickinson University Press, 2000), 60.

15. Cited in Michael A. Morrison, *John Barrymore: Shakespearean Actor* (Cambridge: Cambridge University Press, 1997), 279.

16. *Shaw on Shakespeare*, ed. Edwin Wilson (New York: Dutton, 1961), 179.

17. As Robert Willson Jr. observes; see *Shakespeare in Hollywood*, 63–64.

18. Ace Pilkington, "Zeffirelli's Shakespeare," in *Shakespeare and the Moving Image*, ed. Anthony Davies and Stanley Wells (Cambridge: Cambridge University Press, 1994), 172.

19. Paul Jorgenson, "Castellani's Romeo and Juliet: Intention and Response," *Quarterly Review of Film, Radio, and Television*, Fall 1955, 1–10.

20. Roy Walker, "In Fair Verona," *The Twentieth Century*, November 1954, 464–71; 467.

21. Roger Manvell, *Shakespeare and the Film* (New York: Praeger, 1971), 98.

22. Anthony Davies, "The Film Versions of *Romeo and Juliet*," *Shakespeare Survey* 49 (1996): 153–62; 159.

23. Harry Levin, "Form and Formality in Romeo and Juliet," *Shakespeare Quarterly* (Winter 1960): 3–11; 6.

24. Stephen M. Buhler, *Shakespeare in the Cinema: Ocular Proof* (Albany: SUNY Press, 2002), 141.

25. See Zeffirelli's comments in *Staging Shakespeare: Seminars in Production Problems*, ed. Glenn Loney (New York: Garland, 1990), 244.

26. "As close to neo-realism as theatre could be, Zeffirelli's sets allowed for action cinematic in speed and fluency." Jill Levenson, *Shakespeare in Performance: Romeo and Juliet* (Manchester: Manchester University Press, 1987), 100.

27. Joan Ozark Holmer, "The Poetics of Paradox: Shakespeare's versus Zeffirelli's Cultures of Violence," *Shakespeare Survey* 49 (1996): 163–79; 179.

28. Jack J. Jorgens, *Shakespeare on Film* (Bloomington: Indiana University Press, 1977), 91.

29. Peter Donaldson, *Shakespearean Films/Shakespearean Directors* (Boston: Unwin Hyman, 1990), 146.

30. "Popularizing Shakespeare: The Artistry of Franco Zeffirelli," in *Shakespeare, the Movie*, ed. Lynda E. Boose and Richard Burt (London: Routledge, 1997), 80–94.

31. Ace G. Pilkington, "Zeffirelli's Shakespeare," in *Shakespeare and the Moving Image*, 168.

32. Barbara Hodgdon, "*William Shakespeare's Romeo + Juliet*: Everything's Nice in America?" *Shakespeare Survey* 52 (1999): 88–98; 89.

33. James Loehlin, "'These Violent Delights Have Violent Ends': Baz Luhrmann's Millennial Shakespeare," in *Shakespeare, Film, Fin de Siecle*, ed. Marc Thornton Burnett and Ramona Wray (New York: St. Martin's, 2000), 121–36; 124.

34. Loehlin, "Violent Delights," 123.

35. Courtney Lehmann, "Strictly Shakespeare? Dead Letters, Ghostly Fathers, and the Cultural Pathology of Authorship in Baz Luhrmann's *William Shakespeare's Romeo + Juliet*," *Shakespeare Quarterly* 52 (2001): 189–221; 208.

36. Kenneth Tynan, *Tynan Right and Left* (New York: Atheneum, 1967), 50.

37. G. Blakemore Evans, ed., *Romeo and Juliet* (Cambridge: Cambridge University Press, 1984), 44–45.

38. Loehlin, "Violent Delights," 130.

~

CHAPTER FOUR

In and Out of Hollywood:
Shakespeare in the Studio Era

The American studio era comprises the period from the beginning of the "talkies" to the end of the 1950s (conveniently, 1930–1960) and is wedded to the soundstages and back lots of greater Los Angeles. By the early 1930s, the Hollywood studios, having made the necessary adjustments required to incorporate synchronized sound and having created a self-regulating code to coordinate and institutionalize their handling of sensitive moral and political content, had arrived at the form that they would maintain and strengthen, with minor variations, for the next quarter century. Only three major Holly-wood Shakespeare films were made in this period: *A Midsummer Night's Dream* and *Romeo and Juliet* in the 1930s, and *Julius Caesar* in the 1950s. (The Fairbanks/Pickford *Taming of the Shrew* [1929] appeared during the transition between silent and sound.) Each was a major studio undertaking (Warner Bros. and MGM), and each contributes to our understanding of the interaction of Shakespeare and American culture, broadly considered, as well as to the larger histories of American cinema in the studio era.

Neither Orson Welles (in particular) nor Laurence Olivier saw himself as a Hollywood filmmaker, but both of them directed and starred in three Shakespeare films, each in the period under consideration, and both might be said to be working either against or under the influence of Hollywood styles and modes of production. Welles's *Macbeth* was filmed on the sound stages and back lots of Republic Pictures, a minor Hollywood studio; *Othello* and *Chimes at Midnight*, on the other hand, were filmed in Europe and North Africa, far away from Southern California. Olivier's films, *Henry V*, *Hamlet*, and *Richard III*, were made in Great Britain, but all three reflect filmmaking styles and practices associated with Hollywood. *Hamlet* has the distinction of being the first "foreign" film to win an Academy Award for best picture (Olivier himself won the Oscar for best actor). Welles and Olivier had a love/hate relationship with Hollywood (and perhaps with each other); each found success as well as failure there at various points in their careers (in Olivier's case, as an actor rather than as a filmmaker), and neither was able entirely to ignore the lure and the rewards promised by the American film industry.

A *Midsummer Night's Dream* (1935) and *Romeo and Juliet* (1936) were made at a particularly difficult time for Hollywood. The Great Depression was cutting deeply into box office receipts, and the recently enacted Production Code (published in 1930 and enforced from 1934) was being tested in an atmosphere of moral outrage at the excesses of films and film people. As John Collick asserts, A *Midsummer Night's Dream* "was produced as a conscious exercise in prestige building, not necessarily with any cynical motives but rather as an attempt to consolidate Warner's reputation as a socially responsible company with both the public and the Hays Office."[1] It would be a mistake, however, to assume that films are put into production only according to market considerations or social pressures. MGM's *Romeo and Juliet*, for example, although it was an exercise in cultural respectability (something MGM, Hollywood's most prestigious studio, needed less than Warners), came about at least in part for reasons having to do with individual human needs and desires. For Irving Thalberg, the legendary (and overrated) MGM production chief, *Romeo and Juliet* was an opportunity to showcase his wife, Norma Shearer, in a role she very much wanted to play. Both films were box office failures.

The production of A *Midsummer Night's Dream* at Warner Bros. and *Romeo and Juliet* and even the later *Julius Caesar* at MGM can be seen as characteristic, each in its own way, of the studio's approach to filmmaking. A *Midsummer Night's Dream* blends a variety of preexisting genres, including the elaborate backstage musical à la Busby Berkeley and the proletarian comedy/drama, and tries to appeal to all audiences. For the core Warner Bros. audience, the presence of Dick Powell, James Cagney, and Joe E. Brown promised comic energy and light entertainment. At the same time, the name Max Reinhardt, the famous German producer-director, signaled European "Art" and theatrical spectacle of a particular kind. Throwing dancer Nini Theilade and choreographer Bronislava Nijinska into the mix further invited the "arty," highbrow set, while the antics of Mickey Rooney's Puck and the flying fairies might be expected to appeal to children.[2] *Romeo and Juliet* fits well into MGM studio's romantic costume drama mode—tales of tragic love ending in death (*Anna Karenina, Marie Antoinette*, etc.). The film's star was Norma Shearer, who was associated with "serious" parts and costume roles (roles often drawn from the theater, like Elizabeth Barrett Browning in *The Barretts of Wimpole Street*), and she carried some of that association with her into *Romeo and Juliet*, as did director George Cukor, most recently responsible for *Little Women* (1933) and *David Copperfield* (1935). The style, tone, and meticulous attention to elements like set decoration and costuming place *Romeo and Juliet* into the "literary adaptation" genre as a self-conscious, not incidental, element. By the early 1950s, when the earlier generic categories lost relevance, MGM began to rely more and more on biblical and historical epics. *Julius Caesar*, released in 1953, clearly borrows some of this generic identity. Made at the end of the studio era, it can serve to exemplify Hollywood's approach to putting Shakespeare on film.

Film Gris: *Julius Caesar* (1953)

Producer John Houseman may have affected MGM's choice of *Julius Caesar*. Houseman, together with Orson Welles, had staged the famous modern dress, antifascist *Caesar* (subtitled "Death of a Dictator") on Broadway in

Mixing Genres

The Shakespeare film is always a mix of generic categories. The texts on which it is founded guarantee this impurity. As already noted, the literary adaptation can itself be considered a genre, so that other generic influences become add-ons to that primary generic identity. It is not always easy, however, to differentiate among genre, mode, cycle, and style. Nor is it simple to define these terms. MGM's *Romeo and Juliet* easily fits the category of the costume film, whereas Warner Bros.' *A Midsummer Night's Dream* does not, in part because of stylistic consistency. The costumes and settings of *Romeo and Juliet* are all of a piece and belong to a recognizable historical period—fifteenth-century Italy—painstakingly reconstructed on the basis of Renaissance paintings and architecture. The "look" of *A Midsummer Night's Dream*, in contrast, involves a hodgepodge of styles and periods, a deliberate confusion of pseudo-Elizabethan, baroque, art deco, and more or less timeless kitsch reminiscent of Goldwyn's *Roman Scandals* (1933) and the Marx Brothers' *Duck Soup* (1933). Whereas *Romeo and Juliet*, as stylized as it may be, appears to take place in a specific time and place, *A Midsummer Night's Dream* anchors itself neither to time nor place: its home is never-never land.

1937, and he had successfully produced *The Bad and the Beautiful* (1952) for MGM. Although the MGM film makes no attempt to reproduce either the bold style or the precise purpose of the 1937 *Caesar*, Houseman was undoubtedly influenced by his earlier experience with Shakespeare's play. Apart from Houseman himself, several cast members had connections to the Mercury *Julius Caesar*: John Hoyt repeats the role of Decius Brutus, and Edmond O'Brien (Casca) and Tom Powers (Mettelus Cimber) had played Antony and Brutus, respectively, in Mercury touring companies. Both stage production and film were certainly intended to be read in the context of contemporary political realities, though the connection was far more direct and obvious with the 1937 production. Commenting on the film, Houseman noted that "without ever deliberately exploiting the historic parallels, there were certain emotional patterns arising from political events of the immediate past that we were eager to evoke."[3] Though the film is set in ancient Rome, various elements of the Joseph Mankiewicz–directed production at least allude to recent history, including the Albert Speer–like architecture, underlined by the black-and-white photography, and the performance of Marlon Brando, who portrays Antony as a charismatic but cynical manipulator. The "forum" scene visually echoes moments from Leni Riefenstahl's *Triumph of the Will* (1935): all steps and massive blocks, with Marc Antony an isolated figure whose demagoguery is inevitably reminiscent of both Hitler and Mussolini.

As is true of nearly all Shakespeare films, especially those made in Hollywood or in the Hollywood mold, *Julius Caesar* is a product of a variety of compromises, large and small. Most obviously, the casting involved a complex balance of aesthetics and economic realities, melding studio contract players (Louis Calhern, Deborah Kerr, Greer Garson), a notable British Shakespearean (John Gielgud), a freelance, semi-independent Hollywood star of British origin (James Mason), and an up-and-coming method actor with little classical training (Marlon Brando). That this mélange of acting styles works at all is surprising, especially since no attempt apparently was made to divide the performers by nationality in any clear-cut fashion. One might argue that the more or less "fascistic" characters, exponents of "Caesarism," are Americans (Calhern's Caesar, Brando's Antony), with the Britishers Gielgud and Mason leading the conspirators. But Edmond O'Brien (Casca) is a very American conspirator, as are, for example, John Hoyt, Tom Powers, and Ian Wolfe (the Apothecary seventeen years earlier in MGM's *Romeo and Juliet*). The mob is led by Americans, notably Lawrence Dobkin and Paul Guilfoyle, who frequently appeared in cop and crook roles. George Macready best known to audiences for his icy gangster role in *Gilda* (1946) and most recently the sleazy abortionist in *Detective Story* (1951), plays one of the first opponents of Caesarism we see.

Shakespeare wrote *Julius Caesar* in such a way that only a perfect balance of skillful performers would achieve his intended effect. The play's stage history suggests that this balance has seldom been achieved or even desired. If the company's lead actor chooses to play Antony, the chances are good that it will be Antony's play. To claim that Shakespeare balances the main characters is not to say that he fails to take sides. The balance is a dramatic device that allows Caesar, Brutus, Cassius, and Antony to have powerful theatrical moments where they can count on the audience's sympathies. Houseman's and director Joseph Mankiewicz's casting strategies were clearly designed to construct such a balance, but through contrast rather than equivalence. This is achieved in part through contrasting styles of performance, in part through an emphasis on the extremes each character exhibits. Louis Calhern's Caesar is both vainglorious and vulnerable, arrogant and avuncular, while John Gielgud's Cassius, neurotically intense, projects a deep cynicism not unmixed with touching sincerity and emotional need. James Mason as Brutus combines a powerful sense of duty with a too easy reliance on his own judgment and integrity. Brando's Antony provides us with perhaps the sharpest sense of contrast. He employs his trademark coiled indolence in the early scenes, adding passionate intensity and manipulative cynicism for the forum speech. Brando's Antony is ultimately the true fascist: cold, ruthless, and unsentimental.

The casting of Marlon Brando as Antony is of particular interest for a number of reasons. Like other actors trained or influenced by "the Method," he most often played characters whose words were inadequate to the feelings he wanted to express—hence the broken sentences, half-finished thoughts, and, particularly in Brando's case, the supposed "mumbling." In *Julius Caesar*, however, Brando is called on to play a character for whom language is a subterfuge designed to keep his true feelings from showing at all. Furthermore, contrary to the fears of many, Brando gives Shakespeare's lines their necessary rhetorical weight, even if the rhythm and breath control are sometimes off kilter. With the soliloquy ("O, pardon me, thou bleeding piece of earth") over Caesar's body (filmed in three unbroken shots), Brando brings a furious, not altogether disciplined passion into the film, not necessarily of a greater intensity than the passion of Gielgud's Cassius, but less contained, more naked and unselfconscious, more "modern" and less "Roman." The effect of Brando's performance is to underline the fact that Shakespeare wrote the role of Antony in such a way that we are never entirely certain of his sincerity or lack of it.

Julius Caesar can also be seen as a compromise between the epic and the domestic, sliding from long shots of Rome and Roman crowds to moody close-ups reminiscent of urban crime thrillers. Even the music contributes to this effect: Miklos Rosza, who scored *Quo Vadis* and *Ivanhoe* and would go on to write epic scores for *Ben-Hur* and *King of Kings*, also composed distinctive music for urban noir classics like *The Killers*, *Naked City*, and *The Asphalt Jungle*. Consequently the film echoes some of the anachronisms of Shakespeare's play: a story and characters at once ancient and modern, Roman and English, based on the historical record but answering to contemporary realities. Much of this was no doubt conscious and deliberate, though some of the specific effects may have been incidental if not entirely accidental by-products of purely commercial decisions.

The ultimate compromise, perhaps, was the negotiation among cultural tastes and distinctions active in 1950s America: the ongoing high-, middle-, and lowbrow discourse. Here again, "Shakespeare" was a fluid commodity. How high was his brow? To what audiences might he appeal? *Julius Caesar*, perhaps not surprisingly, had long played a special role in American culture. "As a work of literature," John Ripley writes, "*Julius Caesar* was much read and admired by eighteenth-century American intellectuals."[4] The attraction presumably was related to the play's perceived "republicanism," a point underlined by its American stage history, which favored the roles of Brutus and Cassius over those of Caesar and Mark Antony. The filmmakers were covering their bets, at least to an extent, by choosing *Julius Caesar*, a play with a "populist" history, a single, straightforward plot, set in the distant past but capable of energizing contemporary concerns. In a number of ways one of Shakespeare's most accessible plays, *Julius Caesar* was, partly for that reason, firmly ensconced in the American secondary school curriculum. It was the one Shakespeare play that virtually every high school student was assigned to read in 1953 (and had been since the late nineteenth century). MGM could thus count on school groups to provide some box office potential and subsidiary commercial value on the 16-millimeter market. The film was featured in publications aimed at educators, like the *Audio-Visual Guide*. (It was from similar motives that the young Orson Welles edited a school version of the play in 1934.) In this context, the casting of Marlon Brando could be seen as an extra fillip for the teen audience (his other 1953 film was *The Wild One*), captive though many of them would be. As an additional incentive to the studio, leftover sets from *Quo Vadis* (1951) could be redressed, thereby saving money at a time when MGM's revenues were steadily declining. This last point relates as well to questions of genre: *Julius Caesar*, as noted earlier, contributes to the early 1950s cycle of biblical and pseudobiblical epics like *Quo Vadis*, *Samson and Delilah* (1949), *David and Bathsheba* (1951), and *The Robe* (1953).

Although some have described MGM's *Julius Caesar* as "theatrical," it would be more accurate to see the film as "televisual." At the same time that Hollywood was attempting to find ways of distancing itself from television, it was emulating some of the techniques and effects of the rival medium. The relatively long takes, the heavy reliance on close-ups, the employment of what appears to be a unit set, and even the black-and-white photography, all are associated with the style and the "look" of live television drama.[5] In spite of the film's epic pretensions (which, in fact, are minimal—Miklos Rozsa's score provides much of the film's sense of grandiosity and pomp), *Julius Caesar*'s mise-en-scène, its reconstruction of preimperial Rome, is stark and spare: "The Rome of the movie is a hard place that chokes off all tenderness."[6] According to Jack Jorgens, "the grayness and lack of contrast . . . added to the lack of depth caused by the flat lighting, give [the film] the appearance of a frieze, and its starkness and ambivalence are heightened by the absence of reaction shots and point-of-view shots."[7] Mankiewicz, as Samuel Crowl observes, "explicitly refuses to give us the spectacle version of Rome we might expect from Hollywood to concentrate instead on a tightly focused formalist approach eager to explore the play's irony and ambiguity."[8] As John Houseman explained, "Our sets are architectural: some small, some massive, but all, we trust dramatically effective. . . . Our main stage . . . has the line and scope of great stage design."[9]

The several crowd scenes, particularly the opening sequence depicting the Romans going about their business, do not distract from the fact that the setting was designed primarily as an acting space, only energized when completed with performers reciting Shakespeare's words. Rome, in other words, comprises several important, highly symbolic places (the marketplace, the senate, the forum, the Colosseum) where the key actors—Brutus, Cassius, Caesar, and Antony—play out their personal and political drama, employing carefully selected props (the busts of Caesar and of Brutus's ancestor, Junius Brutus, the steps and platforms of the forum, Pompey's statue). These objects and places in turn exist to be used by these performers as they play their historical roles. The bust of Caesar we see in the opening scene, a particularly lifeless reproduction reminiscent of a death mask, strewn with garlands and attended by numerous pigeons, foreshadows Caesar's fate and prefigures his later egotistical boast that he is "unshaked of motion." Busts, statues, and monuments become absent presences during the first colloquy between Brutus and Cassius, reminding us simultaneously of Caesar's power grab (he wants to place himself among Rome's ancient heroes) and Brutus's noble lineage, represented by the bust of his Republican ancestor, Junius Brutus (the identity is made clear with Cassius's line, "There was a Brutus once that would have brooked / Th'eternal devil to keep his state in Rome / As easily as a king.")[10]

The visual style of *Julius Caesar* has sometimes been associated with film noir, and, as already noted, there is some justice to this characterization. The storm sequence in particular, as Jack Jorgens observes,[11] provides an opportunity for noirish effects, including rain-swept streets, low-key lighting, and sharp contrast of bright and dark. Edmond O'Brien, who throughout the late 1940s and early 1950s appeared in such noir and near noir films as *The Killers*, *DOA*, and *White Heat*, contributes to the generic identification. But if film noir represents a low-key, shadowy world of people at the end of their rope, morally bankrupt and easily seduced, a world of what Vivian Sobchak

In Joseph Mankiewicz's *Julius Caesar*, Louis Calhern's Caesar is a complex mix of strength and vulnerability.

memorably termed "lounge time,"[12] the style and significant action of *Julius Caesar* might more aptly fit the film into a category one critic identified as "film gris," gray cinema. It would be a serious misreading both of Shakespeare's play and of Mankiewicz's film to see it as yet another exercise in noirish gangsterism. (Catherine Belsey, on the other hand, reads the film as "a direct descendant of the classic western, and its central conflict is between two individuals, Brutus, honest, liberal, possibly misled, and Antony, subtle, devious and self-seeking.")[13] That the gangster elements are present is undeniable, particularly in the casting of several key characters: Louis Calhern as Caesar and, as I have noted, Edmond O'Brien as Casca. But too much can be made of this as well. Calhern, after all, had most immediately played Shakespeare's King Lear on the stage for John Houseman, and O'Brien, though a staple of crime and noir films, was often cast as a policeman or a detective.

The noir milieu is there, but it needs to be more closely defined. Visually, as I have already noted, *Julius Caesar* is far more gris than noir; indeed, the word "gray" is frequently employed whenever the film is discussed. The term "film gris," or an equivalent, has been employed by several students of 1940s and 1950s cinema, most notably Thom Anderson.[14] In his reading, film gris is associated with leftist filmmakers investigated by HUAC (the House Un-American Activities Committee) and the films they produced from 1947 to 1951 (some blacklisted and some, interestingly, graylisted). Houseman and Mankiewicz, though they avoided the blacklist, were both well-known liberals, Mankiewicz having had a notable run-in with the red-baiting Cecil B. DeMille. My point is that *Julius Caesar* fits, to an extent, Anderson's discovery of "greater psychological and social realism" film gris than was usually the case with film noir. The left, as James Naremore writes, was "greatly interested in stories about fascist or authoritarian personalities."[15] Film gris, to generalize, often involves the question of moral choice; in film noir, the choice was made long ago.

Associating *Julius Caesar* with film gris inevitably leads to a consideration of how this film fits into its Cold War context. Any attempt to see *Julius Caesar* as a Cold War parable, however, immediately runs into difficulties. Anthony Miller rightly argues that "the film's political suggestions are open-ended, elastic, and reversible."[16] Of course, these may be precisely the qualities that would identify the film as a Cold War document. It is more difficult to see the film as "leftist" in any meaningful sense, in spite of the left credentials of both Houseman and Mankiewicz. Nor is it self-evident that *Julius Caesar* "engages fully the audience's sympathies with James Mason's Brutus,"[17] any more than we need agree that the film upholds the idea that "social disruption was produced by unscrupulous individuals in quest of personal power."[18] For someone who wants to make an unambiguous political statement, Shakespeare's play is probably not the best vehicle. Which is not to deny that *Julius Caesar* is, almost to the exclusion of any other categorical description, a political play. As such, it necessarily opens itself to theatrical interpretations that may have little or nothing to do with either the specifics of preimperial Roman history or the politics of the Elizabethan monarchy. No production of *Julius Caesar* has, to my knowledge, aroused the same kinds of passions excited by several productions of the more inflammatory *Coriolanus*, but playgoers, readers, directors, and critics could hardly ignore the words spoken by Cassius after the assassination of Caesar: "How many ages hence / Shall this our lofty scene be acted over / In states unborn and accents yet unknown?" (3.1.111–13). Shakespeare may here be thinking as much of the hoped-for theatrical afterlife of his play as of the fall of tyrants, but his words certainly invite future audiences to seek parallels in the political turmoil of their own times.

A great virtue of the MGM *Julius Caesar* is that it complicates our response to the play rather than determines it. Shakespeare has created characters who are inconsistent with themselves in word and deed. Antony provides a perfect instance of this. The Antony who loves plays and carouses late of nights is talked about but not much seen. Brando first appears in his athlete garb, half-naked, sensual, and deferential to Caesar. Antony the sensualist and Brando the sexual icon are introduced simultaneously, but the remainder of the film pretty much ignores this side of Antony's personality. We see the Antony who "loved his friend" and sincerely mourns Caesar's death (how else but sincerely can we interpret his impassioned soliloquy over Caesar's dead body?). Antony the rabble-rouser is clearly in evidence in the forum scene, where Caesar's body becomes a prop in Antony's repertoire of tricks, while Antony the ruthless cynic dominates the so-called proscription scene. The next time we see him, he is expressing contempt for Brutus and Cassius. Then, at the end of the play, inexplicably, he is eulogizing Brutus as "the noblest Roman of them all." As a character in the psychological sense, Antony self-destructs.

John Gielgud's rhetorical mastery serves to underline Cassius's own skills as a persuader. Cassius's resentment of Caesar is strong, but it is not allowed to become merely personal. Gielgud's focused performance marshals everything as evidence, each detail a calculated contribution to the pattern of denunciation he is weaving for Brutus's benefit. Roy Walker, who saw Gielgud's stage Cassius, finds "a dangerous implacability in his film performance that impresses me as even finer than his stage interpretation."[19] If there is a neurotic edge to Gielgud's Cassius, it stems not so much from his envy of Caesar as from his fear that Brutus does not value him as highly as he might. His performance constantly modulates between passion and calculation, each register moderating the effect of the other. Louis Calhern's Caesar is a complex mix of strength and vulnerability, combining an awareness of his all too human fears with a pride in his own accomplishments that encourages him to a dangerous vanity. Even his most outrageously pompous statements seem aimed at convincing himself as much as others.

James Mason's thoughtful, low-key Brutus fits Orson Welles's description of the character as he played him in the 1937 Mercury production, "the bourgeois intellectual who, under a modern dictatorship, is the first to be put up against the wall and shot."[20] Although Houseman claimed that "James Mason's Brutus is the hero of our tragedy. . . . It is for him, in Hollywood parlance, that you should be rooting,"[21] Brutus's heroic role is highly compromised. His stoicism and reliance on logic, as Mason projects these qualities, seem rather inhuman. And just as Brutus allows himself to be seduced by Cassius and beaten by Antony, Mason seems satisfied to allow the more flamboyant performers, Gielgud and Brando, to take the film away from him. In part because of Mason's reticence, Brutus's forum speech has seldom seemed as specious as it does here. It becomes an appeal to reason that consists of illogical connections and false options that Brutus appears not to believe himself. Brutus is further undercut by Mankiewicz's mise-en-scène. The soliloquy that begins "It must be by his death" (2.1) is filmed in such a way that, as Brutus walks around in his garden, the latticelike bare tree branches photographed from a high camera angle suggest that he is constructing a verbal web that will entrap not only Caesar but himself as well. For Samuel Crowl, the imagery in this scene reflects "the tangled nature of Brutus's tortured reasoning."[22]

The assassination scene is strangely muted. The killing of Caesar becomes a private, almost domestic act—the other senators barely respond, a passive audience to a strange ritual. The conspirators, for their part, perform on cue, taking up their positions according to plan, and even Caesar appears to be acting out a predetermined role, puffing himself up in arrogance so as to be all the more appropriate a victim. Once again, the minimalism of the setting places the focus squarely on the actors, who move in a nearly abstract space. Here as throughout the film, Mankiewicz generally avoids reaction shots or shot/reverse shot patterns, and concentrates instead on grouping the actors and significantly blocking their movements in counterpoint to other elements of the mise-en-scène. In Brutus's orchard, for example, the actors are positioned and moved to construct a continuing tension between the image of Brutus standing alone and Brutus among the conspirators, Brutus and Cassius together, and then apart. At several points, a large urn separates Brutus from the others. Other highly charged objects energize this scene: the bust of Junius Brutus (a variation of the one we saw in the Colosseum) and a sculpture (sometimes we see only its shadow) of the she-wolf that suckled Romulus and Remus. Although these objects could be seen as the set decorator's shorthand for "Rome," they serve the more specific function of placing the conspiracy in the larger context of Rome's founding and Brutus's double-edged republican heritage.

That important character "the crowd" is here almost comically fickle, which is perhaps a fault of direction rather than the result of conscious design. The stop-and-start nature of their movement turns them into marionettes, their strings continually jerked by Antony. Hollywood's capacity to provide numerous extras may work against the play's dramaturgy. Shakespeare, having to rely on a handful of actors (he gives lines to only four plebeians), created specific voices for each of his citizens. It is quite likely that the remainder of the citizens were the Globe audience (as was the case in the 1999 production in the restored Globe). In film, however, the several hundred extras cease to project any individuality. They are an undifferentiated mass, and the citizens Shakespeare has given lines to now become rabble-rousers ("ugly, sexless, and hysterical," one viewer found),[23] rather than stand-ins for the people. In consequence, the film takes on a distinctly anti-populist bent, aided by the casting of tough-guy or comic character actors like Lawrence Dobkin and Paul Guilfoyle in the "citizen" roles.

If MGM's *Julius Caesar* seldom seems as cinematically exciting as one would hope, it remains a powerful if low-key interpretation of Shakespeare's play: straightforward, well crafted, and at times a bit dull. It successfully employs charismatic performers who, in spite of very different backgrounds and training, work together convincingly as an ensemble. Both a "respectful" mounting of Shakespeare's play and a film of its time, serious and rather grim, *Julius Caesar* is an ultimately pessimistic take on the inevitable corruption of political action. Released as it was at a moment when the Hollywood studio system was coming to an end, MGM's Shakespeare film nicely summarizes the studio's pretensions to "Ars Gratia Artis" ("art for art's sake"—MGM's motto) versus the commercialism that in reality had guided its activities for a quarter of a century. In the end, *Julius Caesar* made only a small profit for the studio, perhaps justifying the commercial instincts of a Louis B. Mayer, the longtime MGM studio chief and "vulgarian" who had been forced out of his position in 1951, before the film went into production, to be replaced by the liberal New Deal Democrat Dore Schary.

Laurence Olivier: Shakespeare and the "Art Cinema"

The three Shakespeare films directed by Laurence Olivier are in part notable for how different each is from the other two, which suggests that, as a film director, Olivier did not have a particularly strong personality; more a producer than a director, he assembled disparate creative talents without imposing an overarching "vision" on them. Each film, of course, was made under specific and differing cultural and material circumstances. *Henry V* was a contribution to home-front morale in the last years of World War II, at once celebrating military prowess and England's Great Poet. *Hamlet* was made at a time when the British film industry seemed poised to challenge Hollywood's hold on English-speaking markets with "quality" films like David Lean's *Brief Encounter* (1945), *Great Expectations* (1946), and *Oliver Twist* (1948); Powell and Pressburger's *The Red Shoes* (1948); and Carol Reed's *Odd Man Out* (1946). *Richard III* (1955) was made under less propitious circumstances and depended for its production grosses on actual and potential television exhibition. All three films were, to a greater or lesser extent, well received in the United States and even welcomed by the Hollywood establishment. Clearly, Olivier's Shakespeare films were no particular threat in the American market.

All three films are focused on and anchored by Olivier's performances in the title roles, performances that reveal different aspects of his acting personality. In *Henry V*, he starts out as the matinee idol, romantic leading man he was in the 1930s. He plays Henry more or less straight, allowing his striking good looks and charmingly casual physical movements to establish the king's personality. In the central scenes, encased in shining armor, he is an iconic version of the hero, an image more than a man; even in the scene with the common soldiers, his disguised Hal holds on to the exalted vision he has of himself. Only at the end, in the wooing scene, does he depart from the heroic mold, giving a very different performance as the awkward, uncertain lover, at once self-deprecating and proud. But Olivier makes it clear that it is a performance, a charm attack as focused and practiced as any battle. Although Olivier brings comedic skills to the scene, a strong element of coldness and artifice lies behind the mask.

As You Like It

As an actor, Laurence Olivier had an early experience with Shakespeare on film, playing Orlando in Paul Czinner's *As You Like It* (1936), a peculiar film that manages to be by turns charming and leaden, at once vivid and rather too precious. The central performances are wildly disparate. Elizabeth Bergner, newly arrived in England from Germany with Czinner, her director husband, is clearly a skilled actress who is playing the wrong role in the wrong language in the wrong medium. Her Rosaline is much too sophisticated and arch, and she works too hard at being "girlish." Perhaps because of her accent, she speaks with excessive deliberation. Physically, she lends energy to the film with her almost constant but elegant movement (though she seems quite conscious of the effect her figure is making in boy's attire), but even this element becomes overly studied. One critic complained of Bergner's "temperamental inability to stop wriggling."[24] Olivier, as Orlando, is very much the matinee idol, looking almost Italianate, all curly black hair and swarthy skin (in the evenings, he was playing Mercutio in John Gielgud's production of *Romeo and Juliet* at the New Theatre). His acting personality, one senses, is already too strong for Orlando (one of Shakespeare's more unrewarding roles). Although he moves somewhat uneasily between callowness and sophistication, he brings wit and charm to a role not particularly strong in either quality. At times he appears self-conscious, almost as if he would prefer that the camera were not there. Much of the time, he and Bergner seem to be acting in different movies.

Hamlet, perhaps because it is more of an ensemble piece than *Henry V*, is seemingly more of a director's film than an actor's, even though Olivier occupies a perhaps higher percentage of screen time than he did in *Henry V*. As a director, he places his performance of Hamlet in context, as another, albeit important, element of the mise-en-scène. Again, the heroic actor in Olivier overcomes any temptation to sentimentality or excessive introspection. Olivier is every inch the prince. As Holden Caulfield, an astute film critic, lamented, "He was too much like a goddam general, instead of a sad, screwed-up type of guy."[25] Holden, who frequently (and unconvincingly) tells us that he hates "the goddam movies," points to a central element of Olivier's performance, but he leaves something out: though this is a Hamlet who is essentially a man of action, someone who ought to be a general, he despises himself for not being one. Olivier both sustains and plays against the heroic expectations by revealing, in crucial moments, something very like nausea, a nausea directed at himself as much as at Claudius or the corrupt court of Denmark. Although much has been made of the Oedipal aspect of Olivier's film, we have no strong sense that Hamlet particularly loves his mother. Rather, Olivier presents a Hamlet who recognizes his own corruption in a corrupt world. As an actor, Olivier is especially adept at appearing to be dead behind the eyes, and a touch of this effect is evident at several key moments in the film. Essentially, however, Olivier is a Hamlet who fits Ophelia's description: "the soldier, scholar's eye, tongue, sword."

Richard III, on the other hand, is an actor's holiday, and to say that Olivier "hogs" the screen would not be an exaggeration. A. B. Walkeley's description of Sir Henry Irving's manner in the opening soliloquy could just as well fit Olivier: "please make no mistake, I am the villain of this play; sit tight, keep your eye on me, and I will see you get your money's worth."[26] Olivier's Richard is at once frightening and comic, but he is also, like Hal and Hamlet, essentially heroic in spite of his villainy. Even more than Hamlet, this Richard is "a goddam general" who, in an alternate universe, would not need to murder his way to the top—he would be there by right. Like Richard, Olivier ruthlessly eliminated competitors who might draw away from his central importance. Queen Margaret, for example, disappears entirely, and the counterweight of Shakespeare's weeping queens is considerably trimmed. The film Richard is a theatrical construct, and Olivier uses cinematic means such as close-ups, moving camera, and long takes not to detract from, but rather to enhance, that theatricality. And it is not only Olivier the actor who infuses Richard with life, it is also Olivier the director/producer. Shakespeare's Richard is very much the actor manager, arranging every detail of the mise-en-scène and moving characters about at will. The modified Colley Cibber adaptation Olivier uses—an egomaniac's delight, one commentator remarked after seeing Cibber's performance—underlines that aspect of Shakespeare's play.

Olivier always claimed not to have taken film acting seriously until he worked with William Wyler on *Wuthering Heights* (1939). Clearly he was influenced by Wyler's directorial style. A *metteur en scène* more than an auteur, Wyler had a style characterized by composition in depth, which creates tension and meaning in the space between foreground and background action, depth of focus, and carefully worked-out deployment of characters in a highly charged dramatic space, combined with expressive camera movement. Wyler's influence is perhaps more evident in *Hamlet* and *Richard III* than it is in *Henry V*. For his directorial debut, Olivier adapts an eclectic mix of styles, drawn in part from European art cinema (notably Eisenstein's

Alexander Nevsky [1937] for the Battle of Agincourt), in part influenced by medieval art, and in part necessitated by Olivier's desire to reproduce the Elizabethan theater as a way of encouraging viewers to accept theatrical conventions foreign to film. *Hamlet* and *Richard III* are each more of a piece, the former almost entirely studio bound and the latter associated with strong visual continuity, which a "unit set" encourages. All three films, in the words of Anthony Davies, "abound with those moments which bring theatricality to the film and then advance its impact in a way which only cinema can."[27]

Olivier's Shakespeare films appear to belong to an elaborate, interactive Shakespeare museum. Each is a carefully constructed object that captures a Shakespeare set in amber. The amber, in this case, is the cinema, and what the cinema has captured is a timeless, heroic, romantic Shakespeare, a Shakespeare that exists in great part to showcase the star actor. Even though each film can be placed in a specific cultural and social context and "moment," each film at the same time constructs a world of its own, a world that combines, as Jack Jorgens writes of *Richard III*, "a unique blend of realism, theatricalism, and painterliness."[28] Like a Victorian toy theater, Olivier's films appear to have been carefully constructed and built up in every detail. They seem to rely on a vision almost childish in the pleasure it takes in the act of construction. Olivier said that he wanted the Danish rulers to look like the king and queen in a deck of playing cards, suggesting something of the playfulness that lies behind all three films. A grander way of suggesting the effect would be to say that *Henry V, Hamlet,* and *Richard III* are *Kunstwerke*, in the manner of Wagner's operas. Each detail of the mise-en-scène—sets, lighting, makeup, costume, movement of the actor—and cinematography was designed with an eye to the total effect in a manner that seems especially self-conscious and deliberate.

The toy theater analogy points also to the "three-dimensionality" of Olivier's Shakespeare films. Staging in depth and deep-focus cinematography, which Olivier may have learned from Wyler and cinematographer Gregg Toland, necessarily encourage the marshaling of actors and objects in a three-dimensional space. Though the deep-focus, moving-camera, long-take style has sometimes been praised for intensifying the sense of reality, it can, in truth, have an almost opposite effect. This is forcibly evident in *Hamlet*, the most soundstage bound of the three. The world of the film cannot be defined by actual temporal or geographic boundaries. All that we can say for certain, after the first few moments of screen time, is that we are dealing with "pastness," with something primordial and primitive, with a world closer to dream than to waking, existing in night rather than day—a world of dreams.

Depth of focus simply helps strengthen the sense of unreality. In life, we learn to block out whatever elements in our environment do not force themselves on our attention. Part of the unease of Olivier's *Hamlet* comes from the way our attention, like Hamlet's own, is sensitized by the environment. All elements are present at all times. Nothing can be wiped out of either consciousness or memory, and foreground and background, past and present, are one. With *Richard III*, which I want to look at in more detail, Olivier weds the Technicolor artifice of *Henry V* to the moving-camera and deep-focus style of *Hamlet*.

Danse Macabre: Richard III

With *Richard III*, Olivier did not have to face either the patriotic challenge of telling the story of England's most heroic monarch in the midst of World War II or the literary and theatrical challenge of playing Hamlet, a role whose every interpretation is tested and measured against every previous one. Olivier is free to do as he pleases, portraying a character of little depth or dimension, but one who, nonetheless, is made up of a set of characteristics almost purely external, a physical presence—hunchback; limp, shrunken arm (to which Olivier adds a pointed nose and a sleek black wig)—and a verbal facility and range—comic, threatening, sardonic, intimate, rhetorical—that encourages a display of the full range of the actor's repertoire. Already very much a vehicle for Richard, Shakespeare's play becomes even more focused on its central character in the transfer to film. Even the film's deployment of space encourages us to see the world itself as Richard's / Olivier's platform, podium, and stage—large, empty rooms, antechambers, and passageways, places in which we so often find Richard alone, ruminating, scheming, plotting.

The camera is drawn to Richard's presence as by a magnetic force, an effect established early on as a large door, closed by a servant, magically reopens to allow the camera to enter and find Richard, alone, waiting for it—and for us. The production and costume designers (Roger and Margaret Furse and Carmen Dillon), as they did with *Henry V*, provided strongly rendered elements of deep, saturated colors for both sets and costumes, though here the royal blues, reds, and golds are complemented by browns and blacks. Unlike *Henry V*, the space in *Richard III* is three-dimensional, and the deep-focus style, enhanced by the fine resolution of the large negative area of VistaVision, helps construct an effect of empty spaciousness. The sets are designed as essentially blank walls of one color decorated with bas-reliefs of contrasting colors—window frames, fireplaces, and so on—that give an impression of Wedgewood china. The colorfully dressed actors stand out against these attractive but only slightly sketched-in backgrounds. Doors, windows, and arches are the primary decorative elements, framing actors and pointing up entrances and exits.

Olivier appears to have borrowed elements of Tyrone Guthrie's production of *Richard III* with Emlyn Williams at the Old Vic in 1937: "The set was made up of a group of windows and doors (like a triptych) which opened and closed to suggest various settings."[29] In the opening soliloquy, the throne, together with pillars that "frame" it on either side, and the crown suspended from the ceiling, form an "inner" stage for Richard, and even the lighting, as in the theater, changes with Richard's mood as well as with his position on the set. The effect is to suggest that we, as a cinema audience, are watching a film that is not theater but *contains* theater, that the various actors are playing roles *within* the world of the film, occupying sets and being "onstage." As Russell Lees remarks on the commentary track to the Criterion laser disc edition, Shakespeare has already treated a number of the scenes in *Richard III* as minidramas ("The Fall of Hastings," for example) within the larger drama. Olivier takes this a step further, constructing a play within the play within the film.

From beginning to end, *Richard III* resembles a *danse macabre*, with Richard leading and almost everyone and everything else following, harnessed to his will. Alone, as in the opening soliloquy, he engages in a pas de deux with

The Fall of Hastings . . . a play within a play within Laurence Olivier's film *Richard III*. Copyright © 1955 London Films.

the camera, while Olivier the director at once maintains the "theatrical" tension of time wed to space while using the moving camera to "edit" Richard's presentation of self in a range from close-up to long shot. When Richard is not alone, his bent body, balanced into a forward trajectory, continually violates the private space of other characters, and especially of Anne, who is both repulsed and attracted by his physical presence; as Jack Jorgens notes, Richard's "list to one side often makes him the most pronounced diagonal in the frame."[30] The effect is evident as well in the staging of Shakespeare's 1.3, which might be called "Richard with the Queen and Her Relatives." In two takes, the first a minute and a half, the second three minutes, Richard, addressing each character in turn and berating Queen Elizabeth and her family and supporters even as he shares little jokes and double entendres with his allies and toadies, remains in perpetual motion, imposing his interpretation of motives and events through sheer dynamism. Even the film's unit set functions to strengthen the sense that Richard is the controlling intelligence behind all that we see and hear. Specific locations appear, almost as if by magic, where and when he needs them to appear. The council chamber, for example, is a few steps away from the cells of the Tower of London, and doors and windows exist primarily to serve his bidding, opening and closing according to his immediate needs, as if he were "a puppet-master displaying his manipulative skills."[31]

Given what we know of Richard's character, his winning of Anne, though on one level hard to credit, is nonetheless charged with erotic "frisson." Just as "Richard" invites his audience to recognize the handsome, charming, charismatic Laurence Olivier behind the fright wig and false nose, so Richard seduces Anne with the same Jekyll/Hyde personification, conquering her with a sexual magnetism the audience is encouraged to feel as well. In preparing for the film, Olivier later recalled, he was aware that "Richard would be flirting with the camera—sometimes only inches away from his eyes—and would lay his head on the camera's bosom if he could."[32] The charm and attractiveness, however, are balanced by the sudden flashes of anger and cruelty. Olivier, as Constance Brown writes in her excellent essay on the film, "has incorporated ample suggestions of sadism and power as a sexual object into his film."[33] For Richard, achieving the throne is a form of sexual conquest; having won his prize, he appears to sink into a postcoital funk.

Having eliminated Margaret from the film, Olivier gives Richard no really worthy adversaries. The focus, when it is not on Richard, is on Richard's victims. Although Clare Bloom lends little more than pathos to her playing of Anne (Joyce Redman, Olivier's original stage Anne, would perhaps have been a better choice), Clarence is movingly played by John Gielgud, who modulates the character's changing moods and emotions into a strong dramatic vignette (he is, however, deprived of his scene of pleading with his murderers). Gielgud's lyric intensity sharply contrasts with Olivier's hard, eccentric, broken-backed delivery, on the one hand, and Ralph Richardson's sardonic, matter-of-fact manner as Buckingham, on the other. (Olivier later wrote that he made a mistake casting Richardson, who was not "oily enough"; in retrospect, he would have preferred Orson Welles!)[34] Olivier allows both actors and the characters they play to dominate, if only briefly, important thematic and dramatic moments. Clarence's recounting of his dream could be seen as Shakespeare showing off his lyrical and descriptive powers, but it serves a significant purpose as well. It involves us, at least for a brief time, with an imagination at least as compelling as Richard's, though far different in its effect. Clarence's fear of death and his guilty conscience, expressed with finely calibrated emotional force in Gielgud's reading, provides a counterweight to Richard's complete absence of feeling. And Richardson's Buckingham, recounting the failure of his mission to energize the general populace in Richard's favor, appears to enjoy his partner's discomfiture, telling his tale with maddening pauses while he gathers food and drink for a belated dinner. (One might be tempted to find that Richardson steals the scene—essentially a long take during which the camera follows Richardson's movements—from Olivier, were it not that, as director, Olivier has clearly given the scene over to him.)

The severe cuts and rearrangements Olivier and his collaborators performed on Shakespeare's text result in a crucial change of focus. In Shakespeare's play, Richard is ultimately just another victim of what Jan Kott has termed the "Grand Mechanism" of history; he may think he controls fate, but in fact fate controls him. Queen Margaret reminds Richard, as well as the audience, of the inevitable turn of Fortune's wheel. That Richard is in so many ways an attractive and appealing villain is Shakespeare's way of tempting us into a similar hubris, into a belief that the individual can cancel the efficacy of the machine. Cibber and Olivier, as well as many a Richard in between and after, cannot resist the urge to stack the deck in Richard's favor, sensing, perhaps rightly, that Shakespeare had the same temptation. The saintly Richmond, together with the weeping queens, pitiful children, and moaning ghosts, could all be seen as Shakespeare's overdetermined strategy to keep Richard in his place.

In a variety of ways, *Richard III* is more "theatrical" than Olivier's other Shakespeare films. Again, I am not referring to "staginess" but to a certain

kind of "artifice" that has its origins in the theater. One of the most obtru-
sive, perhaps, is the way Olivier emphasizes certain "points," or moments of
high drama. In the nineteenth-century theater, a "point" was a piece of business audiences had come to expect in a familiar play that is signaled by a kind
of "freeze" in the action, often punctuated by loud, sharp chords of music (for
Richard III, many of those "points" were from Cibber). Among these in Olivier's film are Richard's response to York's reference to his humpback; Richard
exhibiting his "newly" withered arm to Hastings and company; Richard forcing Buckingham to kneel and kiss his hand at the end of the mayor scene;
Richard forcing a pillow on Tyrell's face to illustrate how he wants the
princes killed, among others. (Not surprisingly, virtually every one of these
involves actions by Richard.) What appears most theatrical are Olivier's tab-
leaux, an effect more evident here than in his other films. If Richard continually bustles, moving quickly from place to place, from room to room, from
court to tower and back, other characters seem frozen into place, posed as on
a tapestry or in a waxworks display. In the "reconciliation" scene, the sharp,
even-focused VistaVision image allows us to be aware of every character in
the frame, each playing a formalized, foreordained role in the highly ritualized, hypocritical scene of false amity, with Richard alone zipping around
lobbing verbal grenades and in general ironizing the ritual moments. Far from
"stagy," however, this scene is quite precisely "cinematic." The camera is
almost constantly in movement, reframing the action in ways that pointedly
stress the relationships among the various characters, isolating factions and
selecting out temporary alliances as they form and re-form in the course of
the scene. Rather than "uncinematic," Olivier's film needs to be seen as participating in the "long-take" style of directors like William Wyler, Max
Ophuls, Jean Renoir, F. W. Murnau, and, of course, Orson Welles.

Orson Welles versus Shakespeare

The three Shakespeare films Orson Welles was able to complete should ideally be examined in the context of a rich and complex career in theater, film,
radio, and television—all media in which Welles presented, or was involved
in presentations of, Shakespeare.[35] Here it is sufficient to note that *Macbeth*
(1948), *Othello* (1952), and *Chimes at Midnight/Falstaff* (1966) were, like so
many of Welles's projects, made under less than ideal conditions, conditions
partly self-imposed and partly the consequences of Welles's inability to come
to terms with the commercial requirements of the Hollywood studios. All
three films are personal and idiosyncratic and could constitute a small sub-

genre all of their own, the "Welles/Shakespeare film." What they share includes a dynamic interaction between the film stylistics and the literary text together with a sometimes ruthless reorganization of Shakespeare's language and structure into a totally new configuration of words and images. These are films of restless energy and challenging abstraction; they might almost be thought of as works in progress, meditations on and critiques of the plays they interpret, challenges offered up to Shakespeare and Shakespeareans. Like the Shakespeare "collages" of Charles Marowitz, a Welles Shakespeare film "combines speed, discontinuity and dramatic juxtaposition. . . . The effect of this swift, fragmentary method is to generate a surreal style that communicates experience from a subjective standpoint, thereby shifting the focus of events from an exterior to an interior reality."[36]

If we consider Wellesian cinematic Shakespeare as genre, what are the identifying or common points of resemblance? First, a visual style—we may call it expressionistic for want of a better shorthand—that refuses "realism" at almost every level: mise-en-scène, cinematography, sound, performance. The scenery may, as in *Macbeth*, be entirely artificial: soundstage exteriors, papier-mâché sets, inharmonious costumes; or, as in *Othello*, the "real" world of Venice and Morocco; or, as in *Chimes at Midnight*, a combination of real exteriors and constructed interiors. In each instance, the world of the film is presented in a highly subjective fashion. The world of *Macbeth* is essentially distorted in the prefilmic conception, while in *Othello* the real world is fragmented and disassembled by editing and camera movement. In *Chimes* the stylistic emphasis is a matter of camera lenses and lighting. These, of course, are not exclusive categories. The sets of *Macbeth* are reinterpreted through lighting and lens distortion; *Othello* employs sets as well as location photography; and *Chimes*, though it may be in some ways more "realistic" looking than the other two, also employs stylization in its constructed elements. Each film takes place in a unified, specific, and self-consciously fabricated world.

The second generic marker has to do with Welles's handling of Shakespeare's language. Language, in all three films, is a dynamic, not a static, element. In practice, this means that Welles will often sacrifice clarity for dramatic point. Actors in these films are seldom allowed to simply "recite" to the camera. They are involved, more often than not, in action, or action takes place around them. "Most directors either move the actors or move the camera," Keith Baxter, who played Hal in *Chimes*, remembers. "Orson would move both at the same time, and that is tricky."[37] The effect can be disorienting, and the dialogue in all three films can be difficult to listen to or to understand. Not surprisingly, Welles has been accused of not caring about

Shakespeare's language, but Welles cares about both language and cinema; if he can make a point at the expense of the words, he does so. Shakespeare is not only in the language, however counterintuitive it may be to say so: Shakespeare, rather, is in what his language *does*, in the work that language performs, and that work transcends the merely verbal.

Third, Welles's Shakespeare films are unified by a set of thematic markers that borrow from, but are not necessarily identical with, Shakespeare's primary thematic concerns. Welles often transforms a latent thematic strand into a manifest one, drawing on issues in Shakespeare that are particularly meaningful to him: the use and abuse of power, the relationship of love to betrayal, a cold new world replacing a golden, mostly imaginary, past—all themes that inform Welles's oeuvre from *Citizen Kane* (1941) to *Mr. Arkadin* (1955), from *The Magnificent Ambersons* (1942) to *Touch of Evil* (1958). In this way, Welles makes Shakespeare his own, and his fidelity is to the dramaturgic essence and core thematics he finds in each play. A Welles Shakespeare film, in short, is a Welles film and a Shakespeare film: the resulting tension, however uneasily, holds each film together. It is characteristic of these films that their coherence remains partial, provisional, and incomplete. The act of adapting the play to film does not precede the film but is woven into its texture and informs the viewer's experience. For Welles, adaptation is dynamic, ongoing, unresolved. The supposed "fear of completion" that some critics have cited to explain Welles's career is not fear so much as refusal. What Welles has to learn from Shakespeare, or what he wants to tell us about Shakespeare, is never fully expressed in the film text.

Convenient though it may be to consider Welles's three Shakespeare films as constituting a subgenre of the Shakespeare film *tout court*, we must not disguise how different the films are from each other. Unity in diversity most clearly characterizes Welles's filmmaking career. However much he may be drawn to a specific set of themes, to recurring techniques (deep focus, long take), and to recognizably similar characters, each Welles film is distinctive in almost every way. And this is particularly true of his Shakespeare films. *Macbeth*—airless, claustrophobic, "theatrical," the style of a single-set play, the look of a traveling Shakespeare troupe fallen on hard times. *Othello*— sunlight, movement, its characters deliriously flowing, image by image, through time and space, a documentary, a travelogue. *Chimes at Midnight*— cold exteriors, warm interiors; a film of texture; wide-angle lenses capturing a mise-en-scène of Brechtian simplicity, a film epic in its effects and intimate, wistful, personal. Each film captures a different Shakespeare, a different Welles, while all three are undeniably Shakespeare, undeniably Welles.

And each exhibits signs of haste, material inadequacy, and confusion, of tensions between ambition and achievement; each, at some point, disappoints even as it exhilarates. All three films can be characterized as Welles characterized *Macbeth*, as charcoal sketches of works painted in oils or, perhaps, variations on a theme. In music, it is perfectly acceptable to rethink a classic piece in a new idiom, to break down and reassemble the original, to "play" with familiar musical ideas. This, in a sense, is what Welles performs on Shakespeare: variations on a theme. A closer look at *Macbeth*, Welles's one genuine "Hollywood" Shakespeare film, illustrates some of the ways Welles transforms "Shakespeare" into something very much his own.

Shakespeare on a Budget: *Macbeth* (1948)

Welles's *Macbeth* went against the expectations of "Shakespeare films" as Hollywood had earlier constructed the genre. *A Midsummer Night's Dream* and *Romeo and Juliet*, as we have seen, were prestige productions, created with the facilities of a large, wealthy studio, starring well-known performers in both major and minor roles, and aiming for, if not entirely achieving, an epic grandeur. Both of the earlier films, though not moneymakers, brought prestige to their respective studios and to Hollywood itself. Both drew on late-nineteenth- and early-twentieth-century theatrical practice and, in doing so, associated themselves with the respected "legitimate" theater, under whose shadow Hollywood felt itself oppressed. Both *Romeo and Juliet* and *A Midsummer Night's Dream* (the latter especially) mixed high culture, "theatrical" elements with low culture, "cinematic" elements in order to draw a large, varied audience. Each film was, at least potentially, accessible. *Romeo and Juliet* wanted to be recognized as a "class" act, and it strove to provide viewers with a cultural experience offered in the mode of Hollywood gloss and romance. *A Midsummer Night's Dream*, less culturally ambitious, aimed to reproduce Shakespeare as popular entertainment. Welles's *Macbeth* failed to satisfy on either level.

Macbeth had its origins in Welles's notorious 1936 voodoo production in Harlem, sponsored by the WPA (Workers Progress Administration), which featured an all-black cast and a nineteenth-century Haitian setting. In preparation for the Republic film, Welles staged the play in 1947 at the Utah centennial celebration in Salt Lake City. As with the film, Welles for this production restored the Scottish setting and had the actors employ a distinctive brogue. Though Welles later claimed that there was no connection between the Harlem staging and the Republic film, both employed a similar unit set (as did the Utah production), both emphasized the occult and supernatural elements of Shakespeare's play, and both edited the text in essentially the same fashion. Welles shot the film in three weeks at Republic Studios, a feat considerably helped by the Utah "tryout." Critics of the initial release, focusing in particular on the "incomprehensible" accents, were sufficiently negative to frighten Republic executives into pulling the film out of circulation. Under pressure, Welles's rerecorded much of the sound track and reedited the visuals, in the process shortening the film and adding a spoken prologue, after which *Macbeth* was rereleased in 1950. European critics were more impressed than their American counterparts, and Welles's film found a significant cult reputation abroad.

In *Macbeth*, Welles highlighted the brutalism and primitivism implicit in the world Shakespeare depicts as well as the contradictions he left unresolved. His Lord and Lady Macbeth are very much as Brecht characterized them in the *Messingkauf Dialogues*, "petty Scottish nobility, and neurotically ambitious."[38] Whereas Shakespeare portrays the Macbeths as an aberrant element in a world of order and harmony and as the inevitable product of a world of violence, bloodshed, and betrayal, Welles clearly opts for the brutality. (He even goes back to Holinshed, Shakespeare's source, as when he shows Macbeth leading the soldiers who kill Lady Macduff and her children.) The "king-becoming graces" of which Malcolm speaks are little in evidence in Welles's film. James Naremore makes the point well: "Welles . . . chooses to set *Macbeth* in the heart of darkness, emphasizing not psychology but rather the struggle between a ruthless desire for power and a rudimentary, elemental need to maintain order."[39] Welles's mise-en-scène contributes to this sense of a primitive world, at once ancient—people seem to live in and around caves—and modern.

However much Welles's visuals were predetermined by the facilities and budget available at Republic Studios, the effect is to collapse past and present time, interior and exterior space. The execution of Cawdor takes place, against all logic, in the courtyard outside of Macbeth's castle while Macbeth and Lady Macbeth embrace nearby, forcing the connection between their sexual union and Macbeth's bloody road to the throne. Insofar as Shakespeare was deliberately historicizing his material, stressing its pastness, forming an implicit contrast between Macbeth's reign and that of another Scottish king, James I, Welles violates Shakespeare's intention and universalizes Shakespeare's essay on power and betrayal. But if we see the idealization of monarchy as Shakespeare's calculated attempt to slip his vision of power past the authorities, then Welles simply made explicit what is implicit in

Orson Welles as Macbeth. Copyright © CORBIS.

Shakespeare's text, and in that sense his *Macbeth* prefigures the Jan Kott–inspired vision of Roman Polanski's 1971 film.[40]

The primitivism of Welles's *Macbeth* was a logical continuation of his earlier experiment in Harlem, and it is this very primitivism, Richard Halpern claims, that is the sign of its modernity: "one of the things that distinguishes the modernist reception of Shakespeare from the late Victorian one . . . is the frequency with which it deploys the discourse of modernism."[41] One critic's primitivism can be another critic's tackiness, however. For Joseph McBride, "the scene of Duncan's arrival . . . cannot, for all of its details of pagan drummers and horrific costumes, avoid the distracting appearance of a sound-stage with painted backdrop of sky, constructed rocks, and so forth."[42] But this points to a different strand of modernism, that represented by the theatrical practice of Bertolt Brecht and his *Verfremdungeffekt*, whereby elements of mise-en-scène exist in part to evoke the constructed nature of the theatrical performance. Welles presents a stripped-down, idiosyncratic view of Shakespeare's play, one that draws on the original but is in no way bound

Polanski's *Macbeth* (1971)

The combined energies of director Roman Polanski, executive producer Hugh Hefner of *Playboy* magazine fame, and the waspish critic Kenneth Tynan, listed in the credits as artistic adviser and coauthor of the screenplay, promise something more outré than the frequently dynamic but rather straightforward and conventional film we see. Though influenced by Polish critic Jan Kott's particularly nihilist reading of the play, Polanski carefully locates his film in medieval Scotland and pays close attention to the text. His major innovation, apart from a nearly nude sleepwalking scene for Lady Macbeth and a higher degree of onscreen bloodshed than is usual in a Shakespeare film, was to cast attractive young performers as the murderous protagonists and allow them to exhibit unmistakable passion for each other. Polanski, however, makes no attempt to get inside his characters, and one suspects that he chose these particular actors because, at least at this moment in their performance careers, they were primarily skilled at "keeping close." John Finch, in particular, lacks affect—his face is precisely *not* "a glass wherein one may read strange matters." Francesca Annis, who showed fuller aspects of her acting personality in BBC dramas some twenty years on, is almost equally inward seeming. However attractive they may appear, and however much their youth may be seen as explaining the force of their ambition, there is nothing empathetic about either of them (or, indeed, about anyone else in the film). We get very little sense of the all-admired Macbeth of the back story, and Finch either cannot or will not project the anguish of Macbeth's tragic disintegration. In the end, Macbeth and his Lady seem as mysterious and inexplicable as they did at the beginning.

by its text or by traditional interpretations of it. Shakespeare drew from his sources a Jacobean morality play of ambition, murder, and ultimate justice, from which Welles, in part reading between the lines, intuited a drama of primordial impulses and modern horrors. In his version of the early scenes, Welles's compressions and outright cuts have the effect of diminishing the valor, loyalty, and dignity with which Macbeth is endowed by the testament of others. We cannot know, even in the play, the extent to which this is a matter more of appearance than of reality. As Bernice Kliman has noted, "Those who want a terribly heroic, a satanically compelling, even a noble Macbeth ignore those details in Shakespeare's text that contradict that supposed grandeur, as reflected in the poetic images,"[43] though we can be certain of Macbeth's strength and courage, whatever his motives and loyalties.

Welles also cuts most references that sustain the sense of a natural order and a social contract, most notably Macbeth's acknowledgment of Duncan's reward: "our duties / Are to your throne and state, children and servants, / Which do but what they should by doing everything / Safe toward your love and honor" (1.4.24–27). Shakespeare's emphasis on the host/guest relationship is pretty much absent from the film. Picking up definite hints from Shakespeare's ambivalence, Welles turns Banquo (Edgar Barrier) into a decidedly sinister figure. He is not *l'homme moyen sensuel* Shakespeare seems to have had in mind; immediately suspicious of Macbeth, he is clearly ambitious himself. Some of his more thoughtful lines are given to the newly created "Holy Father" character, in consequence of which Banquo loses what little he has of moral authority. His act 3 soliloquy ("Thou hadst it now") is spoken as a direct threat to Macbeth. Welles's fluid mise-en-scène allows for a world where characters and actions intertwine with ease, and where, as Michael Mullin finds, "the mind of the speaker, the world around him, and the world we see, are all one."[44] The witches, for example, are not presented as supernatural intrusions into the world of the play, seen only by Macbeth and Banquo. Now everyone sees them. That Macbeth and Banquo had some traffic with them—though it may cast some suspicion on their subsequent actions—is nevertheless unremarkable. Evil is familiar and always at hand.

Welles handles time and space as indefinite, an effect intensified by his employment of what is essentially a unit set: outside and inside are not clearly delineated, and time seems an unbroken, present moment. Although it has become conventional to refer to Welles's film as "expressionist," there are elements of the surreal as well. In his description of the setting, Jorgens invokes "a solipsistic world of dizzying heights, jagged rocks, moonscapes, gnarled dead trees, fog, and Rorschach-test floors from which there is no escape."[45] Welles's film often looks like a charcoal sketch: outlines that are not filled out, lines corrected without being fully erased, smudges and stray marks whose significance is not altogether clear, details left to the imagination. And this sketchiness is thematic as well as visual, helping to produce a drama that, as Joseph McBride notes, "avoid[s] nuance of character in order to more effectively present the clash of extreme emotions and actions and free us into the world of nightmare."[46]

In reassembling and reshaping elements of Shakespeare's play, Welles adds, combines, and eliminates characters at will, conflates scenes and locations, transfers lines from one character to another, all without violating the essential architectonic of the original. By creating the composite character of the Holy Father, whose lines are borrowed from Ross, Banquo, and even

Macbeth, Welles highlights a theme Shakespeare presented obliquely and implicitly: the struggle between witchcraft and Christianity, the primitive and the civilized, the profane and the holy. Welles's treatment of this conflict is not unambiguous, however. The Holy Father is a sinister character, and Welles relishes his Grand Guignol execution at Macbeth's hands. The witches reappear at the end (as they had in the Harlem production) to speak the last words ("peace, the charm's wound up"). In this film Christianity is simply one power structure supplanting another. None of the characters in Welles's film is unambiguously good or bad. If this greatly simplifies Shakespeare's Macbeth, it is an interpretation available in it. Welles, in choosing to keep the so-called England scene (4.3), often heavily cut in stage productions, acknowledges the ambiguity in Shakespeare's design. We see and hear the play's "good" characters—Malcom, Macduff, and Ross (here replaced by the Holy Father)—engaging in odd mind games and accusing Macbeth of vile crimes of which we have seen nothing while at the same time presenting the past as a golden age, something for which we have little evidence.

In the end, Welles created a wildly uneven film in which scenes of remarkable imaginative force alternate with banality. The Birnam Wood scene, for example, begins in a pedestrian manner, with a soundstage forest being cut down by unconvincing extras, but the payoff shot of branches barely visible, swaying in slow motion through the fog, is magical in its simplicity. At times, Welles reverts to a more or less straightforward style and conventional lighting and editing, as in much of the sequence of Macbeth's first conversation with Banquo's murderers, moments when the mise-en-scène appears the least evocative. At its best, however, Welles's long-take, deep-focus style intensifies the play's sheer theatrical power. The murder of Duncan is photographed by Welles in a continuous shot of slightly more than ten minutes, in the course of which the relationship between Macbeth and his wife is delineated through the play between foreground and background, high and low, large and small. The camera almost becomes a third character as it probes and traces the dynamics of their interaction. Wide-angle lenses and depth of focus create perceptual anomalies. At one point, on Macbeth's line about the "multitudinous seas incarnadine," Lady Macbeth appears to be standing in Macbeth's outstretched hand, becoming one with the blood that stains it. Welles's editing can be equally memorable, as in the dreamlike moment when clouds invade Macbeth's image as, in a slow dissolve, he disappears just as his voice begins to speak the "tomorrow and tomorrow" soliloquy, as if he were already bereft of solidity and mass, already a spirit meditating on the world he has lost.

The differences in tone and style in the Shakespeare films of Welles and Olivier are clear enough. "For both [Olivier and Welles]," Leo Braudy writes, "Shakespeare is like a genre . . . that offers material for a contemporary statement." Olivier, however, "sticks clearly to the language and form of the play itself," so that "we judge Olivier finally by Shakespeare, but we judge Welles by other films."[47] What may not be so obvious are the similarities. Looking today at *Macbeth* and *Hamlet*, films that were gleefully played off against each other when they were released almost at the same moment over half a century ago, we can more easily note the elements they share. Both Welles and Olivier employ low-key, black-and-white images, and both films are evidently studio bound. Both feature highly stylized sets, constructed as labyrinths and seemingly cut from stone. Both films rely on a combination of voice-over and direct, onscreen speech for soliloquies; both greatly streamline and simplify the plays on which they are based; and both are guided by a strong directorial hand. If, at the time, Olivier's *Hamlet* won the contest hands down, today it is Welles's achievement that appears the greater. Looking at the films without preconception, however, one would have to say that *Hamlet* and *Macbeth* are powerful, deeply flawed films, moments of brilliance alternating with longueurs and bizarreries of various kinds. Both films are constructed around the central performances of their director-actors. Both, finally, could be described as charcoal sketches of the Shakespeare originals. Even if *Hamlet* is more polished, more various and rich in production detail (in part because it is more expensive), there is, nonetheless, a sense of "illustrative moments from Shakespeare" about Olivier's film as there is about Welles's *Macbeth*, something unfinished, an invitation to the viewer to fill in the gaps.

Notes

1. John Collick, *Shakespeare, Cinema, and Society* (Manchester: Manchester University Press, 1989), 83.

2. For a thorough discussion of the background and generic affinities of Warners' *A Midsummer Night's Dream*, see Robert F. Willson Jr., *Shakespeare in Hollywood, 1929–1956* (Madison, N.J.: Fairleigh Dickinson University Press, 2000), 32–50; Jack Jorgens provides a generous and careful evaluation in *Shakespeare on Film* (Bloomington: Indiana University Press, 1977), 36–50.

3. John Houseman, *Entertainers and the Entertained* (New York: Simon & Schuster, 1986), 86.

4. John Ripley, *Julius Caesar on Stage in England and America* (Cambridge: Cambridge University Press, 1980), 100.

5. According to Houseman, "Unlike most productions which are designed in black and white, *Julius Caesar* was designed and executed in monochromes." Houseman, *Entertainers and the Entertained*, 86.

6. Maurice Charney and Gordon Hichens, "On Mankiewicz's *Julius Caesar*," *Literary Review* 22 (1979): 433–59; 443.

7. Jorgens, *Shakespeare on Film*, 101.

8. Samuel Crowl, "A World Elsewhere: The Roman Plays on Film and Television," in *Shakespeare and the Moving Image: The Plays on Film and Television*, ed. Anthony Davies and Stanley Wells (Cambridge: Cambridge University Press, 1994), 146–62; 149.

9. John Houseman, "This Our Lofty Scene," *Theatre Arts*, May 1953, 26–28; 28.

10. For a detailed discussion of the use of busts and statues in the film, see Willson, *Shakespeare in Hollywood*, 149–52.

11. Jorgens, *Shakespeare on Film*, 102.

12. Vivian Sobchack, "Lounge Time: Postwar Crises and the Chronotope of Film Noir," in *Refiguring American Film Genres*, ed. Nick Browne (Berkeley: University of California Press, 1998), 129–70.

13. Catherine Belsey, "Shakespeare and Film: A Question of Perspective," *Literature/Film Quarterly* 11, no. 3 (1983): 152–58; 152–53.

14. Thom Andersen, "Red Hollywood," in *Literature and the Visual Arts in Contemporary Society*, ed. Suzanne Ferguson and Barbara S. Groseclose (Columbus: Ohio State University Press, 1985), 141–96.

15. James Naremore, *More Than Night: Film Noir in Its Contexts* (Berkeley: University of California Press, 1998), 125.

16. Anthony Miller, "*Julius Caesar* in the Cold War: The Houseman-Mankiewicz Film," *Literature/Film Quarterly* 28, no. 2 (2000): 95–100; 95.

17. John H. Lenihan, "English Classics for Cold War America," *Journal of Popular Film and Television*, Fall 1992, 42–51; 42.

18. Belsey, "Shakespeare and Film," 154.

19. Roy Walker, "Look upon Caesar," *Twentieth Century* 154 (1953): 469–74; 472.

20. Interview in the *New York Post*, November 24, 1937, Mercury *Julius Caesar* clipping file, New York Public Library for the Performing Arts, Lincoln Center.

21. Houseman, *Entertainers and the Entertained*, 94.

22. Samuel Crowl, "'Our Lofty Scene': Teaching Modern Film Versions of *Julius Caesar*," in *Teaching Shakespeare into the Twenty-First Century*," ed. Ronald E. Salomone and James E. Davis (Athens: Ohio University Press, 1997), 222–31; 227.

23. Charney and Hitchens, "On Mankiewicz's *Julius Caesar*," 435.

24. Cited in Roger Manvell, *Shakespeare and the Film* (New York: Praeger, 1971), 31.

25. J. D. Salinger, *Catcher in the Rye* (Boston: Little, Brown, 1991), 117.

26. Cited in Julie Hankey, ed., *Plays in Performance: Richard III* (London: Junction, 1981), 10.

27. Anthony Davies, *Filming Shakespeare's Plays* (Cambridge: Cambridge University Press, 1988), 65.

28. Jack Jorgens, *Shakespeare on Film* (Bloomington: Indiana University Press, 1977), 147.

29. Scott Colley, *Richard's Himself Again: A Stage History of Richard III* (New York: Greenwood, 1992), 166.

30. Jorgens, *Shakespeare on Film*, 143.

31. Hugh M. Richmond, *Shakespeare in Performance: Richard III* (Manchester: Manchester University Press, 1989), 58.

32. Laurence Olivier, *On Acting* (London: Weidenfeld & Nicolson, 1986), 206.

33. Constance Brown, "Olivier's *Richard III*: A Reevaluation," *Film Quarterly*, Summer 1967, 23–32; 27.

34. Olivier, *On Acting*, 207.

35. For a detailed discussion of Welles's career as a Shakespearean, see Michael Anderegg, *Orson Welles, Shakespeare, and Popular Culture* (New York: Columbia University Press, 1999).

36. Charles Marowitz, *Recycling Shakespeare* (New York: Applause Theatre Book Publishers, 1991), 32.

37. Bridget Gellert Lyons, ed., *Film in Print: Chimes at Midnight* (New Brunswick, N.J.: Rutgers University Press, 1988), 270.

38. Bertolt Brecht, *The Messingkauf Dialogues*, trans. John Willett (London: Methuen, 1965), 85.

39. James Naremore, *The Magic World of Orson Welles*, rev. ed. (Dallas: Southern Methodist University Press, 1989), 138.

40. Alan Sinfield, "*Macbeth*: History, Ideology, and Intellectuals." *Critical Quarterly* 28, no. 1–2 (1986): 63–77.

41. Richard Halpern, *Shakespeare among the Moderns* (Ithaca, N.Y.: Cornell University Press, 1997), 16.

42. Joseph McBride, *Orson Welles* (New York: Viking, 1972), 110.

43. Bernice Kliman, *Shakespeare in Performance: Macbeth* (Manchester: Manchester University Press, 1992), 128.

44. Michael Mullin, "Orson Welles's *Macbeth*: Script and Screen," in *Focus on Orson Welles*, ed. Ronald Gottesman (Englewood Cliffs, N.J.: Prentice-Hall, 1976), 136–45; 143.

45. Jorgens, *Shakespeare on Film*, 26.

46. McBride, *Orson Welles*, 113.

47. Leo Braudy, *The World in a Frame: What We See in Films* (Garden City, N.Y.: Anchor, 1977), 202.

CHAPTER 5

◠

Branagh and the Sons of Ken

Kenneth Branagh's relatively brief career as a Shakespearean filmmaker has featured a rise and fall that, though perhaps not of the scope of Shakespearean tragedy, illustrates some of the difficulties likely to be encountered by any filmmaker who has a modest popular hit that he or she tries to duplicate by making films with increasingly larger budgets.[1] Branagh began by setting himself up, with *Henry V* (1989), as the heir to Sir Laurence Olivier, an heir who does his predecessor one better. Part of the interest and excitement *Henry V* generated had to do with the saga of its young creator's remarkable success: a Belfast boy who made good in London and starred as Shakespeare's warrior king at the Royal Shakespeare Company (RSC) at the age of twenty-three. Against the odds, he was able to raise the money for a film of *Henry V*, both directing and playing the title role. Shakespeare's narrative, fortuitously, parallels the young filmmaker's success, as Hal and Branagh both prove themselves to a skeptical world. The overall sweep, the freshness of approach, the neo-Brechtian simplicity of the mise-en-scène, clearly "worked" to introduce *Henry V*, with its tension between realism and heroism, to a whole new audience. *Much Ado about Nothing* (1993), Branagh's next Shakespeare adaptation, filmed on location in Italy and featuring American as well as British actors, was a notable box office success, reportedly grossing $22 million on an $8 million budget.[2] With *Much Ado*, however, Branagh indulged in popularizing gimmicks—slapstick overcomes sophistication, some of the casting choices are bizarre, and the more subtle dimensions of the comedy are ignored.

With *Hamlet* (1996), Branagh's ambition grew with his budget. Filmed in 70 millimeter, cast with international stars, and presenting the fullest possible text of Shakespeare's longest play, *Hamlet*, though generally well received by the critics, was a commercial flop. In many ways an extraordinary and courageous film, *Hamlet* exhibited some painful errors of judgment. With a running time of over four hours and an uncut text, it might have been wiser to operate within a smaller framework and keep the emphasis on the interpersonal dynamics of the play. Instead, Branagh decided to create an epic, a film "event" of a kind not seen since the days of David Lean's *Lawrence of Arabia* and *Dr. Zhivago*. But the film did not find an audience; or, rather, the audience it found was too small to justify the expense and scope of the project. The Branagh phenomenon began to unravel even as he announced preproduction on at least three new Shakespeare films. The first, a musical version of *Love's Labour's Lost*, was so marginal a product that it barely received a release in the United States, where it managed to gross $300,000. The film's dismal box office silences talk of *As You Like It* and *Macbeth*, the other two items in a proposed trilogy. Once again, we have ample proof that there is nothing certain about Shakespeare on film. In the meantime, however, Branagh's initial success encouraged other filmmakers to make Shakespeare films of their own, and the late 1980s and early 1990s saw a flurry of Shakespeare adaptations—including Oliver Parker's *Othello*, in which Branagh, playing Iago, gives his most compelling Shakespeare film performance, and Trevor Nunn's *Twelfth Night*, produced by Branagh's own Renaissance Films.

Like those of Olivier and Welles, Branagh's films necessarily reveal a wedding of his directorial and acting personalities. With Branagh, something like restless energy is at work with both roles. As a director, he is fond of circling, elaborate camera movements; he wants to turn everything into action and spectacle. As an actor, he likes movement and "business"—his Hamlet is nearly always walking or running; he seldom stands still. Both as director and as actor, Branagh can be extremely literal: he doesn't want anything to remain unexplained or mysterious, and his penchant for effect can be ludicrous: the earth cracking open for the appearance of the Ghost in *Hamlet* is only one instance of his reach for the obvious. In short, Branagh can be both a powerful interpreter of Shakespeare and a ham-fisted vulgarian, both sharply focused and all at sea, both a moving and powerful actor and a performer who strains for effect, an adapter in awe of the text one moment and completely casual about it the next, a director simple and straightforward in one scene and intoxicated by the cinematic apparatus into unseemly tricks at another time. His casting strategies can reveal a healthy disregard for traditional Shakespearean acting—Denzel Washington as Don Pedro, Billy Crystal as the First Gravedigger—or a misfired reach for box office clout—Robin Williams as Osric, Michael Keaton as Dogberry, Gérard

Depardieu as Reynaldo, Jack Lemmon as Marcellus. His desire for clarity and "realism" can lead to sharply delineated and revealing moments as well as to simpleminded exegeses of ambiguous and complex scenes.

An Accessible Shakespeare: *Henry V* (1989), *Much Ado about Nothing* (1993), and *Love's Labour's Lost* (2000)

Henry V exhibits a freshness and formal simplicity, a "clarity" as both a narrative and a dramatic text, not thus far recaptured in any of Branagh's subsequent films. Virtually every scene is carefully etched, the dialogue and speeches projected with full understanding, the actors interpreting the verse even as they speak it. Branagh happily allows the essential dynamics of Shakespeare's play to govern the flow and rhythm of the film. He avoids, to an almost dangerous extent, establishing shots and explanatory business, encouraging the audience to collaborate in constructing the narrative. Among the very few exceptions are the inserts and flashbacks, but these are not so much attempts to construct a "back story" as they are a means of characterization—especially of Henry. The minimalism of the sets and props, the subdued elegance of the costuming, effectively support the spare script. The "long take" style, something of a Branagh trademark, is here dictated perhaps as much by economy as by choice and is skillfully employed. Particularly striking, in addition to the four-minute "non nobis" sequence on the battlefield, is the less showy scene where the tavern characters speak of Falstaff's death (it too is nearly four minutes long). Branagh places the Hostess, Bardolph, Nym, and Boy on three levels of stairs. As the dynamics of the scene develops, the camera almost imperceptibly moves closer and closer to the Hostess, allowing Judi Dench to make the most of her moving eulogy of Falstaff. As Dench concludes, the camera pulls back to again include the other characters and reestablish a sense of ensemble and camaraderie. In a sense, the "non nobis" long take performs a similar function, that of uniting, by maintaining the integrity of time and space, all of the combatants in a common lamentation of the death and destruction of war.

The long take, though a specifically cinematic technique, contributes to the film's play with the tension between "theater" and "cinema." In some ways, Branagh's film may be more theatrical than Olivier's. We never really leave the soundstage on which we began, and the Chorus's reappearance at the conclusion, closing the doors he opened at the beginning, reminds us of the "closed" atmosphere we have felt throughout. Certain details of the mise-en-scène, too, are theatrical in the sense of having been created for effect both within and outside of the diegesis. Henry's "entrance," for example, takes the form of a sinister, larger-than-life silhouette (variously identified by reviewers as Batman or Darth Vader); almost immediately, however, we have the contrasting, "cinematic" close shot of the young king, hair tousled, unprepossessing in appearance, sitting in a casual, relaxed posture on the throne. These contrasting stylistic approaches give us contrasting views of Henry, and the tension between them will govern our understanding of the character throughout.

In spite of Branagh's attempts to differentiate his *Henry V* from Laurence Olivier's, the films are surprisingly similar.[3] Branagh keeps slipping into an homage to his predecessor, even providing Henry with a white horse for "Once more unto the breach," and his heroic pose and energy in this scene seem just as strong and assured as with the earlier Henry. Like Olivier, Branagh cannot resist introducing Falstaff into his scenario, although, unlike Olivier, he links the rejection of Falstaff to his own betrayal at the hands of the conspirators. What differences there are between Olivier's and Branagh's *Henry V* center, to a large extent, on the issue of masculinity. Branagh presents a hero at once tentative, unostentatious, and emotional (as others have remarked, this may be one of the weepiest Henrys ever),[4] though one who is at the same time capable of quick anger and harshness. Unlike Olivier, Branagh includes the king's order to execute his old tavern companion Bardolph, but he softens the point. In the play, Henry gives no indication that he recognizes the name; the film provides a flashback making it all too clear that Hal not only knows who it is he is sentencing to death but is tormented by the knowledge. The Hal of Shakespeare's *Henry V* appears, on the surface, to be very much in control, to be full and complete as he is, even in moments of self-doubt and vulnerability. Olivier plays this version of the king to the hilt. Branagh, on the other hand, reads back into the role, at least as subtext, the Hal of the *Henry IV* plays, a Hal who is at once focused on the future and uncertain of his destiny. This is a king who, in Peter Donaldson's words, "must earn his success like a son of the artisan or merchant class making a go of the family business."[5] Branagh, furthermore, has a habit of grimacing and contorting his face at moments of high emotion; whether intentional or not, this too differentiates him from Olivier, whose Henry never loses an even keel, exhibiting throughout a sangfroid suggesting that this Henry knows perfectly well how to be a king.

The vulnerability and pluck of Branagh's Henry versus Olivier's emerges most expressively in the scene with the common soldiers and the rumination and prayer that follows (4.1), while his uncertainly and modesty are empha- sized in the courtship of Katherine (5.2). In the former scene, Branagh's per- formance is understated and controlled. The boyishness of the opening scene disappears, and the somewhat aristocratic disdain for the populace we sense in Olivier's Henry becomes, with Branagh, a genuine envy of those who do not have to carry the responsibilities that fall on the king. In the courtship scene, Branagh's Henry is modest and awkward: this is not, as it is in Olivier's film, an act—at least not entirely. With Olivier, we sense throughout that Henry is performing, that he sees the courtship role as simply another mask to put on, part of a job he knows how to handle, and he exhibits the same ease and easy assurance he revealed at the very beginning of the film, when he casually tossed his crown around a post at the back of his throne.

Much has been made of Branagh's *Henry V* as a post–Vietnam War film (in the British context, post-Falklands as well), but the analogy seems less forceful as time goes on.[6] On the one hand, the film's gestures in the direc- tion of pacifism are not compelling: we certainly learn that war is hell (Agin- court is bloody and muddy; the threats at Harfleur are chilling), but any war film, even as it revels in the carnage, tells us that.[7] On the other hand, the potential jingoism of *Henry V* is tempered by Branagh's emphasis on the per- sonal development of the king: it is almost as if the war exists primarily to test Henry's mettle (or, as the trailer puts it, "a king who defied the odds to prove himself a man"). As James Loehlin observes, "it seems, finally, that the film endorses Henry's war as an occasion for him to earn, and display, his heroism."[8] The film's equivalent to Shakespeare's act 1, scene 2, the prepara- tions for the invasion of France, is staged and performed to enforce the idea of Henry manipulated by both the church and the nobility: he goes to war with France almost as if his life and crown depended on his decision. This is an interesting reading, but Branagh fails to pay off on it—it is not clear that Henry has really won anything by the end of the film. Are we to see Henry as victim, or is it he who has manipulated his elders? That old men send young men into battle is an undoubted truth; that the film challenges that truth, or truly presents what Branagh saw as "an uncompromising view of politics and a deeply questioning, ever-relevant and compassionate survey of people and war,"[9] is not as clear. In fairness, it should be noted that these matters are not altogether clear in Shakespeare's play either. Whatever we may finally think of his editorial choices, political goals, or performance as Henry, Branagh's success as a first-time filmmaker is undeniable. Branagh does not, any more than Olivier did, give us Shakespeare's *Henry V* in all of its ambiguity and complexity, but he succeeds in bringing out a good deal of the play's imaginative force. Even Patrick Doyle's music, which becomes overemphatic in later Branagh Shakespeare films, here ideally combines, often in the same melody or phrase, the epic strains reminiscent of William Walton, Olivier's composer, at his most fulsome, with a strong undercurrent of poignancy and regret, a tension that characterizes much of the film's thematics.

   Much Ado about Nothing, on the other hand, though it may be, as Samuel

---

Editing the Text

In the course of explaining how he went about adapting *Henry V* for the screen, Kenneth Branagh provides a variety of justifications for his prunings. "It seemed clear that a great deal of the text would have to be cut," he writes, "as I was determined that the film should be of a commercial length." "In any case," he adds, "the cuts dictated themselves." First to go were the "more tortuous aspects of the Fluellen/Pistol antagonism, culminating in the resoundingly unfunny leek scene." Also dispensable were the "double-edged exchanges between Henry and the Duke of Burgundy in Act V [which] . . . failed to advance the plot, and added little to the aspects of the play that we wanted to explore." Branagh also did away with "Elizabethan obscurities, particularly in the language of the Boar's Head scenes, with only the most delicious-sounding phrases escaping sacrifice on the altar of instant understanding." Finally, "Plot repetitions and excessive flights of fancy were ruthlessly excised."[10] Branagh makes a number of judgments in the course of his brief catalog, finding that comic scenes that are "unfunny," rhetorical flights, and scenes that fail to advance the plot are more or less dispensable. One may well wonder, however, whether these are justifications before or after the fact. (Notably, none of these reasons, or any similar ones, is mentioned in Branagh's introduction to the "full-text" *Hamlet.*) One might argue, contra Branagh, that, for example, "flights of rhetorical fancy" are in part what *Henry V* is about; that Shakespeare's comedy is always problematic for a modern audience and that a director needs to find ways to come to terms with it; that the Henry-Burgundy exchange is in fact crucial to expressing much of the realpolitik atmosphere of the original. In the end, of course, it matters little if the cuts and alterations were the consequence of forethought or the necessity of afterthought. Branagh's choices have consequences and, presumably, they are the consequences he sought.[11] Branagh's explanations to the contrary, his own practice suggests that no cuts are inevitable.

Crowl sympathetically describes it, "the most successful version we have of a Shakespearean comedy on film,"[12] and though it is undeniably lovely to look at, fails in significant ways to come to terms with the rich and complex wit of Shakespeare's play. Comedy, one suspects, is not Branagh's forte. The melodrama of the Hero/Claudio plot clearly engaged his interest far more than either the Beatrice and Benedick romance or the Dogberry scenes. Robert Sean Leonard as Claudio and Kate Beckinsale as Hero provide the innocence and vulnerability that ensure the success of their scenes, whereas Branagh as Benedick and Emma Thompson as Beatrice only intermittently find the emotional core of their characters. Too often slapstick substitutes for comic finesse, as when Benedick is made to struggle with a folding chair. Very little is earned in this film—we are continually being told how to respond, what to think and feel.

Too many moments in *Much Ado about Nothing* feel pumped up and exaggerated, sometimes to the detriment of common sense. The credit sequence, featuring slow-motion images of galloping horses and scurrying women, takes us into the realm of the action/adventure film (in Branagh's own words, "heat haze and dust, grapes and horseflesh, and a nod to *The Magnificent Seven*") but this results in a mood and tone that has little or nothing to do with what follows. Branagh appears unable to let the text do its work. That Claudio should see a man at his fiancée's bedroom window and from such slim evidence draw the wrong conclusion is one thing; that he should see

The abortive wedding in Kenneth Branagh's *Much Ado about Nothing*.
Copyright © CORBIS.

Boraccio humping Hero is quite another. Although similar inserted business has been presented on stage (though none as explicitly venereal), John Cox, for one, finds that "the value of such a sequence is an open question."[13] "It seemed that if we saw this [the deception of Claudio] occur on screen, it would add a new dimension to our understanding of Claudio," Branagh claims,[14] but that "new dimension," unfortunately, is one that, in the words of Samuel Crowl, "asks us to understand the wounded lover's anger and to sympathize with Claudio rather than judge him."[15]

A similar misjudgment governs Branagh's handling of the comic policeman Dogberry, played by Michael Keaton. In his introduction to the published screenplay of *Much Ado about Nothing*, Branagh writes that "the difficulty for actors lies in not putting things in between themselves and . . . reality—a funny voice, a walk, an unconscious treatment of the character that suggests he or she is from another planet."[16] Given these sentiments, one wonders why Branagh allowed Michael Keaton to give such a forced, eccentric, irritating, and in every way "unnatural" performance, one that destroys any sense we might have that Dogberry, in spite of his malapropisms and thickheadedness, might nevertheless be, at some level, a human being. In the script, Branagh describes Dogberry as "a psychopath," a concept that neither makes sense in the context of Shakespeare's play nor serves any observable function in Branagh's film. Since much of what Keaton says and does is almost entirely incomprehensible, Dogberry and the Watch could just as well have been left out, especially since the action is set in an isolated villa, which would not seem to need a police force.

Branagh is at his best in *Much Ado about Nothing* at moments of dramatic intensity, when his direction can be straightforward. The coda to act 4, scene 1, in which Beatrice and Benedick reveal their love for each other at the same time that she asks him to kill his friend Claudio, benefits from a tight framing within an enclosed space. After an establishing shot, the scene resolves into a sequence of over-the-shoulder shot/reverse shots in the most academic of styles (the four-minute scene involves six camera setups arranged into forty-one shots). Although flawed by the strains of Doyle's highly repetitive score, the scene otherwise provides, once again, an ideal wedding of essentially "theatrical" and essentially "cinematic" elements— the theatrical is transformed into the cinematic. The editing at once keeps the couple separate and together in a way only editing can do: each shot singles out one character, but each also includes a sign—if only a wisp of Beatrice's hair—of the presence of the other. The slandering of Hero, which eventually brings these two together, initially keeps them apart. The pattern is broken in Beatrice's declaration of love for Benedick (which follows his declaration of love for her). Branagh only then cuts to a two shot of Beatrice and Benedick kissing.

Almost immediately, the original pattern, employing the same setups, is reintroduced for "Kill Claudio." On the line, "you kill me to deny it," we return to the "kiss" two shot, but now the shot emphasizes separateness, as Beatrice struggles and finally succeeds in freeing herself from Benedick's embrace (this happens twice in the shot). We then cut, on Benedick's "Beatrice," to a new close shot of Benedick, then back to the two shot. On "by this hand," Branagh returns to Benedick, initiating a new series of shot/reverse shot close-ups, but now the "other" is absent from the shot. On "and so, farewell," we return to a close shot of Beatrice and a new setup that includes the back of Benedick's head in the frame. In the course of this shot, Beatrice walks offscreen and Benedick turns to look in her direction, toward the camera. A reverse shot shows Beatrice walking away. Branagh then cuts back to the shot of Benedick as he walks off and the scene ends. The dramaturgy here is elegant and economical, the character dynamics precisely delineated, and the emotional conflict convincingly rendered without resort to emphatic pointing. Unfortunately *Much Ado about Nothing* as a whole only infrequently rises to a similar standard of clarity and economy.

Branagh's choice of *Love's Labour's Lost* as his next Shakespeare project after *Hamlet* appears in every way peculiar: the play is, in the words of its latest editor, "distinctly odd and difficult,"[17] one that, in the words of another editor, "has less story interest than any other play that Shakespeare ever wrote."[18] Unlike *Much Ado, Love's Labour's Lost* lacks a tightly interlocked "comic" and "serious" narrative line. The various sets of characters are related to each other very loosely, and almost everything of interest in the play stems from Shakespeare's overflowing pleasure in his own linguistic facility. Given the challenges posed, Branagh's idea of making a musical film intensifies the artificiality of the original material. As film, *Love's Labour's Lost* appears underfed: the characters are imprecisely located, neither inhabiting a recognizable world nor fitting into a consistently stylized universe. The "prescripted" songs add to the disconcerting sense that we are nowhere in particular, a sense in no way modified by the newsreel clips we from time to time witness that are meant to remind us of the war and in general of the late 1930s context, while at the same time filling in missing plot developments. The camera setups appear more as necessities than choices: the feeling is one of severe economic constraints that have not been imaginatively engaged, especially when we recall what Branagh achieved with the modest budget for *Henry V*.

The dancing and singing, performed entirely by the lead actors, seldom rise to a level above the amateurish (the main exception to this is Adrian Lester, as Dumain, and Nathan Lane's rendering of "There's No Business Like Show Business"). The effect may be what Branagh intended: within the diegesis of the film, amateurishness could be seen as the authentic expression of feeling in contrast to the artificial, stultifying oath of celibacy the young men have taken. At times, the music and dance reinforce or at least complement the characters and action, as with the "Dancing Cheek to Cheek" number, in part because the modified ballroom choreography makes less demand on the performers than, say, tap. Equally effective is the use of "They Can't Take That Away from Me," each verse sung by a new character as the men and women part from each other. For the most part, however, the songs and dance numbers fail to become elements in the overall design of the film. In his desire to re-create the Hollywood musical, Branagh may have forgotten that, for example, Gene Kelly and Frank Sinatra in *On the Town* are only *pretending* to be sailors on shore leave: in reality, they are Gene Kelly and Frank Sinatra.

Even more problematic, however, Branagh's *Love's Labour's Lost* is difficult to follow, which may be in part explained when we look at the scenes that were filmed and then cut, as we can do on the DVD edition. Both the "Muscovite" scene, in which the young men appear to the young women disguised as Russians, and most of the "Nine Worthies" pageant, in which the low comic and eccentric characters provide court entertainment, were eliminated from the theatrical release version. The "Nine Worthies" scene, in particular, is undeniably dull as Branagh filmed it—a series of disconnected moments presented without energy or comic force that make little sense. Branagh evidently believed he could simply do without two relatively elaborate scenes he had already shot, thereby shortening an already relatively short film, which suggests that he was essentially unsympathetic to the dynamics of Shakespeare's comedy. Here as elsewhere in his oeuvre, Branagh's easy familiarity with Hollywood genres may itself be a hindrance to comprehension. A Branagh film is often a stylistic hodgepodge that draws on a variety of sources but fails to integrate them into a concordant whole. Considered as yet another subgenre of the Shakespeare film, the Branagh film may be most notable for generic confusion and instability.

The Shakespeare Film as Costume Epic:
The "Complete" *Hamlet*

Branagh's *Hamlet* takes the Shakespeare film enthusiastically into the nearby genres of costume film and epic: it must be the grandest, most colorful, most populated Shakespeare adaptation of all. In so many ways "cinematic," it at the same time alludes to the elaborate theatrical pageants of nineteenth-century actor-managers Henry Irving and Herbert Beerbohm Tree. It is a Victorian, or at least an Edwardian, *Hamlet*, both in its period setting and in its impulses to spectacular effect. Unlike most Victorian Shakespeare, however, *Hamlet* has the distinction of being the only major Shakespeare film to employ the "full text"—or something very much like the full text—of Shakespeare's play. What we hear in Branagh's film is probably more than any audience in Shakespeare's time would have heard, as Branagh has "conflated" the First Folio (F1) text of 1623 with the significantly different Second Quarto (Q2) version of circa 1604.[19] Branagh's decision to film *Hamlet* uncut was no doubt influenced by his having acted in an uncut version both on stage and in a BBC Radio production (the latter featuring Derek Jacobi as Claudius). The choice was a characteristically bold one, and the rewards of seeing so full a *Hamlet* are many.[20]

Compared with other film and most stage versions, Branagh's film delivers a higher ratio of *Hamlet* vis-à-vis the Prince than is usually the case, and we are necessarily drawn to the extraordinary performances of Derek Jacobi as Claudius, and (in her far fewer scenes) Julie Christie as Gertrude, as much as we are drawn to Branagh's performance of Hamlet. The full text, when enacted, has the effect of placing Hamlet in context: he is still the center of attention, of course, even when "off-stage/screen" (all of the other characters are fixated on him one way or another), but he is not necessarily or always the center of *our* attention. Unlike the nineteenth-century actor-managers, Branagh, in part for box office reasons, surrounds himself with skilled players and performers who are "stars" in their own right, willingly embracing the possibility that a high-powered cast may engulf or at least overshadow his own performance. Although some of these performances are misjudged or stand out too ostentatiously from the overall tone (Jack Lemmon, Gérard Depardieu, Robin Williams), others forcefully and sharply flesh out even small roles: Charlton Heston as the First Player and Billy Crystal as the First Gravedigger provide Hollywood star power; Michael Maloney as Laertes and Simon Russell Beale as Second Gravedigger connect the film to the RSC/National Theatre nexus.

In Kenneth Branagh's *Hamlet*, Julie Christie's Gertrude is clearly a woman who has repressed what she knows or fears to be true. Copyright © 1996 Castle Rock Entertainment.

If one criticism of Laurence Olivier's *Hamlet* is that he gives us the other characters exclusively from Hamlet's point of view, this cannot be charged to Branagh: both Claudius and Gertrude, as well as Polonius, have lives apart from Hamlet's understanding of them. Jacobi constructs a portrait of a completely plausible ruler. There is nothing cynical about Claudius's opening speech, nothing perfunctory. His words may, in fact, be genuine expressions of his thoughts and feelings: this is a Claudius who does not acknowledge the extent to which he is a hypocrite. Gertrude is a woman who has repressed what she knows or fears to be true, but she is guiltless of her husband's death; past her prime but still highly sensual, her youthful self, one intuits, has been reawakened by the doting affections, if not the passions, of her second husband. The Polonii family (Polonius, Laertes, and Ophelia) too are given their due. Polonius, as Richard Briers plays him, is no fool, but neither is he as clever as he thinks. He can be ruthless when necessary, and he knows and willingly accepts the manner in which Claudius came to the throne (as does most of the court), but he can be tender as well. He picks up and hugs Ophelia after Hamlet abuses her; earlier Laertes, played with his usual intensity by Michael Maloney, is clearly moved and even a little disturbed by the strong fatherly affection that lies behind the "to thine own self be true" advice. Kate Winslet, though she exhibits less vulnerability and pathos than had Helena Bonham Carter in Zeffirelli's film, is a strong, sensual, and appealing Ophelia. Her mad scenes, always a danger point in any production of *Hamlet*, are quietly but poignantly underplayed (apart from a striking but perhaps too obvious moment when she mimes the sex act). Ophelia wants to control her madness, not exhibit it.

Branagh's film makes especially clear the extent to which *Hamlet* is a struggle between "mighty opposites," though this owes as much to Jacobi's brilliant performance as to the fact that Claudius retains all of his lines. Furthermore, this *Hamlet*, in sharp contrast to Olivier's or Zeffirelli's films, is a political as well as a private play. Hamlet's choices have public consequences, and we are never allowed to forget that a kingdom is at stake. Watching Branagh's film, we can more easily understand why the Danish court would want stability at all costs and would happily turn to the strong and plausible Claudius rather than summon home a student prince from Wittenberg. The full text gives us moments often not seen even in the theater, such as the droll and nicely performed exchange between the Clown/Gravediggers (Billy Crystal and Simon Russell Beale) at the beginning of 5.1. And some lines that make little sense in other productions—Polonius's "This is too long," often spoken after the First Player has gotten half a dozen lines out, here is at least understandable, even if Charlton Heston turns the recital into a convincing piece of high-style rhetoric.[21]

Throughout the film, Branagh oscillates between carefully structured scenes and sequences that serve to clarify language and action and other moments when his visual exuberance threatens to obscure meaning altogether. He wants the eye to be fed even as the ear's attention is most required. A number of passages, crucial to an understanding of the political situation or in other ways of thematic importance, are either sufficiently complex or obscure that they require careful treatment. Horatio's twenty-five-plus-line explanation of the political situation in 1.1 (ll. 80–107) needs to be clarified for both the audience in the play (Marcellus and Bernardo) and the audience watching the play. Branagh, however, films the speech in a long tracking shot as the actors are in motion (where they are walking to is unclear), and the dual movements (camera and performers) distract significantly from the words. Horatio needs to shape his speech, to break it up into digestible units, and to use the reaction of his listeners as an excuse to provide precision and explanatory pauses, especially for the film audience. Instead, Nicholas Farrell gives us the lines all at once as if anxious to get it over with. The speech virtually demands close-ups of Horatio, but Branagh never provides them. At the other extreme, Branagh can at times make too much of a relatively minor moment. Particularly irritating is his handling of the Polonius/Reynaldo scene. Turning Reynaldo, clearly a servant to Polonius, into a pimp, providing a prostitute for Polonius, and then casting a seemingly puzzled (does he understand English?) Gérard Depardieu as Reynaldo, unnecessarily complicates what is a fairly straightforward revelation of the extent to which Denmark is a world of distrust between parents and children, a world where spying is a favorite occupation. As Russell Jackson, the film's Shakespeare adviser, commented in his film diary, "Eventually, the scene seems like part of a (lost) Balzac novel."[22] But Balzac, at least here, has little to tell us about *Hamlet*.

One of Branagh's more questionable choices is the inclusion of what his script identifies as "flashbacks" and formalist film theorists would more accurately term either "displaced diegetic inserts" (we see, out of chronology, something that either has happened or is imagined by a character). It is a natural temptation for filmmakers to show the viewer what a speaker is telling. Olivier's *Hamlet* includes several flashbacks: the poisoning of Old Hamlet, Hamlet's mime for Ophelia ("As I was sewing in my closet"), Ophelia's death, and Hamlet's fight with the pirates (Branagh, interestingly, chose not to illustrate the last two of these). Kosintsev's *Hamlet* (1964) includes scenes of Hamlet making up new orders for Rosencrantz and Guildenstern, as do the Gade/Neilsen (1920), Zeffirelli (1990), and Almereyda (2001) films. But no other director of Shakespeare film engages in this technique as frequently as Branagh—who, given the length of the film, has more opportunities than most. It could be argued that these inserts are not "true" flashbacks. Old Hamlet, for example, could not have a memory of his brother poisoning him, since he was asleep at the time; Horatio is not likely to know what Fortinbras looks like; and neither the First Player nor Hamlet, most obviously, was present at the sacking of Troy. At other moments, however, what we see is clearly meant to be a flashback, as when Ophelia sees herself in bed with Hamlet.

These "Hamlet and Ophelia in bed" moments are the most problematic, not because they necessarily violate Shakespeare's text—Ophelia's mad scenes, after all, are pretty clear on this subject—but precisely because they make obvious what need not be explicitly spelled out: the ambiguities of the Hamlet/Ophelia relationship are in the end more interesting than a literalization of it. Branagh even creates a new "scene" of Hamlet reading the "Doubt thou the stars are fire" poem to Ophelia as they are in bed—which is, of course, nonsensical since this is in a letter Hamlet clearly sent to Ophelia in his recently adopted "mad" mode, not when he and Ophelia were still lovers. The text at the very least leaves room for ambiguity here, which, in one sense at least, Branagh closes off. More puzzling, however, is the problem of exactly whose flashback this is—Ophelia has left the room and Hamlet is not present in this scene. It must therefore be a flashback for Polonius, Claudius, or Gertrude, and yet it seems very unlikely to belong to any of them, except as a prurient projection.

What does Branagh the actor make of *Hamlet*, finally? His performance has mixed results. He is, as one critic of his stage performance remarked, an "impressively princely Hamlet,"[23] very much in the mold of Olivier. In appearance and demeanor, this is the Hamlet of Ophelia's idealization. In terms of individual moments and specific speeches, however, Branagh quite precisely "overacts," not in the sense of giving a too broad, "theatrical" performance, but in the sense that he finds intensity in far too many moments: he is, at times, merely hyper rather than responsive to specific stimuli. His interpretation of the character, as distinct from the specific qualities of his performance, can be best defined according to the choices he avoids. This is not an overtly Oedipal Hamlet, especially when compared to Olivier and Zeffirelli: his relationship with his mother is affectionate but not sexual.[24] Nor is Branagh's Hamlet a vacillating or particularly melancholic intellectual. He would act, one gathers, if a clear opportunity arose, but because Claudius is a genuine opponent, the opportunities are few. This is a Hamlet who, whatever he may say ("To be or not to be"), is not eager to sacrifice his own life at the altar of revenge. Nor does Branagh's Hamlet ever seem genuinely mad. The closest we come to gauging the extent of Hamlet's disorder is in the Fishmonger scene. Here Branagh acts out various forms of "craziness," breaking out into eccentricities: mugging, employing "funny" voices, exhibiting rapid shifts of mood and emphasis. We may finally wonder if his "acting crazy" is really an act, or if "acting crazy" is a consequence of really being crazy. Branagh performs Hamlet performing madness, but, for the most part, this Hamlet appears quite sane.

And what does Branagh the director have to tell us about *Hamlet*? As already noted, by providing a full text, Branagh ensures that *Hamlet* retains its dual focus on interpersonal dynamics and the larger world of dynastic politics. Even here, however, it is by no means obvious just what Branagh's political interpretation might be. Claudius does not appear notably corrupt or heavy-handed, and Denmark gives every appearance of being a properly ordered, successful society. We have no reason to believe that Hamlet would make a better ruler than Claudius, or that he would be more effective in dealing with the threat from Fortinbras. If Denmark is a prison, it appears to be a rather pleasant one, more like the Ruritania featured in several movie versions of the *Prisoner of Zenda* than the stony and grim police state we see in, for instance, Kosintsev's film, to mention as stark a contrast as possible.

A Victorian Hamlet

Branagh's Hamlet hearkens back—in moments, at least—to the first significant film Hamlet, Sir Johnston Forbes-Robertson. His 1913 performance not only re-created, in a fifty-nine-minute adaptation, that actor-manager's way with the play and with the role (which he had first assayed in 1897) but also sums up much of the Victorian era view of Hamlet in the theater. As played by Forbes-Robertson, Hamlet is the star not only of the film but in the world of the play itself. This is no melancholy Dane, sulking in a corner, but a prince, courteous and comfortable with the Danish court. When, in the first scene (Shakespeare's 1.2), Laertes prepares to leave for France, Hamlet bids him farewell, and Laertes kisses Hamlet's hand. Forbes-Robertson creates a Hamlet who is first and foremost a gentleman. His acting is carefully detailed and precise, his movements at once large and subtle. However "theatrical" its origins, this is a performance by an actor instinctively attuned to the film medium. In the "recorder" scene (near the end of 3.2), Forbes-Robertson mimes his interchanges with Rosencrantz and Guildenstern with clear, uncluttered gestures and finely calibrated facial expressions. Hamlet never loses our sympathy or our admiration. Forbes-Robertson does not give us a complete Hamlet, of course, but it is one we seldom see. Only recently (2000), with Simon Russell Beale at the National Theatre, has the stage given us a Hamlet who might be characterized as being in a number of ways in the Forbes-Robertson mold.

The final images—soldiers tearing down the monumental statue of Old Hamlet—suggest the fall of the Soviet Union and its satellites (though it could just as well suggest the end of czarist Russia), but in the context this has very little resonance. If Old Hamlet represents, say, the Romanian dictator Ceausescu, who does Fortinbras represent? And why Old Hamlet's statue? Aren't there any statues of Claudius available? And wasn't Old Hamlet a king who, if we believe his son, ruled a "well-tended garden" now gone to seed under Claudius? In the end, Douglas Lanier finds, we have "not a triumph of popular community" the film seems to promise "but the fall of paternal icons and the utopian potential they signify."[25] Which may be another way of saying that, like a number of Branagh's clever ideas, this one seems less than coherent.

Commenting on the goals of his screenplay adaptation, Branagh writes that "its intention was to be both personal, with enormous attention paid to the intimate relations between the characters, and at the same time epic, with a sense of the country at large and of a dynasty in decay."[26] In practice, he is more successful with the first goal than the second. As a positive consequence of Branagh's approach to *Hamlet*, nearly every scene, every speech, every moment is given a pointing, a psychological underpinning that at best results in sheer dramatic intensity. On the other hand, there are moments when Branagh fails to integrate the meaning of the words with the expression he wishes to give them or the effect he strives to achieve. A striking instance of mistaken goals is the handling of "How all occasions do inform against me," perhaps the most straightforward and "sensible" of Hamlet's soliloquies. In Michael Pennington's words, "There is a new lucidity in Hamlet, undeceived, no longer intellectually evasive, that anticipates the simplicity at the end of the play, by which time he will at last give a straight answer to almost any straight question."[27] Branagh chose to turn this moment into a cinematic tour de force, a pre-intermission bit of dazzle. In one take, the camera pulls farther and farther back as Hamlet's voice continuously rises in volume, ending the shot with Hamlet, at the top of his voice, now a small figure in the depth of the shot. It is as if Branagh wanted to do the Olivier method of filming speeches—tracking back instead of tracking in—one better. Although it makes sense to pull the camera back for a rousing speech like "Once more unto the breach" (*Henry V*), one that rises climactically line by line and point by point, it makes less sense to do so here: to shout out, at the top of his voice, the final resolve ("Oh from this time forth / My thoughts be bloody or be nothing worth, " 4.4.65–66) seems more than a little ridiculous. A whispered injunction to himself would be more effective (this is precisely how Branagh says the line in the BBC Radio production). But even if we accept Branagh's interpretation, we cannot really follow Hamlet's words when we are marveling over the technical accomplishment of the camerawork.

In Branagh's Wake: *Othello* (1995), *Richard III* (1995), *Twelfth Night* (1996), and *A Midsummer Night's Dream* (1999)

Kenneth Branagh's initial commercial success encouraged other filmmakers to tackle Shakespeare in the 1990s, and each film reflects something of Branagh's "realistic" approach to the play text. In contrast to Baz Luhrmann's imaginative and flamboyant rendering of *Romeo and Juliet*, directors Oliver Parker, Richard Loncraine, Trevor Nunn, and Michael Hoffman chose a conventional, more or less straightforward handling of mise-en-scène, editing, and cinematography, very much in the Branagh mold. Branagh's influence on these films is variously evident. In Oliver Parker's *Othello*, Branagh plays Iago, and two actors associated with him—Michael Maloney and Nicholas Farrell—play, respectively, Roderigo and Montano. Trevor Nunn's *Twelfth Night* was produced by Renaissance Films, the company Branagh founded; Hoffman's *A Midsummer Night's Dream* adopts a Tuscan setting, much like *Much Ado about Nothing*; Loncraine's *Richard III* mixes British and American actors and alludes to various Hollywood styles and genres. All of these films tend to favor location filming as a way of anchoring themselves to "reality," but each is stylized to a greater or lesser degree.

Oliver Parker's *Othello*, with Laurence Fishburne in the title role and Branagh as Iago, released in the wake of the notorious and drawn-out O. J. Simpson trial (the verdict was announced on October 30, 1995, and the film was released in December)[28] appeared to some critics an opportunistic use of Shakespeare. Parker, however, has adapted Shakespeare's play in a relatively straightforward, albeit compressed, manner, his naturalistic approach working against some of the more lurid aspects of the drama. Expository details, including Roderigo's infatuation, Iago's resentment, the secret marriage, and the Turkish fleet, for example, are immediately sacrificed to action and excitement, and we lose any clear sense of character relationships together with the charged imagery Shakespeare initiates in his early scenes. In this sense, at least, the opening of Parker's film echoes Orson Welles's fast and loose treatment of the first act, but without the compensatory visual and audio panache of the earlier film. Later, Parker eliminates the storm that begins act 2 (and begins Verdi's opera), thereby sacrificing the anxiety over Othello's safety as well as the opportunity to exhibit Iago's fatally dangerous ability to insinuate himself into any social interaction he chooses. Even if we grant the film's right to forget Shakespeare, there is something far too casual and sketchy about the transition from Venice to Cyprus—the tragic dynamic of subsequent events depends, to a significant extent, on the "atmosphere" of Cyprus, the outpost and war camp: Parker gives us pretty pictures but little else. The greeting ("My fair warrior") of Othello and Desdemona has little impact because the danger involved in their separation has not been established. If the budget did not allow for a realistic depiction of ships in a stormy sea, imagination could have provided a substitute: this is what differentiates between a skilled and a merely adequate filmmaker.

Fishburne, the first African American to play Othello in a mainstream film, is dignified and forceful. He looks and sounds right (though at times his costuming verges on the ludicrous), but his performance lacks an inner core. Crucially, Fishburne's Othello is strong without being dangerous, dignified but not fear-inspiring, hurt but insufficiently angry. We wait, throughout, for the explosion that never comes; the depth of his sense of betrayal can only be guessed at. This is what critic Helen Gardner (approvingly) terms "The Noble Moor" with no trace of F. R. Leavis's more flawed hero.[29] We sense throughout the film an unwillingness on Parker's (or is it Fishburne's?) part to allow the nearly burlesque elements of the play to have any sway; no one wants to allow the black man to become "the fixed figure for the time of scorn / To point his slow unmoving finger at" (4.2.53–54). At the same time, Parker dangerously plays up the "black stud" stereotype. The wedding night sequence, especially, has unfortunate overtones of a male predator and his (albeit willing) victim. Othello is the aggressor, moving toward Desdemona, who backs away as if in fear—that she backs away to the bed does not entirely erase the implication of rape.[30]

In part because of Fishburne's contained performance, the film exacerbates a danger present in Shakespeare's play that Iago, with his soliloquies and ruminations of various sorts, will simply overshadow the unselfreflective Othello. Welles guarded against this by taking the drastic step of eliminating virtually all of Iago's soliloquies and never giving him the opportunity of addressing the camera directly. (Laurence Olivier, in his National Theatre performance, played Othello in such a powerfully eccentric manner as to overwhelm Frank Finlay's Iago; when the production was filmed, however, the balance was somewhat redressed.) Parker not only allows Branagh to retain Iago's soliloquies but invariably presents them in close-up, as intimate conversations between Iago and the camera. Branagh, for his part, takes full advantage of the opportunities offered him, giving his most powerful and convincing performance in a role that allows his intelligence to shine while keeping his emotionalism and tendency to "overact" in check.

Branagh's Iago believes himself in charge of events at the same time that he is at their mercy, a man either uncertain of his own motives or unwilling to face their nature. His "plausibility" is never entirely free of resentment. He does not, as some Iagos do, work very hard to charm or seduce those he wishes to manipulate. He performs the minimal gestures in that direction, but little more. In his intimate colloquies with the camera, he behaves little differently than he does in his dialogue scenes; he is not particularly respectful of the audience he appears to address. At one point, having deliberately burned himself by grasping a smoldering brand, he puts his hand over the lens of the camera, as if he were embarrassed and angry at having revealed his masochistic tendencies. The key to this Iago is, interestingly, in line with Olivier's 1938 stage performance—unrequited love for Othello. The homoerotic subtext is made clear in the "bonding" moment in 3.4 ("I am your own forever") with Iago and Othello in a tight embrace. In truth, however, very little has prepared us for this. Iago's motivation is neither clearly worked into the fabric of previous scenes between Othello and Iago nor coherently integrated into a larger interpretation of the play.

The film's rhythm is insufficiently governed by the linguistic patterns evident in the text. Much of the climactic force of, for example, the so-called brothel scene (4.2) is dissipated by the failure to achieve a proper tempo that would help explain why the characters cannot find a moment of mutual understanding. Othello's accusations are so monstrous that Desdemona can only offer shocked and uncomprehending responses to them even as the violence of his verbal attack prevents her from fully communicating her innocence of his charges. To slow the pace or lessen the intensity at this point can only destroy Shakespeare's daring balancing act. Indeed, as the film reaches its climax, it begins to lose rather than gain intensity. One would expect the accelerating disintegration of Othello and the increasingly desperate improvisations of Iago to speed up the tempo of scenes and sequences, but this never really happens. The murder scene too is awkwardly staged and edited, with Desdemona a passive victim who takes little care to save her life. Having both Othello and Desdemona sitting down—he in a chair, she on

In Oliver Parker's adaptation of *Othello,* we wait, throughout, for the explosion that never comes; the depth of Othello's sense of betrayal can only be guessed at. Copyright © 1995 Castle Rock Entertainment.

the bed—defuses the tension just at the point where it should be at its height.

Perhaps most problematic are the interpolated "flashbacks" and visions Parker employs (as Branagh had in *Henry V* and would in *Hamlet*), inserts that may represent what has actually happened, what a character imagines will happen, and, presumably, what has not and will not ever happen. The last-mentioned category includes the moments when Othello "sees" Desdemona and Cassio making love. In a dramatic structure that is always in danger of blaming the victim, of finding Desdemona at least potentially guilty—as a woman, as a Venetian—of what Iago intimates and Othello comes to believe of her, these inserts are particularly bothersome. The effect is problematic in part because the provenance of the image is at times uncertain, at least initially. One insert is presented in a way that violates classic point-of-view editing: Parker cuts from an image of the floating handkerchief to Desdemona in bed with a man who, though not immediately identifiable, is clearly not Othello. Only then does Parker cut to Othello, establishing this shot, retroactively, as his point of view and not, or at least not only, our own. Only several shots later are the images of Othello, Desdemona, and Cassio (now clearly identified) shown to be Othello's nightmare. This is valid enough as a way of making the viewer share Othello's psychological state, but the implications are nonetheless highly disturbing in that we are allowed, if only momentarily, to incriminate Desdemona as an adulteress. As Carol Chillington Rutter rightly concludes, the effect of these inserts is to make "women somehow at fault for male fantasies."[31]

Richard Loncraine's *Richard III* is based on, though not a reproduction of, the 1992 National Theatre production directed by Richard Eyre. It is set, even more single-mindedly than the original, in the 1930s, with Richard (loosely modeled on Sir Oswald Mosley) as a homegrown fascist demagogue.[32] In line with other "realistic" Shakespeare films, the mise-en-scène, though more stylized than in Parker's *Othello*, takes advantage of real locations that, together with the constructed sets, have been carefully chosen to provide the pre–World War II feel. The period style provides sufficient historical distance to justify the poetic language and enough "modernity" to make Shakespeare's Plantagenets into contemporary figures. As James Loehlin convincingly argues, "*Richard III* can also be read as an inspired conflation of two principal cinematic genres: British 'heritage' film and the American gangster movie."[33] Ian McKellen repeats his stage performance as Richard, though with some significant differences in conception and execution. An actor seemingly without personal vanity, McKellen, who also cowrote the adaptation with Richard Loncraine, gave himself a particularly sinister appearance, something like a basset hound that had gotten the worse of it in a dogfight—his features are askew, his haircut is unflattering, his teeth are bad, his mustache is thinly sinister, and his body is awkwardly bent. This is a sharp contrast to his stage performance, where he kept his natural good looks and combined them with a ramrod-straight bearing; he had deformities, but he controlled and even hid them through sheer willpower. In the film, McKellen plays Richard as almost completely transparent. No one is fooled by him—there is no plausible exterior for him to wear in public. Richard always wins precisely because his acts of piety and modesty are never convincing. McKellen makes Richard into an essentially sour and bitter man who cannot truly enjoy his triumphs. In the Nuremberg Rally scene, it is notable that Richard has nothing to say. The physical trappings of power, rather than words of inspiration, are all he brings to the populace.

The McKellen/Loncraine script greatly condenses the various elements of Shakespeare's play, eliminating, as Olivier had done, the character of Queen Margaret, the only opponent Richard seems to fear, some of whose lines are given to Richard's mother, the Duchess of York. Lines from one part of the play are combined with lines from other parts, sometimes in a seemingly arbitrary manner. Various insults ("poisonous, bunch-backed toad") spoken behind Richard's back are now spoken to his face, resulting in a new relationship between Richard and his opponents that the film fails to exploit. The compression of the Richard-Anne scene makes the courtship even more improbable than in Shakespeare, where it is already a hard pill to swallow.

On film in *Richard III,* Ian McKellen was both funnier and less attractive physically than he had been on stage. Copyright © 1995 United Artist Pictures Inc.

Richard III and Hitler

Viewing Richard of Gloucester as a proto-Hitler goes back to Donald Wolfit and Laurence Olivier, who both played the role in wartime Britain, but it becomes a central element in the Ian McKellen Richard both at the National Theatre and on film. The parallel is not really apropos, however, either as regards Shakespeare's play or these actors' interpretations. Olivier's Richard, in particular, cannot be equated to the humorless, shrill, puffed-up, seeming nonentity that was Hitler. Nothing could be further from the "banality of evil" than Olivier's Richard. In Shakespeare, it is the "good" who are banal, the evil—Richard, of course, but also Buckingham—who are attractive, or at least enjoyable. Some critics of Olivier's stage and film performances thought the actor was providing audiences with too much fun, but Shakespeare certainly prepared the way. Ian McKellen, on the stage at least, went the other way. The Hitler analogies were stressed, and McKellen made Richard *seem* banal ("a beautifully executed study of the banality of evil"),[34] though the force of his acting personality to some extent belied his interpretive strategy. On film, McKellen was both funnier and less attractive physically than he was on stage. In the National Theatre production, he was cool, controlled, and sleek; he made little effort, in the opening soliloquy, to charm or seduce. His deformities were painstakingly hidden under his military greatcoat and an iron will that appeared to "straighten" his crooked limbs. Although allusions to Hitler can provide a historical frisson to almost any post–World War II production of *Richard III*, they are ultimately irrelevant to Shakespeare's Richard, who has no program, no sense of national destiny or purpose, and no rhetoric to inspire his followers. Hitler, at some level, believed the words he spoke; Richard believes only in his will to power.

Not surprisingly, much of the rhetoric is sacrificed: here, however, the sacrifice is almost fatal. It is precisely through a rhetorical attack that Shakespeare's Richard overcomes Anne's defenses; her attempt to match his sallies, to play by his rules, defeat her. In the film, the give-and-take almost disappears, and Anne's capitulation seems at once foreordained and arbitrary. And Kristin Scott Thomas, in any case, is too much the woman of the world to be taken in by Richard's tricks. Which, of course, may be the point: on the losing side of a civil war, Anne is smart enough to know where her creature comforts lie.

Often the compression and rearrangement of text can be effective. The Fall of Hastings scene, one of Shakespeare's finest little "playlets" (albeit it owes much to Thomas More, a crucial if indirect source for Shakespeare's play), though curtailed, is constructed and played to emphasize that everyone, even Buckingham, is embarrassed by the sheer nakedness of Richard's hypocrisy: no one even pretends to believe that he has only now become crippled. At times the script adroitly recombines lines from different scenes or moments in the play. After Richard rejects Buckingham (4.2), for example, we find Buckingham together with Anne, who, talking more or less to herself, complains that "never yet one hour in his bed / Did I enjoy the golden dew of sleep, / But with his timorous dreams was still awaked" (4.1.83–85), to which Buckingham responds, or appears to respond, with the non sequitur "Let me think on Hastings and be gone" (4.2.104). The effect verges on theater of the absurd—it makes perfect sense at the same time that it seems surreal. These are Shakespeare's words, reconstituted into a non-Shakespearean collage.

Though enjoyable on a number of levels, there is ultimately something too easy and glib about the film—all the rough spots have been smoothed out and little is left to challenge an audience. Richard becomes yet another in a long line of postmodern figures (Freddy, Michael, etc.) from horror films who have no clear motivation and no real affect, who act entirely on impulse and as a response to the mechanism of the narrative in which they find themselves. Without some sense of the chain of political and personal betrayals and counterbetrayals that precede his ascension, Richard's ambitions exist in a vacuum. The various "roles" he plays in Shakespeare's complex of relationships—Vice, Scourge of God, buffoon, nemesis—are flattened out into a single, incomprehensible embodiment of sheer malignity. In the final sequence, which not accidentally plays like a *Die Hard* or *Terminator* film, it is unsurprising that Richard becomes a monstrous machine whose destruction takes place in a fiery industrial landscape.

The Trevor Nunn *Twelfth Night* and Michael Hoffman *A Midsummer Night's Dream*, though each has its defenders, together exhibit some of the drawbacks to a "realistic" approach to Shakespearean comedy. Neither film has anything to match the visceral pleasures of Parker's *Othello* and Loncraine's *Richard III* at their best. Nunn, a brilliant stage director, signally fails to breathe life into one of Shakespeare's richest and most carefully designed plays. The temporal and spatial dynamics of the film medium, surprisingly enough, here seem to have hampered an essentially theatrical imagination. The challenges of what Peter Brook termed "the empty space" can quicken the imagination, whereas the far too crowded space available to film can smother it. Nunn's usual flair has been virtually atrophied by the allure of the shot/reverse shot, the easy shifts in time and place, and the unearned scenography of location filming. The imaginative possibilities of the play run counter to Nunn's highly conventional desire to be "cinematic." The problem is not that Nunn sacrifices theater to cinema but that the cinema he produces is far too conventional.

The acting in *Twelfth Night* suffers as well from the "naturalistic" approach. Ordinarily skilled performers like Helena Bonham Carter (Olivia) and Imogen Stubbs (Viola), who was a remarkable Desdemona in Nunn's RSC *Othello*, make little impact here. Similarly, the scenes with Sir Toby, Sir Andrew, and Feste have almost no comic life: Mel Smith's Toby, in particular, is unfunny, Richard E. Grant fails to get the full measure of Sir Andrew, and Ben Kingsley cannot find the right tone for Feste, whose bitterness is poorly motivated. On the other hand, Nigel Hawthorne, though he starts out inauspiciously (Nunn keeps him mainly in long shot in his first scene with Olivia), grows into the role as the film progresses. He is particularly good in the "yellow stockings" sequence, though even here the scene would have been funnier had Hawthorne been directed to bring out the "Puritan" aspect of Malvolio more clearly. Though some of the surefire moments work (the duel scene, the brother/sister recognition at the end), the various parts are not integrated into a comprehensible whole.

Hoffman's *A Midsummer Night's Dream*, though more visually striking than Nunn's *Twelfth Night*, relies excessively, as did Branagh's *Much Ado about Nothing*, on its Tuscan setting—a particularly odd choice for a play that is so clearly English. Shakespeare did not pore over maps or immerse himself in Latin culture in order to compose his romantic comedies. *A Midsummer Night's Dream* no more takes place in "Athens" than it does in "Paris" or "Moscow": the Lords and Ladies are Elizabethan gallants; the Mechanicals are London or Warwickshire workmen; the Fairies are straight out of British folklore. The absence of specificity is one key to the play's dynamics—which is why director Peter Brook could, in a famous production, place it in a white box and make it work. Insofar as he has lovingly re-created the texture of late-nineteenth-century Italy (including various references to and excerpts from opera), by so much do we lose much of what is truly magical about Shakespeare's play. Hoffman gives us an overly explicit fairy world that at the same time lacks all unity. As Stephen Buhler remarks, "Victorian-style fairies . . . seem out of place amidst the Ovidian satyrs and nymphs . . . populating Hoffman's forest world."[35] "Realism" here only serves to makes the magic disappear.

Hoffman provides a strangely soporific reading of a play full of action and movement. There is little energy or sense of fun, and the forward thrust of the narrative is slowed down at almost every step by irrelevant business (wine poured on Bottom's head, Puck fiddling with a bicycle, frolicking fairies, etc.). The play may have the word "dream" in the title, but this should not be a license for everyone to sleep—Puck (Stanley Tucci) and Oberon (Rupert Everett), who lie or sit a good deal of the time, appear to suffer from lethargy; the former lacks spirit, the latter lacks authority (as does Theseus, played by David Straitharn). Turning Bottom (Kevin Kline) into a handsome, hen-pecked dandy makes little sense of the character—why wouldn't he be a suitable sexual partner for Titania? Indeed, apart from Michelle Pfeiffer as Titania, who at the least lends the film some sexual warmth and dynamism, only Roger Rees as Peter Quince makes much of his character (but why cast Bill Irwin, the wonderfully inventive "postmodern" clown, as one of the Mechanicals and then give him virtually nothing to do?). "Why *A Midsummer Night's Dream?*" Michael Hoffman asks. He then answers: "For its magic, its innocence, its comedy, its poetry, the untarnished soul of Peter Quince, the mythic power and beauty of Titania—to be part of the four-hundred-year-old pageant that is Shakespeare in performance."[36] Unfortunately, only the last of Hoffman's reasons appears fully realized in his film.[37]

Coda: Branagh Redux?

At different points in his relatively brief career, Kenneth Branagh, consciously or subconsciously, has provided readers and viewers with self-portraits. His autobiography, *Beginning* (1989), which, given the author's tender age, occasioned some ridicule, is the most explicit. Almost as self-referential is the character played by Michael Maloney in *The Bleak Midwinter* (U.S. title, *A Midwinter's Tale*), which Branagh directed in 1995 while planning and raising money for *Hamlet*. The film presents a highly idealized view of the director as enthusiast. Though neurotic to the point of being suicidal, he is nonetheless a heroic figure, manipulating people into doing what he wants them to do even as he exhibits kindly concern for all. His one explosive loss of control is perfectly understandable—a moment of self-indulgence that in no way undermines the overall positive image that is almost always in evidence. (Characteristically, Branagh has difficulty maintaining an overarching tone for the film. His script careens from genuine feeling and earned humor to silliness and self-indulgence. Much of the comedy is sophomoric and forced, and the central conceit—putting on *Hamlet* with a cast of marginal performers and misfits—is more interesting as a con-

---

"Strange and Admirable": Adrian Noble's *A Midsummer Night's Dream*

Paradoxically, a number of the most "cinematic" Shakespeare films are those that give full play to the theatrical grounding of the original play. Adrian Noble's *A Midsummer Night's Dream* (1996), though little noted or appreciated on its release, is an imaginative and fluid remounting of his 1994 RSC stage production. Noble makes no attempt to provide the kind of cinematic realism that fellow RSC director Trevor Nunn employed in *Twelfth Night*; everything in this production takes place clearly "onstage," though just as clearly not the "real" RSC stage. Noble's film is theatrical in the primary sense that it relies on clear and minimal visual concepts—multicolored umbrellas, bright, naked lightbulbs, big soap bubbles, Dali-like floating doors, and so on—that are reused and reconfigured in a variety of ways. An eclecticism in costuming—ranging from pajamas for the lovers, to frock coats for the authority figures, to 1930s garb for the Mechanicals—and a variety of anachronisms (Bottom's motorcycle) are also signs of "theater." A productive byplay exists between the freedom of camera movement, photographic lenses, actor positioning, stylized sets and costumes, candy colors, and so on. The key is an elegant simplicity, a refusal to allow too much specificity to bury the play in "realistic" detail. Hoffman's *A Midsummer Night's Dream* constructs a world all too substantial; Noble gives us formalized sketches of a purely imaginary world.[38]

---

cept than it is in the execution.) Fancifully, one might suggest that Branagh's performance in the 2002 Channel 4/A&E biopic, *Shackleton*, is a self-portrait as well, this time of a survivor. Much of the early part of the film finds Shackleton, at a low point in his career, desperately raising money for one last expedition. On the journey itself, having lost his ship as well as any hope of succeeding in his goal of crossing Antarctica, he snatches some kind of victory from the jaws of defeat, his stubbornness and grit saving his men from almost certain destruction. Branagh is entirely convincing in this role (he was nominated for an Emmy), giving a restrained and moving performance of a man who is at almost every moment at the end of his rope.[39]

Notes

1. For a detailed overview of Branagh's career, see Sarah Hatchuel, *A Companion to the Shakespearean Films of Kenneth Branagh* (Winnipeg: Blizzard, 2000).

2. Hatchuel, *Companion*, 13.

3. James Loehlin makes a similar point, remarking that "the overwhelming impression I had from watching the two films was how much they are the same." James N. Loehlin, *Shakespeare in Performance: Henry V* (Manchester: Manchester University Press, 1996), 128.

4. For Graham Holderness, these tears are more "a liturgical collusion with the ideology of patriotic war than an emotional interrogation of its values." "'What Ish My Nation?': Shakespeare and National Identities," *Textual Practice* 5, no. 1 (1991): 74–93.

5. "Taking on Shakespeare: Kenneth Branagh's *Henry V*," *Shakespeare Quarterly* 42, no. 1 (1991): 60–71.

6. See, e.g., Susanne Collier, "Post-Falklands, Post-Colonial: Contextualizing Branagh as Henry V on Stage and on Film," *Essays in Theatre* 10, no. 2 (1992): 143–54; the political context is examined as well in, among many other essays, Curtis Breight, "Branagh and the Prince, or a 'Royal Fellowship of Death,'" *Critical Quarterly* 33, no. 4 (1991): 95–111; Robert Lane, "'When Blood Is Their Argument': Class, Character, and Historymaking in Shakespeare's and Branagh's *Henry V*," *ELH* 61 (1994): 27–52; Chris Fitter, "A Tale of Two Branaghs: Henry V, Ideology, and the Mekong Agincourt," in *Shakespeare Left and Right*, ed. Ivo Kamps (New York: Routledge, 1991): 259–75.

7. For an analysis of the film's "conservative ambivalence," see Donald K. Hedrick, "War Is Mud: Branagh's Dirty Harry V and the Types of Political Ambiguity," in *Shakespeare, The Movie: Popularizing the Plays on Film, TV, and Video* (London: Routledge, 1997), 45–66.

8. Loehlin, *Henry V*, 145.

9. Branagh, Kenneth Branagh, *Henry V: The Screenplay* (New York: Norton, 1997), xvi.

10. *Henry V: The Screenplay*, xv.

11. As Courtney Lehmann, who discusses Branagh as uneasily torn between his Irish and English identity, wittily notes, his "pretense of thrift enables Branagh to put Shakespeare on a diet, cutting the scenes that accentuate the 'breach' between frontier and mainland." Courtney Lehmann, "Kenneth Branagh at the Quilting Point: Shakespearean Adaptation, Postmodern Auteurism, and the (Schizophrenic) Fabric of 'Everyday Life,'" *Post Script*, Fall 1997, 6–27; 17.

12. Samuel Crowl, "The Marriage of Shakespeare and Hollywood: Kenneth Branagh's *Much Ado about Nothing*," in *Spectacular Shakespeare: Critical Theory and Popular Cinema*, ed. Courtney Lehmann and Lisa S. Starks (Madison, N.J.: Fairleigh Dickinson University Press, 2002), 110–24; 122.

13. John Cox, ed., *Shakespeare in Production: Much Ado about Nothing* (Cambridge: Cambridge University Press, 1997), 156.

14. Kenneth Branagh, *Much Ado about Nothing: The Making of the Movie* (New York: Norton, 1993), xv.

15. Crowl, "Marriage of Shakespeare and Hollywood," 121.

16. Branagh, *Much Ado*, ix.

17. H. R. Woudhuysen, *Love's Labour's Lost*, The Arden Shakespeare, 3d ser. (Walton-on-Thames: Nelson, 1998), 1.

18. G. R. Hibbard, cited in Woudhuysen, *Love's Labour's Lost*, 7.

19. Branagh even added a few words—interjections, mainly—to the Shakespeare text. See Russell Jackson, "Kenneth Branagh's Film of *Hamlet*: The Textual Choices," *Shakespeare Bulletin*, Spring 1997, 37–38.

20. A two-hour version was subsequently released as well, though mainly in Europe. See H. R. Coursen, "Branagh's Two Hour *Hamlet*: A Review Essay," *Shakespeare Bulletin*, Summer 2000, 39–40.

21. The full text, however, poses challenges that Branagh cannot always meet. For one thing, there are—dare one say it?—passages in *Hamlet* that probably ought to be cut in performance (and, in some instances, very likely were cut by Shakespeare himself). The "hard times in the theater" discussion Rosencrantz and Guildenstern and Hamlet engage in (2.2.313–33; not in Q2), which includes passages like "Nay, their endeavor keeps in the wonted pace, but there is sir an eyrie of children, little eyases, that cry out on the top of question and are most tyrannically clapp'd for it" (314–16), can hardly be made sense of without footnotes. This passage remains, on film, well-nigh incomprehensible, especially since, rather than try to clarify it, Branagh chooses to simply get through it: the combination of camera and character movement virtually assures that we will not be able to follow what is being said.

22. Russell Jackson, "Film Diary," in *Hamlet*, screenplay and introduction by Kenneth Branagh (New York: Norton, 1996), 183.

23. Cited in Robert Hapgood, ed., *Shakespeare in Production: Hamlet* (Cambridge: Cambridge University Press, 1999), 14.

24. On the other hand, as Courtney Lehmann and Lisa Starks argue, Branagh's film may be considered "Oedipal" in another fashion: if we go outside the text, we can see how Branagh has in various ways constructed a father–son rivalry with Derek Jacobi: see "Making Mother Matter: Repression, Revision, and the Stakes of 'Reading Psychoanalysis into' Kenneth Branagh's *Hamlet*," *Early Modern Literary Studies* 6, no. 1 (2000): 1–24.

25. Douglas Lanier, "Art Thou Base, Common, and Popular?: The Cultural Politics of Kenneth Branagh's *Hamlet*," in *Spectacular Shakespeare: Critical Theory and Popular Cinema*, ed. Courtney Lehmann and Lisa S. Starks (Madison, N.J.: Fairleigh Dickinson University Press, 2002), 149–71.

26. Branagh, *Hamlet*, xiv–xv.

27. Michael Pennington, *Hamlet: A User's Guide* (New York: Limelight Editions, 1996), 113.

28. Judith Buchanan discusses some of the connections in "Virgin and Ape, Venetian and Infidel: Labellings of Otherness in Oliver Parker's *Othello*," in *Shakespeare, Film, Fin de Siècle*, ed. Mark Thornton Burnett and Ramona Wray (New York: St. Martin's, 2000), 179–202.

29. See Helen Gardner, "The Noble Moor," *Proceedings of the British Academy* 41 (1955): 189–205; and F. R. Leavis, "Diabolic Intellect and the Noble Hero: A Note on *Othello*," *Scrutiny* 6 (1937): 259–83.

30. "In his love scenes with Desdemona, and in its many subsequent tormenting variations in his anxious fantasy, he is both voyeur and predator." Buchanan, "Virgin and Ape," 188; see also Lois Potter, *Shakespeare in Performance: Othello* (Manchester: Manchester University Press, 2002), 194.

31. Carol Chillington Rutter, "Looking at Shakespeare's Women on Film," in *The Cambridge Companion to Shakespeare on Film*, ed. Russell Jackson (Cambridge: Cambridge University Press, 2000), 241–60; 256. For a more positive response to Parker's interpolations, see, also in the Jackson collection, Patricia Tatspaugh, "The Tragedies of Love on Film," 135–59; 148–49.

32. For a useful comparison of the Eyre staging and Loncraine's film, see Samuel Crowl, "Changing Colors Like the Chameleon: Ian McKellen's *Richard III* from Stage to Screen," *Post Script*, Fall 1997, 53–63. Lisa Hopkins details some of the associations between the milieu of *Richard III* and the current royal family in "'How Very Like the Home Life of Our Own Dear Queen': Ian McKellen's *Richard III*," in Lehmann and Starks, *Spectacular Shakespeare*, 47–61.

33. James N. Loehlin, "'Top of the World, Ma': *Richard III* and Cinematic Convention," in Boose and Burt, *Shakespeare: The Movie*, 67–79, 71.

34. Michael Billington, cited in Scott Colley, *Richard's Himself Again: A Stage History of Richard III* (New York: Greenwood, 1992), 261.

35. Stephen M. Buhler, *Shakespeare in the Cinema: Ocular Proof* (Albany: State University of New York Press, 2002), 184.

36. Michael Hoffman, *William Shakespeare's A Midsummer Night's Dream* (New York: HarperCollins, 1999), ix.

37. For a more balanced analysis of Hoffman's film, see Samuel Crowl, "A Midsummer Night's Dream," *Shakespeare Bulletin*, Summer 1999, 41–42.

38. See also Mark Thornton Burnett, "Impressions of Fantasy: Adrian Noble's A Midsummer Night's Dream," in *Shakespeare, Film, Fin de Siècle*, ed. Mark Thornton Burnett and Ramona Wray (New York: St. Martin's, 2000), 89–101.

39. Commenting on Branagh's (mis)fortunes, Richard Burt suggests that "it would not be entirely surprising to find Branagh, like Olivier and Welles before him, ending up doing television commercials for everyday products like camera film and wine." Richard Burt, "To E- or Not to E-? Disposing of Schlockspeare in the Age of Digital Media," in *Shakespeare after Mass Media*, ed. Richard Burt (New York: Palgrave, 2002), 1–32; 15.

CHAPTER SIX

Electronic Shakespeares: Televisual Histories

Television, at least in theory, could be the twentieth-century medium best suited to presenting Shakespeare's plays to a global audience. From its earliest days, television constructed a variety of technological and stylistic parameters that set it apart from both theater and cinema. The development of live dramatic broadcasts in the late 1940s and early 1950s provided audiences with a presentation that was in many ways closer to theater than film. As with theater, a primary emphasis was placed on the spoken word: in television, unlike the movies, the writer was king. To this day teleplays are dialogue driven. In the early days, this was an effect partly of the medium and partly of financial constraints. Not only was the TV image small compared to the projected film image but, perhaps more importantly, the TV camera captured its image with an extremely shallow depth of field (and required an extraordinary amount of light even for that).[1] Consequently it was more practical to produce programming in a studio, in a relatively small physical area and with a strong dependence on close-ups and medium shots. Because the video image was not in itself notably compelling, sound quickly became all-important. Television was and is radio with pictures; we listen to television as much as we watch it. Here is a medium where Shakespeare's highly textured language is not necessarily at a disadvantage. In fact, it would not be going too far to suggest that the language is easier to attend to on television than it often is in the theater.

The economic aspect of this equation worked hand in hand with the technological. Because budgets for television drama were relatively small, sets were minimal and therefore most effective if stylized. Locations were simply and vaguely defined: a whole production could be on one soundstage with interconnecting sets. The methods of live television—continuous action with multiple cameras providing different views on the action—combined the intensity and continuity of the theater with the shifting vantage points of the cinema. The setting could be designed in a theatrical manner and at the same time exhibit cinematic variety. As with radio, the text was presented as a continuous flow, and the constant use of close-ups allowed for a unified, unvarying sound pattern. It is not difficult to see analogies between television and Shakespeare's own theatrical practice: an emphasis on language and symbolic objects; a reliance on stylization in the presentation of both time and space; a minimal but evocative mise-en-scène; a crucial dependence on the actor; an ability to shift rapidly from one location to another; and a dramaturgy based on monologue, duologue, or small ensemble. Television escapes the temptation, almost inevitable in film, to "open up" the space and scope beyond the demands and needs of a theatrical work. No film version of *Henry V* or *Macbeth* can resist giving us Agincourt or Birnam Wood coming to Dunsinane: television can neither present such scenes in a convincingly "realistic" way nor afford to do so in any case. Most of what is "theatrical" in Shakespeare remains theatrical on television, while what might be thought "cinematic" can emerge without too much disproportion.

The generic markers of televised Shakespeare overlap with but are not identical to those that characterize the Shakespeare film. In part, this is because Shakespeare on television is much more clearly a hybrid form, blending the mise-en-scène of the theater with the framing and editing strategies of film. Video productions, consequently, tend to move toward an intimately observed, self-contained, primarily interior (or interior-feeling) world. Unlike a playgoer, the television viewer seldom sees the world of the play "whole"—there is nothing equivalent to the stage itself. What we have, instead, are a variety of stages, of settings, even if (as in the CBC/Stratford, Canada, and American Bard productions) the entire production has been mounted on an actual stage. In the theater, something similar can be achieved through lighting and staging, but the audience can nevertheless see the whole acting area. The effect, which Shakespeare undoubtedly exploited at the Globe and elsewhere, is that no matter where we are in the geography of the play's world, we are always in the *same* place: in the Henry IV cycle, the king's throne and Falstaff's "throne" are one. In the theater too we are conscious that the stage is a space within a space: the house, the theater, is around us so that the stage is indeed *a* space, not *the* space. The theatrical

illusion encourages us to ignore that "other" space we inhabit, but it nevertheless remains there: the stage on which the actors perform is coterminous
with the space in which we perform our role as audience. Neither film nor
television provides that experience.

Television nonetheless exhibits an intensity of its own that differentiates
it from both film and theater. Unlike the tendency in film, television drama
features a virtually continuous dialogue track: montage sequences, lyrical
passages underscored with music, extended action sequences, and silence are
ordinarily absent from television drama. By the same token, a theatrical production, performed for and with a live audience, has a tendency to pick up
rhythm in part from that audience. The intensity is of a different kind in the
theater, where the continuity of word and action tends to be broken up by
scene changes (even if these are merely brief blackouts), rounds of applause,
pauses for laughter, acknowledgment of the audience, and so forth. A stage
production of a Shakespeare play acknowledges, to a greater or lesser extent,
the presence of the audience and thus highlights its own theatricality (in
the 2000 National Theatre *Hamlet*, Simon Russell Beale pats his somewhat
generous stomach on the line "I have lost all custom of exercise" and gets
the expected laugh). The closest analogue to a televised Shakespeare production is neither film nor theater but a radio broadcast or sound recording.

Interestingly (though perhaps not surprisingly) the most successful video
versions of Shakespeare, with some notable exceptions, have been those
founded on a preexisting stage production, for example, *The Merchant of Venice*, with Laurence Olivier and directed by Jonathan Miller (ironically
enough, given the inadequacy of his productions for BBC's Shakespeare Plays
series). Essentially the production staged at the National Theatre by Miller,
the videotape version (1973) was restaged for television, with a "realistic"
set, multiple cameras, and a fluidity almost entirely lacking in Miller's BBC
attempts. A different, even more successful approach was the Royal Shakespeare Company *Antony and Cleopatra* (1975), with Janet Suzman and Richard Johnson. The taping was evidently done on the stage of the RSC,
keeping the simple but evocative settings, as well as, presumably, the blocking and stage business. The prime virtue of this production lay in its refusal
to pretend that it was anything other than theater. And yet the effect was
far from "canned." The camera was given a central role, catching up both
the sweep and the intimacy of the play. One reason for the success of these
televised productions is that they had already been tested and well honed in
the theater. The force of ensemble playing and a cohesive, carefully thought-
out interpretation necessarily finds its way to the videotaped performance.

And, precisely because these are not films, little effort is wasted on attempting to transpose theater into cinema. Once again, a tight budget and a short shooting schedule force a straightforward, economical approach.

Televised Shakespeare, at its best and regardless of its origins, maintains a high degree of the theatrical and does not aspire to cinema. Even a production conceived entirely in television terms will exhibit a theatrical bias in terms of setting, movement, lighting, and so forth. The Granada Television *King Lear* (1983), featuring Laurence Olivier, is a case in point. Taped almost entirely on a soundstage and featuring simple, highly stylized sets, the production has a feel of the theater at the same time that it is constructed of multiple camera setups and flows like a teleplay. The gestures in the direction of cinema are few but telling. The camera can gain a view from any place on the circumference of the action, dissolves are used for transitions, characters who are present at the end of one scene can be present at a different part of the set at the beginning of the next, and so on. Only when the director goes too far in the direction of realism does the production falter (we do not really need or want to see Lear skinning and cooking a real rabbit). Television drama involves a careful melding and balancing of theater and cinema. It is, in its essential mode, a compromise between the two media.

Televised Shakespeare, like filmed Shakespeare, has developed its own generic identities, which can in part be illustrated by considering two significant and distinctive broadcast moments: live U.S. productions from the 1950s and the BBC Shakespeare Plays series from the late 1970s and 1980s. The live Shakespeare broadcasts, especially those on the Hallmark Hall of Fame program, featured various signs of Shakespeare as cultural capital (crowns, musical fanfares, leather volumes, busts of the poet, etc.), with prologues, epilogues, and commercial messages that worked to construct "Shakespeare," and television itself, as both highbrow and accessible. The inevitable result was a middlebrow product. Viewers were being exposed to an enriching cultural experience, which, they were reassured, was nothing to be afraid of. The Shakespeare Plays, although they also indulged in the "aura" of Shakespeare's name and image, exhibited an approach meant to reconfigure Shakespeare *as* television rather than merely exhibit Shakespeare *on* television. Unlike the abbreviated Hallmark productions, these used relatively full texts and made few gestures in the direction of late-twentieth-century theatrical experimentation. In tone and style, the BBC Shakespeare is essentially conservative: the plays are domesticated and contained by the assumed formal constraints of television drama.

Shakespeare Live(s): The Hallmark Years

The key names associated with televised Shakespeare in the United States in the 1950s were Maurice Evans, George Schaefer, and Hallmark Cards. Though Evans appeared in Shakespeare productions not directed by Schaefer, and though Hallmark produced Shakespeare without the director/actor collaboration between Schaefer and Evans, it is the sponsorship of the former and the creative work of the latter that were responsible for five productions of four plays from 1953 to 1960: *Hamlet* (1953), *Richard II* (1954), *Macbeth* (1954, 1960), *Taming of the Shrew* (1956), and *The Tempest* (1960). In this period Hallmark also produced *Twelfth Night* (1957), directed by William Nichols. These Hallmark Hall of Fame productions, ostensibly meant to lend prestige to Hallmark Cards (if not to television itself), were, at least initially, versions of Shakespeare's plays reduced and tamed by the conventions and technological characteristics of 1950s television. Drastically cut, mounted on often less than adequate sets, and marred by the difficulties involved in creating a live broadcast, the plays are frequently in danger of being reduced to inexplicable dumb shows and noise and seldom rise much above the level of a good Classics Illustrated comic book. At their best, however, the Hallmark–Maurice Evans telecasts suggest the range of interpretive and stylistic possibilities for televised Shakespeare.[2]

The Hallmark productions can be considered in two groups: the more or less "realistic" productions, *Hamlet, Richard II*, and *Macbeth* (both versions), which employed an illusionistic, three-dimensional setting anchored in a specific time and place; and the impressionistic productions, *Twelfth Night, Taming of the Shrew*, and *The Tempest*, self-consciously theatrical, set in an abstract or only marginally designed space, and employing "Brechtian" devices such as signboards, direct address to the camera, and so forth. Not surprisingly, the former are productions of tragedies, the latter of comedies. With the first Hallmarks, *Hamlet* and *Richard II*, television Shakespeare was searching for an appropriate form. The comedies are unquestionably more successful, and they remain, for the most part, fresh in the viewing today, whereas the tragedies seem stuffy and dull. Another way of looking at these productions is to divide them into those designed by Richard Sylbert and those designed by Rouben Ter-Arutunian. Sylbert's sets are elaborate and crowded; Ter-Arutunian's are clean and minimalist. Because live television drama depends on choreographing not only the actors but also the multiple—usually three—cameras, the way the set is imagined and constructed determines, to a great extent, how the production will flow. Maurice Evans is a much more compelling performer in the comedies—he is a fine Petruchio and an amusing Malvolio. His Hamlet, by contrast, is unexciting—he recites the role rather than performs it. And his Macbeth is not much more interesting. He plays Richard II with greater conviction, perhaps because the theatricality of the character complements his performance style.

One major problem with the "realistic" productions, especially *Hamlet* and *Richard II*, is that they give us too much to look at. Because the actors are so often photographed in medium shot or close-up in order to accommodate a small viewing area, the frame is crowded and cramped with settings and props. With *Hamlet*, the choice of a Victorian-to-Edwardian setting exacerbates the problem.[3] The decor, in consequence, draws our eye away from the actors. (Kenneth Branagh, choosing a similar period for his *Hamlet* [1997], at least had the advantage of 70-millimeter film meant to be projected on large screens, though his mise-en-scène at times draws attention away from the architectonics of the drama.) *Hamlet*, Shakespeare's longest play, is cut drastically along fairly predictable lines followed in subsequent television and film productions. (The deep cuts can have unintentionally comic or at least bizarre consequences: poor Polonius, for example, has to say "this is too long" after about four lines of the First Player's Hecuba speech.) *Richard II*, though less severely compressed, must have presented audiences with difficulties nonetheless: the complex historical and dynastic issues, the mystery of who is related to whom and who has done what to whom, are certainly increased in a cut version, and the situation is not helped by Shakespeare's decision to thrust us immediately into the historical thickets. This production makes things worse by completely omitting 1.2, a scene of almost pure exposition that partly explains, retrospectively and by anticipation, much of what happens in 1.1 and 1.3 (which are here combined). Any viewer not already familiar with the play would not stay around for very long.

The cultural credentials of the first Hallmark Shakespeare broadcast are made explicit from the outset. *Hamlet*, televised close to the anniversary of Shakespeare's death (April 26, 1953), is trumpeted, in part literally (with a musical fanfare), both as "the first television appearance of one of the theater's most distinguished actors, Maurice Evans" and also as "the first television production of William Shakespeare's *Hamlet*" (actually, the BBC broadcast an abbreviated *Hamlet* in 1947; only a few still photographs document this production). The television camera takes us to the Hall of Fame itself (a grouping of rather modest columns), where we are shown the bust of Shakespeare and told that he "belongs to the ages." Thus we are primed for culture on a medium much denigrated for its lowbrow status. The production itself is to some extent bogged down by its own pretensions. The pacing is slow, the line delivery drawn out. Given the abbreviated play we are getting, it is all the more surprising that the pace was not picked up and that silences are allowed to linger as long as they do (1.4, for example, begins with what feels like a long silence before the first line, "the air bites shrewdly"). But the real problem is Evans himself, who poses and, as critics noted at the time, recites rather than performs the role of Hamlet. As Bernice Kliman writes, "Some viewers may have an aversion to Evans's mannered and declamatory style, with quaver in voice and quiver on lips, a somewhat exaggerated 'Shakespearean' style of acting."[4] Ignoring for the moment that he looks too old for the part (and the issue is one of appearance and manner as much as, if not more than, chronological age—Johnston Forbes-Robertson, who appeared in a film of *Hamlet* at the age of sixty, acts "younger" as Hamlet than Evans does here), Evans provides few clues to Hamlet's inner turmoil. We lose entirely the manic, richly comic aspect of Hamlet's character and are left mainly with the gentleman poet, an amateur melancholic. Evans never seems entirely engaged.

At its best, the Hallmark/Evans *Hamlet* makes virtue of necessity. Like many a *Hamlet* production, this one begins with 1.2. Portions of 1.1 are reintroduced in 1.2 as flashback, a nice trick in live television where the actors who need to appear in the flashback are often on camera in the "present." The sleight of hand is simple and effective: as Horatio tells Hamlet what he saw on the battlements, camera 1 closes in on Hamlet in close-up, allowing Horatio, still conversing with Hamlet, to leave the latter's side unseen and move to another part of the soundstage where he acts out bits of 1.1 for camera 2. We then return to camera 1, still on a close shot of Hamlet, while Horatio moves back into his position at Hamlet's side. The camera pulls back to reveal Horatio and the scene continues. Although the viewer may not realize what is going on, at some level the flashback must have recorded itself in his or her consciousness as a bit of video "magic." The challenges posed by live television, however, prove more unnerving to the *Hamlet* cast and crew than anything presented by either theater or film. The actors must not only, as in the theater, maintain the flow of their performance and avoid mistakes even as they are conscious of the possible mistakes of other players, but they must also, as in film, hit their marks and remain conscious of their relationship to the several cameras even as various stagehands and technicians surround them (in the *Hamlet* broadcast, a member of the crew walks by during one of Evans's soliloquies). No wonder poor Ruth Chatterton, as Gertrude, nearly blows her opening speech: an experienced stage and film actress, she is clearly nervous throughout most of 1.2. Though she eventually settles down, consciousness of her bad start must have haunted her throughout the evening.

Richard II (January 24, 1954), like the *Hamlet* broadcast, begins with a prologue that provides an aura of culture and class. We are shown, successively, a book of Shakespeare's *Works* and a volume of *Richard II*; we hear of Evans's 1937 performance of Richard on Broadway, and we view scenes from the coronation of Elizabeth II, which was a major television event in 1953. As we see the crown placed on Elizabeth's head, a voice-over recites parts of John of Gaunt's "This Royal Throne of Kings" speech from *Richard II*. The conjunction of Shakespeare and royalty reinforces the highbrow, high-class status of the program, an effort conveniently amplified by an image of the sponsor's trademark logo, a royal crown. Shakespeare, Richard II, Elizabeth II, Maurice Evans, Hallmark—a happy convergence. As I have already suggested, however, *Richard II* perhaps too readily fulfilled the expectations such an introduction excited: a busy, cramped, largely incomprehensible production seemingly designed to confuse a television audience.

Evans is better suited for Richard than for Hamlet, in part because the less attractive elements of his acting style (mellifluous line readings, posing, narcissistic self-indulgence) are elements of Richard's character as Shakespeare drew him. On the other hand, he misses the tragic depths and emotional complexities of Richard unkinged. George Schaefer, who did not actually direct the *Hamlet* broadcast though he rehearsed the actors, here attempts to take advantage of the medium, with mixed results. He employs the multiple-camera technique with great fluidity and ingenuity. Other directorial choices are not so happy. Shots from inside a fireplace, matching transitional "cuts" that move from a close-up of an object in one scene to a close-up of a similar object in another scene (although this had not yet become a television cliché), and a frequent employment of unmotivated overhead shots all call attention to themselves without adding anything of interest to the production.

Hallmark presented Maurice Evans in *Macbeth* on two separate occasions, first in 1954 and then in 1960, productions that mark changes that occurred in television broadcasting in six years. The first *Macbeth* was broadcast live (and in color, for those few homes with color sets) on November 28, 1954. The second was a color film, released theatrically in Europe and broadcast on television in the United States (it was later released theatrically in the United States for selected urban exhibition). Both productions depend excessively on the conventional readings of the leading roles provided by

Evans and Judith Anderson (they had played Macbeth and Lady Macbeth in New York in 1937). Evans's Macbeth is weak and vacillating while Anderson's Lady Macbeth is an ogre. In the 1954 production, the compression of even this, the shortest of Shakespeare's plays, placed great weight on the two protagonists. Evans once again appears too mild and "gentlemanly" for the horrors that he causes and of which he becomes the victim. For Bernice Kliman, "He lacks the driving force of evil; a weariness at his center saps the play's energy."[5] Anderson is frightening from the outset—she might as well be one of the witches (and in some productions of the play, she is). The actions and reactions of both characters seem predetermined and predictable. (Only once are we truly surprised: on the line "Things bad begun make strong themselves by ill," Macbeth violently grabs and kisses his wife; unfortunately, a viewer is likely to be more embarrassed than moved by this expression of middle-aged conjugal passion.) For Jack Gould, the production lacked "the underlying excitement, the sense of ambitious urgency" the play demands.[6]

The most effective 1950s TV Shakespeare productions are deliberately anti-illusionistic in manner and style: *Taming of the Shrew* and *Twelfth Night*, for Hallmark, in addition to a very different 1950 *Othello* on NBC. *Taming of the Shrew* (March 18, 1956), which employs a commedia dell'arte style in costume, setting, and stage business, revels in its minimalism. The movements are fluid, the image is uncluttered, and the details of mise-en-scène are harmonized with one another. The effect is to distance the audience from the characters of this highly problematic play, a desirable goal, it would seem, even in 1956. The first meeting between Kate and Petruchio is presented (in a manner that would have delighted Bertolt Brecht) as a boxing match, with "corners" and "seconds" and a "bell" to signal the beginning and ending of "rounds." Baptista, on the line " 'tis a match," lifts up Petruchio's arm and Kate's arm in the manner of a referee announcing the winner. Throughout the production signs are held up to indicate locations and other explanatory information ("meanwhile, back at the ranch"). Literal slapsticks are employed, as is direct address to the camera ("He that knows better how to tame a shrew"). The moon (or is it the sun?) is a cardboard disc. Both Evans as Petruchio and Lili Palmer as Kate experience and project pleasure in their performances. "Suddenly Evans," Bernice Kliman notes, "who in 1953 looked too old to be a credible Hamlet, in 1956 at fifty-five is as youthful a Petruchio as one would want, illustrating that perception is based on style rather than form."[7] The supporting cast brings the subplot to life as well. Diane Cilento manages to turn Bianca into a wise and witty foil to her sister,

TV Bloopers

Live television, notoriously, was plagued by a variety of mistakes and technical foul-ups that had the unintended effect of reminding viewers that what they were watching was occurring in "real" time and that the represented world on the television monitor was a human construct. Indeed, the shadows cast by microphones and camera booms are so pervasive in early television broadcasts as to become an almost acceptable element of the mise-en-scène. It is nearly impossible, for example, in the Maurice Evans *Hamlet*, to tell when a shadow might be deliberately placed and when it is an accident. Just as a theater performance, no matter how realistic or illusionistic its intentions, is always in danger of spilling over into the audience space, so live television, passing by in real time, threatens to exceed the boundaries of the frame. Cables snake offscreen, stagehands go about their business in full view, and sounds and shadows point to a world elsewhere. Fifties television broadcasting in general fulfills the "anti-illusionistic" theory and practice of playwrights like Bertolt Brecht. The low-resolution, black-and-white (but mostly gray) image, poor depth of focus, small viewing area, and commercial interruptions, together with the viewer's situation (watching, from some distance, a piece of furniture placed in the corner of a frequently fully illuminated room), effectively made it difficult, if not impossible, for the mimesis to compel full engagement from its audience. In watching live television, we are simultaneously caught up in and distanced from all that appears on the screen.

and Philip Bourneuf as Baptista projects a droll eccentricity in spite of being masked as a Pantaloon figure throughout.

The importance of the scenic design to the success of these productions is reinforced by a production designed by the Soviet-born Armenian Rouben Ter-Arutunian, who brought European design ideas (he was trained in Berlin) to American television and theater. (He later designed a flexible, permanent set for the first two seasons of the American Shakespeare Festival in Stratford, Connecticut; his basic concept was used for six Shakespeare productions over two summers.)[8] *Twelfth Night* (December 15, 1957) employed a design motif drawn from the paintings of Watteau. Much of the play is presented as a dream of the clown/singer, Feste, which allows for a fantasy mise-en-scène. A unit set incorporates the various locations the play alludes to. Orsino's palace and Olivia's court are adjacent to each other, part of the same dream landscape. The key, as in *Taming*, is not so much that the performing space is bare (though, in comparison with *Hamlet* and *Richard II*, it certainly is) but rather that it is deliberately nonillusionistic, conceived of as a more or less imaginary landscape, and designed for pleasing visuals and practicality.

One distinct advantage of putting on a Shakespearean comedy is that all involved not only have fun doing it but are seen to have fun. If, as a number of critics have suggested, Shakespeare's plays are all metatheatrical to one extent or another, the comedies bring this element very much to the fore. Both *Twelfth Night* and the earlier *Shrew* revel in their own artificiality and become, in a sense, meta-televisual. Both productions refer to the style of some television commercials, especially those placed in an abstract, dream-land-like space, with young women in filmy pastel costumes selling television sets by dancing around a variety of table models and consoles. *Twelfth Night* borrows performers from the Steve Allen show, Howard Morris and Alice Ghostley, to play Feste and Maria. (Morris had some experience with Shakespeare and with Evans/Schaefer, having played Laertes in their "G.I. *Hamlet*" and Rosencrantz when the production was restaged and recast for Broadway.) These TV comics are joined by a partly British (Evans, Max Adrian, Denholm Elliott, Rosemary Harris), partly American (Dennis King, Lloyd Botchner) cast of stage and television performers—an appropriate mix given the wide range of social classes Shakespeare created for this play.

As an interpretation of *Twelfth Night*, this production can be faulted for being at times too fanciful and lighthearted. The storm and the losses it appears to entail for Viola and Sebastian are downplayed, as is Orsino's vengeful jealousy (his threat to kill Caesario/Viola is cut). Malvolio's experience in the "dark house," on the other hand, is more than usually grim; he is placed in a hanging cage and haunted by surreal dancing figures in black cloaks and white masks. His threat to revenge himself on the whole pack of his tormentors is treated as a final joke when a trapdoor opens under him and he disappears in smoke, like the devil in a miracle play. Evans's wildly eccentric performance as Malvolio, which combines a false nose, bizarre hairstyle, and low-class accent, prevents us from taking Shakespeare's steward at all seriously. Evans follows stage history in much of his "business." When Olivia tells Malvolio to "run after" Viola, he incredulously repeats "run" and then goes off with a comic trot; when he catches up with Viola, he places Olivia's ring, tied in a handkerchief, at the end of his staff as if he were above simply handing it to her—both gags that go back at least as far as the nineteenth-century actor-manager Herbert Beerbohm Tree. Extra business is provided for the "box tree" scene, some drawn from established custom (on the word "revolve," Malvolio turns completely around) and some evidently conceived ad hoc. When Malvolio reads the words "cast thy humble slough," he first pronounces the last word as "sluff," then corrects himself and says "slou," a pronunciation loudly affirmed by the supposedly unheard, invisible Sir Toby. At the scene's conclusion, Malvolio ascends in a balloon! Later he appears to Olivia not only cross-gartered and in yellow stockings, but in a preposterous costume. He chases Olivia aggressively until he is caught in a net and dragged away.

The third and final Hallmark Shakespeare production with Evans and Ter-Arutunian, once again directed by George Schaefer, *The Tempest* (1960), seems less of a piece than *Taming* and *Twelfth Night*. Ter-Arutunian's designs attractively render the mystical aura of Prospero's island without providing the unifying element of his designs for the earlier Hallmark productions. The centerpiece is a rendering of the medieval spheres as a series of overlapping white hoops. This motif is repeated in the globe of intertwined branches above Caliban's den and the woven tree branches inside which Ariel hides to discombobulate the comic triumvirate in 3.2. The design finally has little thematic value, since the "magical" elements are not really picked up by the rest of the production, which seems only mildly interested in Prospero as magus. As with *Twelfth Night*, we once again find casting from the Steve Allen stock company, this time Tom Poston as Trinculo in one of the worst performances imaginable. On the positive side, Lee Remick, another casting choice meant to broaden the production's appeal, embodies a Miranda at once charming, sweet, and sexy. Roddy McDowall, covered in white paint and silver glitter, makes a convincing Ariel in the sylph tradition, and Richard Burton, made up to look something like the Gill-Man from *Creature from the Black Lagoon* (a 1950s icon featured in three films), complete with exoskeleton, scales, webbed feet, and sharp claws, combines the animal brutishness and lyrical power of Caliban, though his performance lacks energy and danger.

Maurice Evans, whose Prospero is benevolent and avuncular, adopts yet another false nose and returns to the safe mode of recitation (a mode the role can easily encourage); he projects little of Prospero's irascibility and anger (we sense that his hostility toward Ferdinand is mostly pretense), and even his admonishments to the young lovers to control their sexual feelings are delivered more or less tongue in cheek. This Prospero would have pleased eighteenth- and nineteenth-century conceptions of the part, audiences for whom "oratorical ability" and "venerable appearance" appear to have been sufficient.[9] That particular mold was broken in the notable 1957 Stratford Memorial Theater production directed by Peter Brook and featuring John

Gielgud. In his third incarnation of Prospero, Gielgud played "a middle-aged, vigorous, and bitter figure" and "made prominent the internal struggles of a flawed human being."[10] Taken as a whole, this production of The Tempest avoids or underplays (or simply cuts) the pressure points of Shakespeare's play—Ariel's powerful yearning for freedom, Prospero's struggle to overcome an impulse to revenge, Caliban's lust, Antonio and Sebastian's malevolence—all of this goes for little. In part because of cuts, everything moves too smoothly to its end; lacking an interpretive center, The Tempest emerges as a series of somewhat unrelated episodes and set pieces.

A more imaginative early Shakespeare TV production, the Othello broadcast on NBC on September 27, 1950, serves as foil to the Hallmark/Schaefer/Evans approach. Unlike the early Hallmark Shakespeares, Othello avoids anything like a realistic setting. Instead, the virtues and challenges of television broadcasting become determining factors in the look of the production. The set, simple to the point of near invisibility, serves multiple functions, being at once interior and exterior, specific and general, Venice and Cyprus; it functions like a unit set in the theater. The cameras (two, sometimes three), together with the selective lighting, focus our attention on specific areas and character groupings. There is very little depth of field, but camera 1 compensates by moving toward the center of action. (The other two cameras are used less frequently, one of them for occasional tight close-ups.) Most unusually, this Othello begins with a narrator who is also a character, and he helps bring the audience into both the play and the playing space. The camera pans over groups of soldiers and citizens, completing its movement on a soldier who turns to the camera and speaks: "On this day and the one following shall you see enacted here on the isle of Cyprus in this year of our lord 1570 the tragedy of Othello the Moor of Venice." The narrator then rejoins the other actors, and we hear Brabantio's voice (a "flashback"?) complain about Othello. The narrator walks around the set, providing a bit more exposition. He comes upon Iago and Roderigo ("Iago, what should I do?"). The narrator says, "And now, the play," and we are back to 1.1 and Venice with the Iago/Roderigo duologue. The narrator reappears at the end of the production, speaking some of Othello's lines from 2.1.

This is a sophisticated, intelligent production of the play (or at least parts of it) that makes virtue of necessity. The acting, if seldom exciting, is more than adequate. Torin Thatcher, an unlikely choice for Othello (a character actor, he often played villains and "heavy" fathers), projects a nobility and forcefulness that convincingly renders Othello's military prowess. He is by no means "black," but he is darker than everyone else (though the murkiness of the existing kinescope makes it hard to tell how dark). Alfred Ryder, as Iago, though frequently melodramatic and perhaps too obvious in his villainy, is nevertheless a compelling presence, intense to the point of hysteria. In continuous movement, alert to everything around him, his hatred founded on a jealousy of everyone, Ryder gives a performance that holds the production together. Because of the truncated nature of this *Othello*, the rest of the cast has little opportunity to establish itself—Cassio, Emilia, Roderigo, and even Desdemona remain throughout shadowy background figures. The text, though heavily cut (no Bianca, no "Barbary" scene, no murder of Roderigo or wounding of Cassio) and bowdlerized ("that cunning whore of Venice" becomes a "harlot"), has been skillfully edited. Though most of act 1 is missing, some of its lines are used elsewhere. "Put up your bright swords" (1.2), for example, is spoken by Othello as he arrives to stop the brawl in Cyprus (2.3). Actions are intelligently compressed. When Othello cashiers Cassio, the latter offers up his sword. Impatiently, Othello snaps his fingers and points to Iago, who receives Cassio's sword. Wordlessly, the transfer of trust has been made. The "seduction scene" (3.3, considerably compressed) employs a single, mostly still camera. As Orson Welles would do in his film, the director, Delbert Mann, chose to sustain the theatrical intensity of this difficult duologue, staged, as is frequently the case in the theater, with Othello and Iago looking over some papers. This seldom noted broadcast demonstrates that a severely abridged production of a Shakespeare play, with little in the way of production values and virtually no self-consciousness about its status as "Shakespeare," can nevertheless bring out the theatrical power and thematic core of the original.

The 1950s American TV productions of Shakespeare oscillated between a presentation of the plays as museum pieces and as living drama, between history and culture on one side and popular entertainment on the other, between theater and film, between image and voice, between past and present, between television's role as broadcaster and as showcase for something like video art, between its role as "medium" and as an end in itself. Very much like the episode of *You Are There* described in chapter 3, televised Shakespeare offered viewers a more or less solemn assurance that they were about to see something "classic" and "authentic," something hallowed by tradition and resonant with truth and/or beauty. A variety of bona fides are exhibited—a bust of Shakespeare, the First Folio, a crown, musical fanfares, and so on. With Hallmark, we sense a special aura that envelops both sponsor and program. Often a voice-over narrator sets the scene, the tone, or both. In some broadcasts, we are advised that commercial interruptions will

The Greeting Card *Hamlet*

Hallmark Hall of Fame's final (to date) Shakespeare production, the Peter Wood/Richard Chamberlain *Hamlet* (November 17, 1970), was in some ways a throwback to its very first Shakespeare, also *Hamlet*: here too we have a nineteenth-century setting (in this case, more Regency than Ruritania) and a "realistic" style. Unlike the 1950s Shakespeare broadcasts, however, this *Hamlet* was not "live"—it was shot on videotape and film. In spite or perhaps because of its attractive sets and pretty costumes, this *Hamlet* never catches fire. This is the Hallmark Shakespeare production that looks most like a greeting card—fussily designed, filled with pretty "sentiments," "tasteful," and completely impersonal. Even with a potentially brilliant supporting cast—John Gielgud as the Ghost, Michael Redgrave as Polonius, Margaret Leighton as Gertrude, and Richard Johnson as Claudius—the force, complexity, and mysteriousness of Shakespeare's play fail to emerge. It is tempting to single out Richard Chamberlain for blame and suggest that this is a *Hamlet* without the prince, but Chamberlain reads his lines with ease and conviction, and he controls the rhythm and pacing. What he does not provide is any sense of pressure, the core of intelligence and wit, of anger and—real or feigned—madness, that underlie the words. His Hamlet is all surface—a smooth, attractive exterior (he looks like a cross between Byron and Shelley) with little of the disturbance beneath. The play's large effects and dramatic highlights go for little, and the text has been edited with no apparent aim or purpose (what is the point, for example, in retaining Hamlet's line "who is it whose grief bears such an emphasis" when poor Laertes has not been allowed very much of either grief or emphasis?) In the end, surrounding Hamlet with seasoned Shakespeareans does not so much diminish Chamberlain as diminish Hamlet.

be few and far between, which may be the ultimate respect American broadcast television can pay Shakespeare. The flip side of all of this, however, is a fast and loose treatment of Shakespeare's text, sometimes bizarre casting of television performers who may or may not be suited to the role they play, as well as sometimes successful, sometimes pointless, updatings and modernizations.

An Anglo-American Venture: "The Shakespeare Plays"

Perhaps the most ambitious project television has ever undertaken, the BBC/Time-Life Shakespeare Plays involved videotaping the entire canon, in relatively full texts, over a seven-year period (1978–1985).[11] The resulting productions, with a few notable exceptions, were far less successful than might have been hoped.[12] Given the British Broadcasting Company's track record for televising both classic and modern drama, the generally mediocre level of these productions is puzzling. No one involved seemed capable of deciding just what form these productions should take, stylistically speaking. That they were not theater was a given from the outset, and no attempt was made to re-create or create new stage productions. Budgetary constraints kept them from being produced on film, with the kind of complicated lighting and single-camera shooting film requires. Videotaping was cheaper and quicker. But the lessons of live television drama, or even the usual BBC mode of staging and videotaping plays (multiple cameras, continuous "live" editing), was also eschewed. Some directors chose to employ long takes and tight shots, presumably to retain something of the continuous action of the theater, while tight framing was thought ideal for television. The result, all too often, was a series of static dialogues, captured with an unmoving camera and with the actors seemingly glued in place for fear of moving out of the camera's range.

The productions directed by Jonathan Miller suffer from this approach, which was especially unfortunate for scenes containing a good deal of exposition, such as the opening scene (the Christopher Sly "Induction" was cut) of *Taming of the Shrew*: Lucentio and Tranio stand fixed in one spot, facing each other, framed in medium close-up; neither they nor the camera moves for some forty lines. It doesn't help that the actors, as if anxious to get this boring part over with, speak as rapidly as possible. No attempt was made to grab the audience at the outset, to lead the viewer into the play, to shape the dialogue. A comparison with a Canadian Broadcasting Corporation broadcast of the 1988 Stratford Festival production is instructive. Although the videotaping was made in front of a live audience, the television director ingeniously used multiple cameras (seven of them) to break the scene into significant units and create a rhythm that matches and amplifies the rhythm created by the original staging. The actors unashamedly play to the audience (the festival audience and indirectly the television audience). The staging allows the actors to be frontal rather than intimate. The exposition, instead of being given all at once in an undigested block, is presented in short, highlighted sections. Consequently the language is comprehensible, the situation clear. As in the theater, the players are admittedly broader than television usually allows, but this is Shakespeare, and a farce to boot.

The conceptual underpinnings of the two productions could not be more at odds. Jonathan Miller chooses to naturalize the play and downplay its farcical elements and flamboyance as much as possible. The Stratford production, set in 1950s Italy, plays up its commedia dell'arte elements and adds some Fellini-inspired stylizations. One is tempted to suggest that the problem here is that Miller's conception was mistaken from the outset (as many have thought), were it not that so many of the productions not produced or directed by Miller suffer from some of the same problems. Cause and effect are not easy to distinguish. Because Miller saw *Taming of the Shrew* as a naturalistic examination of "companionate marriage," he chose a quiet, intimate style to support his thesis. Rather than solve this chicken/egg question, it is enough to suggest that the production, in spite of some striking moments, doesn't really work. When Miller takes a similar approach to *Othello* and *Antony and Cleopatra*, plays that demand some scope and size, some sense of the heroic, the result is close to disastrous.

The BBC/Time-Life series of the Complete Works also chose to function pretty much without stars, though many of the actors who appeared in these broadcasts were well known to British television viewers, if not to viewers in the United States. Even within the British context, however, BBC cast its productions in a highly eclectic manner, relying on television actors more than Shakespeareans. The very first broadcast, of *Julius Caesar*, featured Keith Mitchell as Antony. Although he had some experience with Shakespeare, Mitchell was best known for his portrayal of the king in BBC's highly successful *Six Wives of Henry VIII*. Brutus, on the other hand, was played by Richard Pasco, longtime stalwart of the Royal Shakespeare Company. *Romeo and Juliet*, another first-season broadcast, emulated Franco Zeffirelli by casting unknowns in the title roles. John Gielgud made a brief appearance as Chorus. His only other role in the series was as John of Gaunt in *Richard II*. Overall, the producers seemed more comfortable employing actors and directors who had worked for the BBC before or at least had television experience. This might explain the offbeat casting of John Cleese (of Monty Python fame) as Petruchio in *Taming of the Shrew*. Apart from Pasco, Helen Mirren, Alan Howard, Derek Jacobi, Patrick Stewart, and a few others, BBC did not draw significantly on actors from the Royal Shakespeare Company or the National Theatre. Ian Richardson, Judi Dench, Ian McKellen, Michael Gambon, all active Shakespeareans, were avoided, as were Laurence Olivier, Michael Redgrave, Ralph Richardson, and Alec Guinness. Americans and other non-British actors were almost completely absent, much to the irritation of Joseph Papp, longtime producer of New York's Shakespeare in the Park, and others. Perhaps the most "Shakespearean" production was *Hamlet*, with Derek Jacobi, Clare Bloom, Patrick Stewart, and Emrys James. One of the motivations behind some of the casting choices was to keep the plays "fresh" for an audience unfamiliar with Shakespeare. A punk Puck (Phil Daniels) in *A Midsummer Night's Dream* was calculated to appeal to younger audiences. For the most part, however, the casting was a hodgepodge, featuring aging film stars (Celia Johnson, Wendy Hiller), up-and-coming young actors (Anthony Andrews, Ian Charleson), eccentric one-offs (Cleese, the Incredible Orlando), and, in a few instances, actors associated with a Shakespearean role who here repeat their stage performances, most notably Anthony Quayle as Falstaff and Alan Howard as Coriolanus.

One can imagine a very different approach. What if the plays had been presented repertory fashion, with a central cast of skilled performers acting out a variety of roles over several seasons? This is one of the pleasures of watching Michael Pennington and the English Shakespeare Company in the history plays under the direction of Michael Bogdanov. Based on productions presented onstage in England and on world tour, the video versions were made during actual performances in Cardiff, Wales, near the end of the run. Watching both "tetralogies" (*Richard II*, the two parts of *Henry IV*, *Henry V*, the three parts of *Henry VI*, and *Richard III*), we experience history as a changing parade where the same faces come to occupy new roles, thus making a "theatrical" as well as a "historical" point: as Elizabethan and Jacobean censors feared, we understand theater and history as one. Though there are some anomalies (Pennington in close-up, receding hairline and all, is clearly too old to be running around the Boar's Head tavern as the young prince, Hal), the pleasures are many. We are here seeing something analogous to what an Elizabethan audience might have experienced; we come to know the performers and we marvel at their versatility. In some ways, of course, comparison with the BBC series is unfair. Bogdanov's company, by the time of the taping, had years of performing under their belts (with some casting changes along the way). These actors were comfortable with one another and with the major elements of the mise-en-scène (costumes, settings, props). All of this shows. Because the taping was done in front of a live audience, the interaction between actors and auditors gives the performance extra life. Most importantly, the television director keeps the focus squarely on the actors, not only by keeping them in close and medium close shot, but also by making certain they never become lost in the background of a shot. One of the signal failures of the BBC Shakespeare is how poorly directed so many of the productions are. David Giles, who directed the second tetralogy, has a knack for putting the camera in the wrong place with relation to the actors. In *Henry IV, Part I*, for example, the "play-acting scene" (2.4) was virtually killed in the direction. No wonder critics like Mark Crispin Miller found Anthony Quayle's Falstaff tedious.[13] But it wasn't Quayle's fault (listen to him in the Caedmon audio recordings of the two parts of *Henry IV*); it was, for the most part, Giles's direction of his scenes. When Quayle is given his chance, as with the "Honor catechism" (5.1), shot simply in close up and without distraction, he shines.

The BBC Style: *Romeo and Juliet* and *Hamlet*

Romeo and Juliet, presented during the first season of the Shakespeare Plays, illustrates well some of the virtues and limitations of the entire series. On the plus side, we are presented with a nearly full text, which allows for a complexity and even ambiguity so often lacking in film realizations of the play. Characters who may appear of little account in a severely cut production emerge fully realized. Capulet (Michael Hordern), for example, is allowed to retain the rich mix of drollery, nostalgic musing, randiness, immaturity, enthusiasm, anger, and grief with which Shakespeare endowed him. Hordern's performance style and hangdog appearance perfectly suit the various tonalities of a man at once buffoon, *senex iratus*, and genuinely dangerous patriarch. His anger at Juliet is real enough but not overdone. His care for his daughter is evident, but in this moment, his love is in conflict with his wounded vanity, and he can barely keep himself in check. His exchange with Old Caputet (the veteran Esmond Knight), a character cut in all film versions, becomes a touching moment similar in effect to the Falstaff–Justice Shallow scenes from *Henry IV, Part II*: we are reminded of old age and death even as the young are about to experience love for the first time. As Anthony Davies nicely puts it, this is a production in which "life is no less difficult for the old than for the young."[14]

The fullness of the text should benefit the young lovers, especially, as I have suggested earlier, Juliet. And to some extent, it does. We are given a richer sense of Juliet than in either the Zeffirelli or Luhrmann films, for example. But both of the young actors lack the emotional range the fuller version requires. Though sporadically affecting, Rebecca Sayre's Juliet stays within a very narrow range, incapable of the rapid shifts in mood and tone the language calls for, and much the same is true for Romeo; Patrick Rycart, though young, acts old. He lends to Romeo an unbecoming sense of irony, and he seems too strong and sophisticated for the role, almost as if he were auditioning for Mercutio. Throughout he speaks and acts as if he knew in advance precisely what he was about to say and do. Shakespeare's young lovers continually modulate between spontaneous utterance and carefully wrought conventional sentiment, between innocence and sophistication, between self-consciousness and naked emotion. They are what they are, to paraphrase Mercutio, by art as well as by nature. The tendency in film versions is to cut the sophistication and the self-consciousness in favor of innocence and spontaneity. If, in Zeffirelli's film especially, the lovers are infantilized, stripped of their edge, the BBC *Romeo and Juliet* almost goes in the other direction. Romeo is overly self-aware and reflective. In the balcony scene, an eighteenth-century-style decorum blankets their passion. This is a Juliet clearly in control of her emotions, the tentativeness and anxiety lost. Again, it is neither the age of the characters nor the age of the actors that is at issue here, but rather how "age" is projected.

The production as a whole borrows from theater and film, and it exhibits considerable influence from Zeffirelli. The sets, though conceived of in a "realistic," even "cinematic" manner, are at the same time reminiscent of Motley's designs for the Peter Brook stage production (1947). Like both Castellani's and Zeffirelli's films, the first scene includes the fruits and vegetables of market day in Verona, fast becoming a cliché, one would think, by 1978. (Could any fifteenth-century Italian town have been as "clean" and "pretty" as the settings in all of these productions? Realism should include some dung along with the sweet peppers.) Zeffirelli's influence is most evident in the two central fight scenes. The Mercutio/Tybalt duel seems mostly good fun and includes moments when each is at the other's mercy with no serious consequence. Romeo's concerned interference in this friendly brawl thus makes little sense. As in Zeffirelli, the fight between Romeo and Tybalt is part chase, part clumsy brawl. Both of these work better in film. The more formalized television studio staging and the limitations on time and money guarantee that the fights will look more choreographed, less carefully rehearsed, and therefore not as dangerous as Zeffirelli's. The "theatrical" and the "filmic" impulses work at cross purposes. The one innovation here is Romeo's repeated stabbing of Tybalt, an added touch of realism that turns Romeo, momentarily, into a blood-thirsty avenger.

A more sophisticated and skillfully mounted production than *Romeo and Juliet*, the BBC *Hamlet*, directed by Rodney Bennett, takes advantage of the edge television has over both theater and film in that the focus is almost entirely on the actor and the language. Soliloquies are delivered to the camera, an effect that seems less self-conscious than it does on film, perhaps because, with television, we *expect* to be talked at. Bennett's choice to limit much of his framing to close-ups and two shots in this instance contributes

A Streamlined *Romeo and Juliet*

However desirable it may be to have the full text, even a severely cut version of a Shakespeare play can maintain elements of the original sufficiently to provide a satisfactory experience. The Alan Horrox–Channel 4 (Great Britain) *Romeo and Juliet*, which runs a swift 81 minutes, is in many ways superior to the BBC production, which runs for 2 hours and 47 minutes. In spite of its length, it probably reproduces as much of the text as Zeffirelli's 138-minute film. The text, though cut to the bone, remains central, a continuous stream from beginning to end. Much of this production, which was shot on film, relies on close or medium-close shots, so that the actors, not the decor, are central. Little in the way of extraneous material is allowed to interfere with the quick pacing: the camera is at the service of the actors. Horrox employs continuity editing—one camera, multiple set-ups, shot/reverse shot—which helps to maintain a tight, fast-paced rhythm as well as an intimacy less easily obtained with a multicamera style. Jonathan Firth, even without the full text, is a fully realized Romeo, youthful but strong, passionate without being sentimental. Juliet too is strong; witty and intelligent, she seems worldly wise even when her words betray her innocence. One can almost read her thoughts (this Juliet knows very well that it was the lark, and not the nightingale, in spite of what she says). And she is, like Romeo, unsentimental. These may be the most "sensible" Romeo and Juliet imaginable, aware of their fate even as they embrace it. The fight scenes are quick, forceful, and serious. Because the emphasis is so much on the young lovers, secondary characters suffer in comparison. We are allowed, nonetheless, to get at least a taste of the fuller characters from the brief glimpses we see of Mercutio (Ben Daniels), Friar Laurence (John Woodvine), and Lord and Lady Capulet (John Nettles and Jenny Agutter). Nearly all of the actors at least suggest the more rounded performance they might have given had the opportunity been available to them.

to an intimate directness between performer and viewer. Relatively long takes and minimal camera movement allow us to savor the words and experience the dramatic tension that in part inheres with the continuity of time and space. In this context, Derek Jacobi's mercurial performance, in the tradition of the neurotic, febrile, intensely emotional Hamlets of the late nineteenth and early twentieth centuries (most recently, John Gielgud and Paul Scofield), is especially foregrounded. By no means an "ideal" Hamlet, he is a continually fascinating one. Jacobi's "plummy" voice, much like Gielgud's, registers every possible emotional change the character undergoes.

At times, watching Jacobi's Hamlet is somewhat akin to watching a tightrope walker: one keeps expecting him to fall off, an experience at once thrilling and unnerving. In the nunnery scene, we see Hamlet discover the true madness that underlies the feigned one. Jacobi delivers the line "it hath made me mad" as if this were a sudden revelation. This is a weepy Hamlet, easily caught up in his own emotionalism. The line readings are frequently distinctive, even unique. Jacobi refreshes many a familiar moment with his at times eccentric interpretation, as if he were discovering the meaning of his words as he says them, and he gives pointed, unexpected inflections to the most seemingly innocuous lines ("O, here they come"). In truth, this aspect of his performance becomes problematic. He can put too much into each moment, so that we become sated with Hamlet's intensity and overwhelmed by his continually shifting moods. The intelligence is fierce, certainly, and one relishes Jacobi's own intelligence as a performer. But this Hamlet tires us out, an effect not entirely absent from Shakespeare's play, and certainly the effect Hamlet has on Claudius, Polonius, Rosencrantz, Guildenstern, and even Horatio.

Against the intense neuroticism of Jacobi's performance, Patrick Stewart as Claudius and Clare Bloom as Gertrude provide an effective contrast. Solidly grounded and self-possessed, Stewart's Claudius, essentially "a good man sullied by one bad act,"[15] is seldom fazed by Hamlet's behavior, however insulting and contemptuous. Were it not for the Prayer Scene, where Claudius for the first time confesses his guilt, one might suppose him innocent of his brother's murder. In the "Mousetrap" scene, he laughs at the dumb show that is supposed to reveal his guilt. If his conscience is stricken, he gives no indication of the fact. Even after the trap has supposedly been sprung, his anger appears to be more the result of seeing "The Murder of Gonzago" as a threat than as an accusation. Clare Bloom projects strength as well. She is loyal to her husband (she does not suspect Claudius of murder) almost as much as she is attached to her son. Gertrude's ambivalence becomes the key to Bloom's performance. When she learns the truth, she pulls back from Claudius, but she is unable, as Bloom has herself remarked, to effect a complete withdrawal.[16]

At times, the preoccupation with individual performers, particularly their heads and faces, occludes the dynamic interplay among the various characters. The camera, which shows us precisely what the director wants us to look at, becomes tyrannical, so that the blocking and movement of actors often seem determined by camera placement rather than the other way around. The "crowds" (already minimal in this play) get short shrift. Claudius's court watches the accidental deaths and casual slaughters of the final scene with virtually no reaction. The static nature of the staging and camera work, which contributes to the "stuffed and mounted" look of many of the BBC productions, plagues *Hamlet* as well. Of course, the question of what "works" and what doesn't "work" on television can only have a complex answer, but as the video version of Trevor Nunn's *Macbeth* (1978) shows, a successful production can be constructed almost entirely of close-ups and two shots, minimal setting, and dynamic lighting. With *Hamlet*, however, the similar stylistic choices appear incidental to any overarching conceptual plan. The lighting tends to simply illuminate the acting space and, aside from the Ghost scenes, contributes little to the atmosphere. The sets are realistic and detailed in some scenes (the more or less Elizabethan interiors), semiabstract in others (exteriors, mainly—the battlements and the graveyard), and at other times a peculiar amalgam of both styles. The abstract moments tend to be most effective, as when we see Claudius preparing to pray, isolated against a pure black background, a vivid splash of color emerging from the darkness. Overall, however, specific design choices do not appear to contribute thematically to an interpretation of the play. Why, for example, is Polonius made to look like a banker or goldsmith? And why is Horatio reading in what appears to be a tavern when the sailors find him? Too often, the precise, detailed, domestic spaces, which are characteristic of the BBC series as a whole, provide an unwanted intimacy and "quiet" that dampens the theatrical dynamics of the play.

An Alternative BBC: Jane Howell's *Titus Andronicus*

The BBC productions directed by Jane Howell—the three parts of *Henry VI*, *Richard III*, and *The Winter's Tale*, in addition to *Titus Andronicus*—are significantly more formalist and "Brechtian" in their staging and mise-en-scène than is evident in the house style adopted for most of the Shakespeare Plays series.[17] *Titus*, in particular, benefits from a permanent unit set, nonspecific costuming, and masks (primarily for the senators and soldiers). The set, an amphitheater of sorts, works particularly well in its suggestion that the horrors of the play are a kind of gruesome entertainment for decadent Rome. At the same time, Howell balances the theatricality of her mise-en-scène by employing a number of "cinematic" codes (shot/reverse shot, camera movement, transitional dissolves, and superimpositions) that were generally avoided in other productions. In particular, she seldom employs the tight framing and unmoving camera characteristic of Jonathan Miller.

The stylization is balanced with gestures in the direction of "realism." Howell does not generally flinch from the Grand Guignol elements of Shakespeare's play. The mutilation of Lavinia is not prettified, and we see Titus's bleeding hand as Aaron holds it, although we do not actually see it being chopped off. Through shot-reverse-shot and editing, Howell can have it both ways, showing the gore but also cutting away from it. Lavinia carries her father's hand in her mouth, but we are allowed to see this only briefly. Howell's Lavinia, unlike Julie Taymor's in *Titus* (see chapter 7), puts the stick with which she writes the rapists' names in her mouth, and when she finishes, we see the blood her mouth has left on it. The effects here, one suspects, are not far removed from the kinds of stylization available on Shakespeare's stage. The realism, however, sometimes works against the stylization. Howell does not allow the set to remain a more or less abstract space, several times re-dressing it to create, for example, the woods where Lavinia is raped and the Goth camp—theatrical effectiveness is sacrificed to television realism (in the theater, we would always be aware that we are looking at one set, no matter how dressed for any given scene). The realism, which might be thought of as a move in the direction of the cinematic, becomes self-defeating: the detailed costumes, for example, always look like costumes, and not particularly attractive ones at that.[18] Television lighting is merciless in its tendency to show everything—something that might be great on film can look unimpressive on videotape. However much care was given to detail, the result is an overall "tacky" look: whatever is meant to look particularly "real" does not look real enough.

Even the stylization can seem haphazard, as if Howell and producer Shaun Sutton could not make up their minds whether to adhere to the BBC style or find some other means of expression. The masks for senators and soldiers, though they contribute an eerie note, are not sufficiently integrated into the overall visual design. It is perhaps appropriate that these figures should be featureless, since they appear to have no function but to stand mutely and watch as events unfold. It is a distinctive feature of Shakespeare's play that the populace, unlike the crowds in *Julius Caesar* and *Coriolanus*, have no real function; like the courtiers in the last scene of *Hamlet*, they are but "mutes or audience" to the actions of the principals. But the masks seem to hint at some larger purpose and suggest a choral function that is not developed. The effect is intriguing, but there is no real "payoff." Nonetheless, this is a production of striking moments: the array of burned-down, unlit candles representing the dead sons of Andronicus; Lavinia using her hair to wipe away the names she wrote in the sand; young Lucius trying to stop his father from participating in the blood lust that seems to overwhelm everyone in the final scene.

After the BBC: The National Theatre
King Lear

The production of *King Lear* directed by Richard Eyre and starring Ian Holm (broadcast on PBS on October 11, 1998) notably demonstrates the effective-

Television Staging

A major challenge for any Shakespeare production, whether on stage, screen, or television, is how to manage the dynamic interplay of the actors with one another and with the setting while at the same time giving careful attention to the language and to each actor's own sense of his or her performance. The movement from theater to television often brings this problem into particular focus. As noted earlier, some of the most successful TV Shakespeares have been remountings of acclaimed stage productions: Trevor Nunn's *Macbeth*, Richard Eyre's *King Lear*, and Jonathan Miller's *Merchant of Venice*. It can happen, however, that an acclaimed stage production loses some of its impact when transferred to television. Much of what made Trevor Nunn's National Theatre *Merchant of Venice* (1999; broadcast on PBS October 8, 2001) a critical favorite simply did not transfer to video. Staged in a "traverse" mode, with a Venetian "Cabaret" in the middle, Belmont at one end, and Shylock's house at the other, much of the interest in the production had to do with how space was negotiated by the various characters. Consequently, it did not seem particularly surprising that Shylock shows up at a café to dine with his bitter enemies, Antonio and Bassanio. On television, however, this last touch was surprising and, moreover, unconvincing, in part because we never had a sense of how different locales related to one another. We never see the set as a unit, each location seems to be separate from the others, and the fluidity of the stage production is completely lost. The courtroom scene, on the stage, was played the full length of the traverse, which lent it a weight and significance it could not have in the video version. In "expanding" the stage picture to incorporate all three previous locations, Nunn's production underlines the sense in which all of the trials of the play are now one trial. On television, the courtroom is just another set.

ness of a television production that takes a theatrical rather than a cinematic model, while at the same time it adapts its theatrical elements to the televisual. The mise-en-scène in this production is highly abstract. Lear's three daughters, for example, are identically dressed in pale blue shifts, while the other characters wear costumes designed in a limited range of colors (blacks and reds and purples predominate). The sets feature clean lines and broad areas of color. These effects were inherited from the National Theatre staging, but they are reinterpreted by the television camera, which can emphasize and deemphasize at will. In some ways, Eyre's production is an answer to—indeed, a deconstruction of—the 1982 *King Lear* with Laurence Olivier, a made-for-television production that seems to emerge from a very different era. But that era is not the early 1980s. Rather, the design, tone, and interpretation of the play owe a good bit to the nineteenth-century theater, from the Stonehenge look of the set to the romantic overtones of Olivier's performance as Lear. Olivier's Lear belongs in the line of the great pathetic kings, Olympian in manner but weak and vulnerable from the outset, who is clearly dependent on his love for Cordelia. John Hurt's Fool is Lear's other child, a loving lapdog whose barbed comments are spoken in duty and sorrow.

In Eyre's production, Ian Holm's Lear is acerbic, malicious, ill-tempered, and physically unimposing; he gives very little in the way of easy sentiment. This is a Lear who, in one sense, deserves what he gets, and he inhabits a universe that, unlike the pre-Christian Britain of Olivier, exists outside of history while not being unlike our own world. The opening scene takes place in more of a boardroom than a court. All space is abstracted, all time indefinable. The production, though not as nihilistic as Peter Brook's RSC *Lear* (and subsequent 1971 film), is more interested in shaping each character's sense of self than in dividing the sheep from the goats. On video, the emphasis on characterization emerges powerfully through the use of close-ups that give us such unsettling moments as Goneril's shocked and pained response to Lear's sterility curse. By avoiding the construction of a detailed, three-dimensional space, the production foregrounds the performers. The arrangement of Lear and the Fool facing each other against a dark background with the single light that enters through an open doorway center frame brackets this music hall/vaudeville routine in a particularly pointed way, emphasizing the psychological/theatrical nature of moment when this Fool seems no other than Lear's alter ego. Characters are frequently detached from their surroundings, alienated from one another and from the society they inhabit. The Olivier *Lear*, in contrast, employs the specifically televisual strategy of the multipart unit set to construct a coherent, self-contained, "realistic" environment, replete with a variety of "cinematic" touches—real horses, a dead rabbit, background movement, and so on. Though both productions are powerful and moving renditions of Shakespeare's greatest tragic play, it is the made-for-television version that has the feel of filmed theater, whereas the National Theatre version, paradoxically, features television itself as star.

Is television good for Shakespeare? The question answers itself, since in the end in spite of the distinctions that can be made (see pp. 23–25) among film, video, and broadcasting, everything ends up on a video monitor. Few of us are likely to see (or to have seen) Kenneth Branagh's Hamlet (especially in all of its 70-millimeter glory) or Julie Taymor's Titus in a movie theater. Far fewer have seen Richard Eyre's production of King Lear at the National Theatre in London. All of these productions and, indeed, virtually every Shakespeare production mentioned in this book have been and will be experienced on television, most likely in some digital format. Already, such hitherto unavailable productions as the King Lear videotaped during a live performance in New York's Central Park and broadcast on PBS in 1974 can be accessed on DVD. Digitalization, furthermore, can provide an experience in some ways superior to the experience of the original theater or cinema audience. The Electronovision Hamlet with Richard Burton, for example, looks and sounds better after being "cleaned" via the magic of digital restoration. Shakespeare will never take over prime-time programming, but as television watching becomes more and more individualized, and as the "monitor" or computer screen on which we watch what we want when we want shares at least equal time with broadcasting and cable, Shakespeare's plays, for those who want to see them, will have moved from that "wooden O" on the South Bank of the Thames known to Shakespeare as the Globe to the nowhere and everywhere of a forever expanding universe we know as the global media.

Notes

1. "Unlike the cinema, the TV image is smaller, less well-defined, often watched in the light rather than the dark, and is generally a domestic or social leisure appliance, so that its messages are in competition with the rest of domestic or social life." Sean Cubitt, Timeshift: On Video Culture (London: Routledge, 1991), 29.

2. For information on the genesis of the Hallmark Shakespeares as well as on some of the production challenges involved in live television, see the interview with George Schaefer in Jack Kuney, "The Art of TV Directing: The Hallmark Hall of Fame and Other Drama," Television Quarterly 23 (1988): 21–32.

3. A late-nineteenth-century setting, used for other *Hamlet* productions as well, has perhaps unfortunate connotations: the *Prisoner of Zenda*, in its various cinematic incarnations, comes too readily to mind—Ruritanian romance and swashbuckling derring-do may not be the best reference point for *Hamlet* even if, as seems to be the case, the choice was a conscious one: "We dreamed up a plan of setting [Hamlet] in a sort of Ruritania," George Shaefer, cited in Tise Vahimagi, "'When You Care Enough to Send the Best': Televised Shakespeare and the Hallmark Hall of Fame," in *Walking Shadows: Shakespeare in the National Film and Television Archives*, ed. Luke McKernan and Olwen Terris (London: British Film Institute, 1994), 209.

4. Bernice W. Kliman, *Hamlet: Film, Television, and Audio Performance* (London: Associated University Presses, 1988), 127.

5. Bernice W. Kliman, "The Setting in Early Television: Maurice Evans' Shakespeare Productions," in *Shakespeare and the Arts*, ed. Cecile Williamson Cary and Henry S. Limouze (Washington, D.C.: University Press of America, 1982), 135–53; 145.

6. Jack Gould, "Adaptation of Macbeth Shown on N.B.C.," *New York Times*, November 29, 1954, quoted in *Shakespeare on Television*, ed. J. C. Bulman and H. R. Coursen (Hanover, N.H.: University Press of New England, 1988), 240.

7. Kliman, "Early Television," 147.

8. Dennis Kennedy, *Looking at Shakespeare: A Visual History of Twentieth-Century Performance* (Cambridge: Cambridge University Press, 1993), 227–29.

9. See Christine Dymkowski, ed., *Shakespeare in Production: The Tempest* (Cambridge: Cambridge University Press, 2000), 13.

10. Dymkowski, *Tempest*, 19–20.

11. For a detailed record of the entire project, see Susan Willis, *The BBC Shakespeare Plays: Making the Televised Canon* (Chapel Hill: University of North Carolina Press, 1991).

12. See, e.g., James C. Bulman, "The BBC Shakespeare and the 'House Style,'" *Shakespeare Quarterly* 35 (1984): 571–81; and Martin Banham, "BBC Television's Dull Shakespeares," *Critical Quarterly* 22, no. 1 (1980): 31–40; both of these are reprinted in Bulman and Coursen.

13. Mark Crispin Miller, "The Shakespeare Plays," *The Nation*, July 12, 1980, cited in Bulman and Coursen, *Shakespeare on Television*, 262.

14. Anthony Davies, "The Film Versions of *Romeo and Juliet*," *Shakespeare Survey* 49 (1996), 162.

15. Bernice W. Kliman, *Hamlet: Film, Television, and Audio Performance* (Rutherford, N.J.: Fairleigh Dickinson University Press, 1988), 200.

16. Quoted in Robert Hapgood, ed., *Shakespeare in Performance: Hamlet* (Cambridge: Cambridge University Press, 1999), 221.

17. For an appreciation of Howell's work on the history plays, see Graham Holderness, "Radical Potentiality and Institutional Closure: Shakespeare in Film and Television," in *Political Shakespeare*, ed. Jonathan Dollimore and Alan Sinfield (Ithaca, N.Y.: Cornell

University Press, 1985), 182–201. See also Willis, BBC *Shakespeare Plays*, chap. 6 and, for an on-the-set description of the taping of *Titus*, chap. 10.

18. "For Titus . . . [Howell] felt the best setting of that intense struggle for honor and revenge would be Northern Ireland, but such a contemporary setting was beyond the series brief, so she opted for quasi-historical togas and roman armor," Willis, BBC *Shakespeare Plays*, 172.

CHAPTER SEVEN

Post-Shakespeares

A number of Shakespeare films released in the last decade of the twentieth century and at the beginning of the twenty-first century have been or can be described as "postmodern." Among these are Peter Greenaway's *Prospero's Books* (1991), Richard Loncraine's *Richard III* (1995), Baz Luhrmann's *William Shakespeare's Romeo + Juliet* (1996), Al Pacino's *Looking for Richard* (1996), Julie Taymor's *Titus* (1999), John Madden's *Shakespeare in Love* (1998), Kenneth Branagh's *Love's Labour's Lost* (2000), and Michael Almereyda's *Hamlet* (2000). A slippery concept at best, postmodern means different things depending on who is employing the term. The films so described, whatever they have in common, vary considerably. At times descriptive and at times evaluative, "postmodern" can be used both to damn and to praise. It is easily reduced to a formula. Not precisely a style, a mode, or even an approach to a subject, postmodern, in one formulation, signifies the rejection of modernism as exemplified in the valuing of surface over depth, affectlessness over emotional involvement, and pastiche over parody.[1] A postmodern filmmaker combines periods, cultures, and locations, puts everything in quotation marks, and exhibits a self-consciousness about the creative process that makes criticism redundant. Everything has already been explained, all allusions have been identified, and nothing remains for the critic to discover.

What I have just written is both parody and pastiche, but it does not disguise the creative energy that can be released when an artist, whether consciously or accidentally, takes a postmodern stance in relationship to the Shakespeare text. Nonetheless, in choosing Shakespeare as a subject, a filmmaker works against the postmodern. Shakespeare's plays, however transmuted by the process of filming, energize a high degree of early modern "affect" and "depth." Some so-called postmodern films appear to challenge traditional approaches to Shakespeare even as they reaffirm them. Michael Almereyda's *Hamlet*, set in the corporate world of New York at the end of the twentieth century, remains, in spite of its contemporary look, a witty and at the same time sincere reconfiguration of Shakespeare's text. In some ways more adventurous, Julie Taymor's *Titus* shows its postmodern credentials by taking one of Shakespeare's most bizarre and infrequently performed plays and, employing an eclectic mix of periods, a self-conscious theatricality, and a variety of distancing devices, arriving at a convincing balance of camp sensibility and high seriousness. *Prospero's Books*, adapted from *The Tempest*, may be the most radical of the three. Peter Greenaway's film looks forward into a future of hypertext and multiplying imagistic surfaces and backward to the early-modern era of Shakespeare's last years as well as the beginning of the twentieth century and the founding moments of the cinema. All three films escape the more clichéd parameters of the postmodern even as they find an identity within it.

It's So New, It's Old:
Michael Almereyda's *Hamlet*

In the preface to his *Hamlet* screenplay, Michael Almereyda recalls that Orson Welles's description of *Macbeth* as a rough charcoal sketch of Shakespeare's play "provoked in [him] a sharp suspicion that you don't need lavish production values to make a Shakespeare movie that's accessible and alive."[2] Filmed in Super 16 millimeter in a catch-as-catch-can fashion ("running and gunning," in insider jargon) on a variety of New York locations (including the Guggenheim Museum for Ophelia's mad scenes), Almereyda's *Hamlet* exhibits all of the "tics" of postmodernity: the *mise en abime* of images within images, including "quotations" from other Shakespeare films;[3] allusions to cultural icons, high and low (John Gielgud, James Dean); an eclectic score that cites Brahms and Tchaikovsky as well as Bob Dylan and Morcheeba; and, in general, a deliberate and conscious self-referentiality that puts everything into quotes, including, especially, Shakespeare himself. This is a Shakespeare "After Mass Media," to cite the title of a recent collection of essays edited by Richard Burt, a world where mediation is personal. The minicam and the power book, and even security camera footage, suggest a creative retreat to the amateur, the unslick, the casual, to the accident of documentary. "The Murder of Gonzago" is a collage film, made by Hamlet himself, using a mix of newly shot video and preexisting "found" material.

However "postmodern" on the surface (and what is postmodernism if not surface?), the primary conceit of the film pushes it back to the moment of high modernity. In 1925, three years after the publication of *The Wasteland* and *Ulysses*, Colin Keith-Johnston, dressed like an Oxford undergrad and brandishing a pistol, exhibited the angst of his historical moment in Barry Jackson's modern-dress *Hamlet* in London. Many of the clever updatings Almereyda employs to bring his *Hamlet* into the twenty-first century were anticipated by Jackson and his director, H. K. Ayliff. In a typical postmodern turn, what is most up-to-date in Almereyda's film is what is most passé: *Hamlet* in contemporary dress, with "morning coat, plus-fours, flapper dresses, bobbed hair, revolvers and motor cars."[4] Shakespeare's plot, "hurried along by a series of cuts designed to reduce the philosophical, meditative aspects of the text and by very quick pace, was given the dash and bite of a modern thriller."[5] Ethan Hawke's solipsistic slacker bears more than a passing resemblance to Colin Keith-Johnston's less than princely prince, with "an ugly, violent streak, the 'rebel against home life' common in the drama of the period, a 'prose Hamlet of petulant snarl and unbridled jest.'"[6] This was a picture of "youth at odds with the universe and turned ugly in its anger."[7] Keith-Johnston's delivery was "naturalistic, staccato, unpoetic."[8]

Ethan Hawke's line readings too are awkward and uncertain, but this is not as problematic as it might otherwise be. Both Hawke's Hamlet and Julia Stiles's Ophelia have difficulty playing the social roles they are expected to play; they are outsiders in the corporate world of Denmark industries. For Hawke, "Hamlet was always much more like Kurt Cobain or Holden Caulfield than Sir Laurence Olivier."[9] His Hamlet is more than simply introspective, however. He is almost totally solipsistic, constantly looking at images of himself and listening to his own recorded voice. The world of electronic reproduction seemingly wired into his body, he is a true "cyber" Hamlet.[10] The romantic pair, Hamlet and Ophelia, as performed by Hawke and Stiles, are cool; the actors provide the characters with minimal affect. The poignancy and vulnerability of Ophelia's situation are most evident in scenes, some interpolated, where Julia Stiles has no lines, where she does not have to speak. Having Ophelia "wired" is a nice way of handling the nunnery scene. She is, here as in Shakespeare's play, the bait employed to entrap Hamlet. Even if we don't agree with some critics, and with many an actor, that Hamlet detects Polonius and Claudius in hiding, Ophelia at least knows exactly what is going on, what is being done to her and by her.

The older generation—Polonius, Gertrude, Claudius—lend only slightly more intensity, are only comparatively less cool than the young. Admittedly, the film sounds most like Shakespeare when Claudius (Kyle MacLachlan) and Laertes (Liev Schreiber) are conspiring. MacLachlan and Schreiber, along with Diane Venora (Gertrude), are comfortable with performing something like the tone and shape of a Shakespearean scene. MacLachlan, whose Claudius is a corporate CEO, is cool in another sense: a man not easily moved to reveal his thoughts and feelings, but dominant enough to slug Hamlet firmly in the stomach during the "Where is Polonius" scene. Diane Venora, who in the past played both Ophelia and, interestingly, Hamlet, plays the self-indulgent sensualist who only gradually becomes aware of the extent of Hamlet's difficulties and Claudius's villainy. Her only refuge is in alcohol. Bill Murray as Polonius (at first thought a bizarre casting choice) gives cool an edge, nicely balancing possessive domination with tender regard—much like Eric Porter in the BBC production. After brusquely warning Ophelia to stay away from Hamlet, he carefully ties the shoelace on her sneaker. The comedy, always inherent in Shakespeare's conception of Polonius, here stems in part from what Murray, who at any moment seems about to make a joke, does *not* say and does *not* do.

Although the cutting and rearrangement of Shakespeare's text, when combined with the sometimes distracting mise-en-scène, often results in the "non sequitur effect," in which lines taken from their original context seem to come out of nowhere, Almereyda clearly embraces *Hamlet* in its fullness and plenitude, however much he is forced and/or inspired to film it in bits and pieces, to cut and slash it into a shape he needs and desires. The result, in Almereyda's own words, is "not so much a sketch but a collage, a patchwork of intuitions, images and ideas."[11] The postmodern "surface" does not disguise Almereyda's engagement with Shakespeare's play. The difference— and, to me, it makes all of the difference—between, say, Zeffirelli's *Hamlet* and Almereyda's, is that whereas Zeffirelli, who presumes to "channel" Shakespeare, gives us a tired, dull, "historical" film with little evidence of real engagement either with the text or with what, if anything, that text might mean, Almereyda gives us a *Hamlet* that, for all of its moments of jejune self-indulgence and clever—as well as not-so-clever—tricks, pulses with something that is recognizably life.

"A Wilderness of Tigers": Julie Taymor's *Titus*

Titus Andronicus, one of Shakespeare's earliest attempts at tragedy, tells an increasingly gruesome tale of rape, mutilation, revenge, and horrible death. At the beginning of the play, Titus, returning home from a victory over the

Goths (fighting them, he has lost twenty-one sons), "sacrifices" the oldest son of the captive Goth Queen, Tamora. Soon he slays one of his four remaining sons in anger. His daughter, Lavinia, is then raped and mutilated (both hands and her tongue are cut off) by Chiron and Demetrius, the two younger sons of Tamora, at the instigation of their mother and her lover, the Moor Aaron. And we are only at the end of act 2! In subsequent acts, two more of Titus's sons are decapitated, Titus having cut off his own hand in the hope of saving them; Chiron and Demetrius are killed, baked into a pie, and fed to Tamora; and Titus, Tamora, the Emperor Saturninus, Aaron, and Lavinia meet a violent end, the last-mentioned killed by her father. Not surprisingly, *Titus Andronicus* has a spotty stage history. The difficulties in mounting a convincing performance of Shakespeare's text have often seemed insurmountable.

Stanley Wells succinctly sets out the challenges any production of *Titus Andronicus* will face:

> The play presents a twin problem. How do you stage its horrors—murder, rape, mutilation, cannibalism—without driving the audience over the bounds of credulity into giggling hysteria? And how, on the other hand, do you cope with its self-conscious literariness—the Latin quotations, the extended similes, the long, rhetorical speeches uttered by characters who according to any normal standards of behaviour should be capable of nothing but shocked speechlessness or hysterical incoherence?[12]

The answer cannot be "to stylize or not to stylize." A theatrical or cinematic presentation of any play will necessarily be stylized, and violence can never be present with complete "realism" (short, perhaps, of a "snuff" film, in which the actors are supposedly murdered). The only real question is how to stylize. The 1955 Peter Brook production of *Titus Andronicus* found its solution in symbolism, such as employing red ribbons issuing from Lavinia's mouth and veiled hands to represent stumps. The other extreme would be a detailed depiction of gore (as in several recent "trash" *Titus* films). Either approach demands some moderation of the merely real. Julie Taymor's choice in *Titus* was to negotiate among degrees of stylization, mostly avoiding a fully "realistic" approach. She engages in considerable sleight of hand (so to speak): what we think we see rather than what we actually see. As Taymor told a class at Columbia University (DVD), she wanted to keep the viewer off guard, never knowing for sure how the next horror will be presented, neither immune to the violence nor led into a false sense of security by the avoidance of the explicit. (Grand Guignol effects, it should be noted, can take us further away from rather than closer to realism. If we are asking ourselves "How did they do that?" we are breaking our contact with the real, which is fine, of course, if that is the intention and if the result is effective.)

Titus opens in a "modern" kitchen (1950s or 1960s style, Taymor helpfully notes on the DVD commentary), where a young boy (Osheen Jones, who serves a similar function in Adrian Noble's A Midsummer Night's Dream [1996]), whose head is covered with a paper-bag helmet, plays violently with toy soldiers and various action figures that he more and more frantically mixes up with his food and a bottle of catsup. (One way of looking at this would be to see it as a rock-bottom-budget version of the film we are about to see, with toys for props, "real" catsup for blood, and primitive special effects.) Taymor appears to be making a self-defeating point: that we are all trapped in a culture of aestheticized violence, just as we are about to see a prime example of aestheticized violence, William Shakespeare's Titus Andronicus. If she wants to suggest that her film is the "real" violence, exposure to which will transform a callous young boy into a caring, chastened human being, the film within this film seems a strange vehicle for such a process. Is Shakespeare's tale of ancient Romans more "real" than the ghastly reality any ten-year-old boy living at the turn of the twenty-first century has already been exposed to? This opening begs a lot of questions. A "real," though oddly muted, explosion shatters the kitchen window and injects reality into the young boy's fantasy scenario. He is then rescued (by the same figure who later appears as the Clown who brings Titus the heads of his sons), brought to the center of an empty coliseum, and held aloft (shades of The Lion King, which Taymor staged in New York) to the cheers of the invisible crowds. The clay-covered soldiers that we and he now see are certainly more ominous and frightening than anything in his collection of toy soldiers.

Though her opening sequence appears to be a highly cinematic deconstruction of Shakespeare's text, a notable aspect of Taymor's film is the extent to which it borrows from and incorporates ideas drawn from the twentieth-century stage history of the play. One could easily tick off numerous specific borrowings from, or at least allusions to, earlier production details and themes. Some of these may well be independent discoveries and even logical extensions of what the text already suggests. A description of Laurence Olivier's performance of the play's opening scene for Peter Brook in 1955, for example, clearly fits what we see of Anthony Hopkins: "a battered veteran, stubborn and shambling, long past caring about the people's cheers."[13] This may be the only logical way to play Titus. On the other hand,

Taymor's allusions to Italian director Federico Fellini parallel elements of Trevor Nunn's 1972 RSC production (Nunn even had his cast watch *Fellini Satyricon*). As Taymor would in her film, Nunn provided an unscripted orgy, and his Saturninus, John Wood, was a clear ancestor to Alan Cumming. Benedict Nightingale wrote of Saturninus's "urbanity, irony, pettishness, narcissism, hysteria, and even a strange infantilism," a performance "more entertaining than it had any right to be."[14] The Mussolini allusions too had been anticipated by a 1967 Baltimore Center Stage production by Douglas Seale.[15] Most significantly, Jane Howell, in her 1985 BBC production (discussed in chapter 6), presented the whole play from the implied point of view of young Martius. She staged the killing of Demetrius and Chiron in an abattoir (a kitchen in Taymor), the two men hanging upside down, "gagged and squealing figures,"[16] and costumed Tamora's sons to resemble members of the rock group Kiss. In Deborah Warner's 1987 RSC production, Titus and his sons enter covered with clay (a key element in Taymor's visual design), and Titus at the end is dressed all in white and wearing the hat of a pastry chef. One is more than a little surprised to hear Taymor speak of these and other effects solely with reference to her own 1994 stage production with seemingly no awareness of the extent to which she is following a tradition.[17] Again, this is not to take away from her achievement. Her eclectic borrowings result in something that is more than the sum of its parts. But we once again see that the production history of any given Shakespeare play almost inevitably colors any new production, stage, film, or television.

Taymor's stylized mise-en-scène, her mixture of incompatible periods and wildly inconsistent settings, costumes, and properties, echoes the inconsistencies of Shakespeare's play, which, with little regard for Roman history and customs, mixes together ancient and imperial, republic and dictatorship, the rise and the decline of empire. Taymor's film does not, any more than does Shakespeare's play, provide a coherent context in which the seemingly arbitrary turnarounds of the first act unfold. Taymor makes no attempt to mitigate the sense of pell-mell arbitrariness. In fact, because of cuts in the text and her rearrangement of the action of scene 1 (putting the entry of Titus, the burial of his sons, and the killing of Tamora's son before the orations of Saturninus and Bassanius that open Shakespeare's play), the turnabouts are exacerbated. In both play and film, the audience must create a context out of its own history and experience, though Taymor drops various clues to her interpretation by textual and extratextual allusions to Italian fascism (especially evident in the entrance of Saturninus and Bassanius, which is staged to remind us of the street fighting and demonstrations that helped bring

Why Do Women Love *Titus Andronicus*?

In discussing Deborah Warner's 1987 Swan Theatre production of *Titus Andronicus*, and in particular the long speech Marcus delivers when he finds the raped and mutilated Lavinia, Jonathan Bate finds significance in Warner's gender: "The simple fact that Warner was (to my knowledge) the first woman ever to direct the play on stage itself effects a radical revision: for a start it defuses the argument that a speech written and performed by men cannot begin to make an audience feel what rape is like."[18] Were he writing today, Bate could go on to make the further point that, in addition to Warner's production, we now have Jane Howell's for the BBC/Time-Life Shakespeare Plays and Taymor's 1999 film. None of these productions can or should be described as "feminist" in a one-dimensional way. They are, rather, deeply "humanist" in their examination of the culture of violence and blood lust, what Tamora rightly calls "cruel, irreligious piety," that perpetuates an unbreakable cycle of rape, dismemberment, and death. All three productions make the rape of Lavinia powerful and disturbing (though none of them goes outside of Shakespeare's text to actually show it). Shakespeare, one would want to emphasize, has already made the rape the emotional center of his play, so that it may simply be that women directors are drawn to *Titus* because they recognize the power and sympathy of Shakespeare's treatment.

Asking the question, Why do women love *Titus*? is, perhaps, to walk on dangerous ground. A better question might be, Why do men *not* love *Titus*? Why, in other words, have (mostly male) critics, scholars, and directors, found *Titus Andronicus*, at least until recently, both distasteful and unplayable? The answer, I would suggest, is partly tied up in that central image of the rape and mutilation of Lavinia, an image at once horrible and fascinating, a crime not only odious but a crime that essentially only men— many men—commit. Shakespeare was especially skilled at evoking and dramatizing that moment when desire becomes crime and in portraying men who employ foul means to achieve sexual conquest. One need only consider, in addition to *The Rape of Lucrece*, *Measure for Measure*, *Cymbeline*, and *Two Gentlemen of Verona*. Imagery of rape is strongly evoked in the history plays, especially *Henry V*. It is part of Shakespeare's understanding of rape that he presents the two rapists of *Titus*, Demetrius and Chiron, as simultaneously barbarous Goths and young Elizabethan gallants vying with each other for a lady's favor. That original Rose Theatre audience is not let off the hook.

Mussolini to power), to the war in Bosnia, and, at least in intention, to the Holocaust.[19] Though perhaps too much can be made of this, it seems fair to say that the "wilderness of tigers" Titus alludes to is an all too familiar landscape at the turn of the millennium.

Taymor's style is sufficiently eclectic and offhand to render any specific political meaning highly problematic. Hers is quite precisely a postmodern style as defined by Frederic Jameson, a mix of citation, imitation, and pastiche. We nod appreciatively at the allusions to Fellini, Visconti, and Pasolini (all sources acknowledged by various commentators, including Taymor herself); we know that the film was made largely at Rome's Cinecitta Studios, where these filmmakers also made films; and we recognize the work of her production designer, Dante Ferreti, who worked with both Fellini and the cult horror filmmaker Dario Argento. This allusive texture, however, is double edged. Cinecitta itself is a legacy of Mussolini and fascism, which thought, carried to its logical conclusion, would implicate Taymor's own project in the fascist impulse she wants to comment on. The (admittedly brief) orgy scene, which Taymor discusses in the context of Luchino Visconti's *The Damned* (1969), is another problematic element. Insofar as the fascist project and the performance or horrors are associated with "decadence" and sexual "deviance," as they are in Visconti's film, *Titus* comes perilously close to an exercise in blaming the victim.

The casting of Alan Cumming as Saturninus and the manner in which he interprets the role contribute further to this problematic. Played with camp flamboyance, Saturninus becomes one of the decadent, mad, sexually ambiguous Caesars of Rome's long decline. At times, he is to the empery as the Wizard is to Oz—the insecure little man behind the curtain: here, a dressed-up doll in a big chair. Cumming is at once comic and sinister, and he continually surprises through unexpected, ingenious line readings. He establishes an immediate bond with Tamora by the knowing way he says "a goodly lady, trust me," as he pulls off her animal skin and reveals the form-fitting golden armor beneath. At times, there are overtones of Macbeth and Lady Macbeth in the interactions between Saturninus and Tamora. When he falls apart in front of the senate, she plays the solicitous wife who smilingly attempts to ameliorate the effects of his breakdown. Up to the time of *Titus*, Cumming's best-known roles were as the sexually ambiguous master of ceremonies in the Sam Mendes revival of *Cabaret* on Broadway and as the gay hotel clerk in Stanley Kubrick's *Eyes Wide Shut* (1999). *Cabaret* itself, one might add, is another work that, in its various theatrical and cinematic incarnations, comes dangerously close to associating the nonconformist sexual activities of its central characters with the cause of which the Nazi rise to power is an effect. "Queers," these texts seem to tell us, are either fascist themselves or the cause of a fascist backlash that consumes everyone. Although Saturninus is not necessarily constructed as "gay" (he appears to lust after both Lavinia and Tamora), he is thoroughly associated with a homosexual aesthetic.

The danger of the kind of postmodern allusiveness Taymor practices is that the associations evoked will not be those the artist intends. Too many allusions to a diverse mix of external signs can result in a work that has no ultimate center, no "base" from which the allusions can be launched and controlled. Taymor avoids some of these difficulties by firmly anchoring her film to Shakespeare's text, a text she presents with the utmost clarity and comprehension. Here fidelity is a virtue. *Titus* must be one of the clearest Shakespeare films ever made. Previous knowledge of the play is unnecessary: virtually every line spoken by every actor is delivered as action as much as speech. The influence of the Royal Shakespeare Company verse-speaking style, popularized in the *Acting Shakespeare* television series and exemplified in the work of John Barton ("the single greatest influence on English verse-speaking for three generations of British actors")[20] and Trevor Nunn, is here transmitted by Cecily Berry, listed in the credits as voice adviser, for many years voice coach at the RSC. Nearly every word of Shakespeare's text, so the theory goes, contains an implicit stage direction, encouraging the actor to show as well as tell. In the instance of *Titus Andronicus*, it helps that the language is "lightly packed," at least relative to Shakespeare's later plays. The metaphors are for the most part easy and expansive, the actions clear and ritualized. The characters tell us, often in striking detail, what they have done, what they are doing, and what they are about to do.

Taymor exposes and embellishes Shakespeare's conception whereby the most "villainous" characters (Tamora, Aaron) are the most natural, in the sense that their actions are motivated by passion rather than, as with Titus, an abstract sense of "duty." The culture Titus and his family represent is locked into custom and ritual, such that the killing of Tamora's firstborn son becomes a carefully scripted ceremony, "Honoring the Dead," expressed in chillingly precise language: "Away with him and make a fire straight, / And with our swords upon a pile of wood / Let's hew his limbs till they be clean consumed" (1.1.131–33). Into this formalized action, the passionate intensity of Jessica Lange's Tamora appears as an indecorous disruption of a preordained act. Zestfully played by Jessica Lange, Tamora, a warrior goddess encased in golden armor, is also a woman horribly wronged by patriarchal "justice." She is so sympathetically and powerfully depicted in her first scene that her subsequent behavior, if not condoned, is made at least understandable. Tamora maintains a powerful femininity even as she wreaks horrible revenge on her oppressors.

Harry Lennix (Aaron), the only actor Taymor brought over from her 1994 stage production of *Titus*, gives the most modern, contemporary-seeming performance in the film, one informed by a tragic sense of resentment for living in a world where the color of his skin prevents him from being the hero. His Aaron is smart, self-sufficient, precise in speech and action. A great screen presence, in part because he is allowed to directly address the camera, with his handsome, flamboyantly scarred face and a voice of butterscotch and brandy, his line readings are intelligent, measured, and American. He skillfully maintains the blank-verse rhythm even as he gives the impression of speaking modern prose. Physically dominant, Aaron easily controls, physically and intellectually, Tamora's two bully-boy sons. He does not so much steal the film (a danger often embraced in the stage history of the play) as take it in unexpected, disturbing directions. He is, perhaps, too easy to like, pushing us in the direction of "violence as entertainment," precisely what Taymor claims she wants to avoid.

In contrast, Shakespeare's "good" characters are either ineffective, like Titus's brother Marcus, or driven headlong by the force of nemesis. Even the most seemingly "innocent," like Lavinia, are provided with moments designed to alienate us from what would be a natural sympathy. Here too Taymor intensifies an effect already present in Shakespeare. When Bassanius and Lavinia come upon Aaron and Tamora, their jibes and taunts are enacted with an enjoyment and spite for which, in this universe at least, we know they will have to pay. Taymor ensures that neither James Frayn nor Laura Fraser gives an entirely sympathetic performance, the former round-faced and smug, the latter, with her pale, almost porcelain beauty, cold and vindictive. Much like the rest of her family, Lavinia seems frozen by the demands of ritual. When she comes to join her father in burying her brothers, she brings her tears in a small glass vial and sprinkles them on the altar (the BBC Lavinia did the same thing), an act that abstracts the force of her already highly formalized speech ("Lo, at this tomb my tributary tears / I render for my brethren's obsequies") and denies her the opportunity to display anything like spontaneous grief. Again, however, Shakespeare has prepared the way: *Titus Andronicus* is hardly a play that simply divides its characters into good and bad.

One of the great challenges *Titus Andronicus* offers is to determine how

the role of Titus himself should be performed. Nearly all of the other characters inhabit more or less emblematic roles, however much they may, from
time to time, stray from them—faithful, sensible Marcus, villainous Aaron,
vengeful Tamora, corrupt Saturninus, virginal Lavinia. But Titus plays a variety of roles and undergoes experiences that can be seen as the sum of the
experiences of virtually all of the other characters, and, as often as not, what
he suffers is the direct result of his own choices and decisions. As Anthony
Hopkins plays him, Titus is a man already beaten down as the film begins.
He moves in a kind of haze, desperately clinging to what shreds of honor and
dignity remain to him in light of the enormous sacrifices he has made for his
country. Everything Titus does is "right" and at the same time horribly
"wrong." Hopkins shows us a man who knows how wrong he is even as he
cannot but choose to act wrongly. Each successive irrational act seems to
justify the original error of judgment Titus made. Hopkins's performance
becomes, in the course of the narrative, more richly varied as Titus himself
is humanized and disintegrates in response to his mounting sorrows. The
range of expressions, sounds, and movements Hopkins makes as he parleys
with the seemingly allegorical figures, Revenge, Murder, and Rapine, tells us
that Titus is not as mad as he seems even as he confirms his tormentors in
the belief that he is.

Taymor is particularly effective at maintaining a balance between the
sheer theatricality of Shakespeare's play and the expectations that derive
from the resources of the cinema. The film throughout carefully juxtaposes
formality, stasis, and ritualized action, on the one hand, and an informal,
fluid matter-of-factness on the other. Self-conscious blocking and framing,
deliberate camera placement, on the one hand; rapid camera movement,
speech and action combined, handheld camera on the other. A particularly
"theatrical," self-conscious moment occurs in the "crossroads" scene (3.1),
where Martius stands frame left and foreground, Lavinia frame right background, and in between, standing on different branches of the road, Titus in
background left and Marcus background right, the four characters forming
the points of a trapezoid ("For now I stand . . . Here stands my . . . son . . .
And here my brother . . . [and] dear Lavinia" (3.1.94, 100, 101, 103). The
effect, nevertheless, is effected in part by such "cinematic" means as location
shooting and the use of a wide-angle lens, both of which help create a tension between stylization and realism.

Taymor's DVD commentary and the various public statements she has
made in interviews and seminars provide as good an example as any of the
importance of trusting the tale rather than, or at least in preference to, the

teller. Taymor wants to see her film as making a statement about violence, and in particular abaout what she terms "violence as entertainment." She has, as noted above, made references to the Holocaust, American ghettos, Bosnia ("This could be Brooklyn or Sarajevo"),[21] Rwanda, East Timor, and the school shootings in Littleton, Colorado. The play, she claims at one point, is "about racism." Neither Shakespeare's play nor Taymor's film, however, can be made to carry all of that baggage. The Holocaust allusions are particularly gratuitous, it seems to me. There is no clear correlation between the boots of soldiers killed in battle ("something that echoes the Holocaust in this—the boots of the dead soldiers," Taymor remarks on the DVD commentary track) and the victims of systematic extermination. As soon as one puts the slightest pressure on the analogy, it disintegrates. Shakespeare's play is a revenge tragedy, a classic "the worm turns" narrative in which the horror and suffering of the first two-thirds of the play are nicely balanced by the horrors of the last third and the audience is encouraged to relish the "payback." Fortunately, the film itself generally ignores these intentions (or post facto rationalizations?); only the completely extratextual precredit sequence, the film's one truly false note, supports the ideas Taymor expresses in her various interviews and extrafilmic pronouncements.

Commenting on Deborah Warner's RSC production, Stanley Wells found that *Titus Andronicus* "emerged as a far more deeply serious play than its popular reputation would suggest, a play that is profoundly concerned with both the personal and the social consequences of violence rather than one that cheaply exploits their theatrical effectiveness."[22] And much the same could be claimed for Taymor's film as well as for Jane Howell's BBC production, both of which, in using the young Lucius as a mostly mute observer of the horrors taking place around him, put great emphasis on the cyclical nature of violence and the redemptive possibilities of innocence. Both productions begin and end with young Lucius, though the endings are rather different in emphasis. Howell's Lucius is shocked to discover that his father has slain Aaron's infant son; Taymor's Lucius carries off the live baby to a possibly brighter future. Although Taymor's ending might seem sentimental, it is perhaps closer in spirit to Shakespeare, who gives us no reason to suspect that Martius won't keep his word and spare the child. Howell's "exceptionally bleak, unforgiving ending,"[23] on the other hand, may be more consonant with the overall tone of the play, which concludes not with Martius's healing words ("May I govern so / To heal Rome's harms and wipe away her woe" [5.3.146–47]) but with his order to throw Tamora's body "to beasts and birds

DVD Extras

Today, with almost immediate release on cable and in videotape and digital formats, even a film not particularly successful at the box office can have an active and profitable afterlife. Taymor's *Titus*, though not a moneymaker in its theatrical version, comes in an attractively packaged two-disc DVD set with a rich variety of specials and extras, including audio commentaries by Taymor, music composer Elliot Goldenthal, and star Anthony Hopkins; a documentary on the making of the film; videotape of rehearsal sessions and a question-and-answer session with Taymor and students at Columbia University; articles from *American Cinematographer*; and a costume gallery. The DVD even has its own Internet site in addition to the Fox/Searchlight site for the film. In a long tradition of expert commentary, the DVD packaging includes a print version of an essay on the film by the scholar-critic Jonathan Bate, the editor of the most recent Arden edition of *Titus Andronicus* (closing the circle, my copy of this scholarly edition of Shakespeare's play sports a sticker on the cover quoting Julie Taymor: "A great edition of a great play"). Related tie-ins include an illustrated coffee table book of Taymor's screenplay and another lavish volume devoted to Taymor's theater and film work. One almost feels that the film has become nearly swamped by the *parerga* that accompanies it.

to prey / . . . Her life was beastly and devoid of pity, / And being dead, let birds on her take pity" [5.3.198–89]).

Prospero's Books: From Text to Hypertext

Appearing near the end of the cinema's first century, Peter Greenaway's *Prospero's Books* (1991) provides a useful entry for an inquiry into the work of art in the age of mechanical and electronic reproduction. A text that simultaneously fetishizes the written word (specifically, the words of Shakespeare) and exploits a combination of film/video/computer technologies, *Prospero's Books* engages with theoretical and practical issues that go back to the earliest attempts to come to terms with the nature and function of cinema and at the same time provides a rich field for semiotic/structuralist, poststructuralist, and postmodern discourses. Greenaway's at once ascetic and baroque film becomes a palimpsest that pushes at the limits of what can be said and thought about cinema itself. As an adaptation of *The Tempest* and an Art Cinema product, *Prospero's Books* is clearly imbricated in questions of authorship. "Greenaway's interpretation of the play," Lisa Hotchkiss observes, "relies on the traditional doubling of Prospero and Shakespeare. To this equation, the filmmaker adds [Sir John] Gielgud and, by implication, himself as director and image maker."[24] The resulting film puts into productive tension the competing authorities of Shakespeare; the magus, Prospero; the performer, John Gielgud; and Peter Greenaway himself.

At once an "art film" and something resembling soft-core pornography (these may, at times, seem to be the same thing),[25] a "faithful" adaptation and a free-form interpretation, a slave to verbal textuality and almost overwhelmingly visual, *Prospero's Books* resists all attempts at categorization. A book, a film, a video, a product of computer art, a nexus of competing languages, a history of art and a postmodern pastiche, an homage to an actor and a film that seems at times empty of human presence, Greenaway's film exasperates and exhilarates by turns.[26] What I would like to trace here are some of the ways Greenaway's film, as an incorporation of an early-seventeenth-century text into a late-twentieth-century hypertext, constantly circles back to its origins, along the way recapitulating the history of theater and film, all the while demonstrating that the magic of contemporary technology, no matter how elaborately marshaled, can only approach, not fulfill, the magic implicit in Shakespeare's strange and evocative play.

As Greenaway has himself stated, *Prospero's Books* is "a project that deliberately emphasizes and celebrates the text as text."[27] The primary text is *The*

The entire film version of *Prospero's Books*—with Prospero here played by John Gielgud—is a projection of the conscious and subconscious mind of Prospero, who is at once poet/playright, actor, filmmaker, and magician. Copyright © 1991 Miramax Films.

Tempest, but we have, in addition, the film itself (which includes a multitude of texts in addition to the twenty-four books Greenaway has conjured up) and the book by Peter Greenaway, a book curiously entitled *Prospero's Books: A Film of Shakespeare's The Tempest*. *Prospero's Books*, the film, is at once a reasonably "faithful" adaptation of Shakespeare's text and a virtual smothering, or perhaps drowning, of that text. Greenaway has quite literally covered *The Tempest* with layers of extraneous materials, much of it only recoverable through a reading of the detailed script that is "Greenaway's book." The book, however, is not the film: Greenaway's narrative and descriptive excursions suggest an expansive, centrifugal mise-en-scène, whereas the film is almost obsessively centripetal in its effects. As with any written text or any screenplay, Greenaway's "book" of his film presents a plenitude that film (or any visual medium), no matter how thoroughly the frame is saturated with information, can never fully achieve.

Apart from the subtext provided by the published screenplay, a number of the primary subtextual concerns of *Prospero's Books* are drawn from the critical history of *The Tempest*: Shakespeare's farewell to the stage, a dialogue on Art versus Nature, a self-referential claim for the power of the playwright, and a discourse on colonialism, among others. The primary subtext of *Prospero's Books*, however, identifies Prospero not merely with Shakespeare but also with Sir John Gielgud and with Greenaway himself. The entire film is a projection of the conscious and subconscious mind of Prospero, who is at once poet/playwright, actor, filmmaker, and magician. Shakespeare's play encourages such an approach. As Stephen Orgel writes, the events of *The Tempest* "are largely the products of Prospero's imagination, or of the imaginative re-creation of his memory."[28] (At the same time, we can note another cultural allusion, to the 1956 Hollywood sci-fi adaptation of *The Tempest*, *Forbidden Planet*, in which Caliban is entirely a projection of Prospero's psyche.) Throughout the film, we are at once inside and outside of Prospero's mind, a mind filled with images founded, often anachronistically, on art historical paradigms: the architecture of Piranesi and Michelangelo; the paintings of Rubens, Titian, and Tintoretto; the Indian drawings of John White; and much else as well. We see very little of nonhuman nature in Greenaway's film—even the pastoral scene of Miranda's first viewing of Ferdinand is wonderfully artificial, and nearly ludicrous, in design. Neither the sunshine nor the bright colors are of nature, any more than bales of straw, papier-mâché columns, or white flower petals falling over the soundstage landscape. Nature, here as elsewhere, is simply a construct of human artifice.

Nearly every shot, moment, or scene in Greenaway's film points to other texts, other discourses. A primary reference point is the cinema itself, its history and its sources in the technology of magic and the magic of technology. *Prospero's Books* takes us back to the beginnings of film as material object. With all of the wizardry of computer programming, Graphic Paintbox manipulation, and multimedia fusion,[29] the effects Greenaway produces are remarkably primitive, imitations of precinematic devices: toy theaters, cardboard cutouts, books that open to reveal three-dimensional buildings, zoetropic imagery. Greenaway's explicit use of images drawn from Eadweard Muybridge's locomotion studies underscores the point. Even the dance choreography contributes to this effect. The precisely calibrated, repetitive, "digital" movements of the dancers turn them into the products of a primitive form of animation, an effect intensified by Michael Nyman's mesmerizing, repetitive score.[30]

Apart from the precise nature of the technology involved, many of the magical moments in *Prospero's Books* might have been achieved by George Méliès circa 1905. Prospero's magic is intimately related to the magicians who, especially in France, were among the first filmmakers. As Erik Barnouw has noted, "Most technical devices that became characteristic of motion picture special effects . . . were familiar to the first film magicians from a century of scientific magic."[31] In short, our awareness that sophisticated computer technology has constructed these images in no way prevents them from looking precisely like the products of turn-of-the-century (of the twentieth century, that is) mechanical inventions. Greenaway's computer-generated, high-definition video imagery, nested within the 35-millimeter film frame, frequently foregrounds mise-en-scène at the expense of nearly everything else, so that as it recapitulates the history of film, *Prospero's Books* also—and this very self-consciously—recapitulates the history of Western art. Specifically, Greenaway is drawn to compositions inspired by European large canvases of the seventeenth and eighteenth centuries: David, Rubens, Veronese. And the resultant tableau effect, which is central to his visual design, may remind us of an earlier theatrical mode—nineteenth-century melodrama, for instance, and, more to the point, the Stuart Masque.

A newly popular, though not new, theatrical form in early-seventeenth-century England, the masque, "a rich and nobly foolish line of courtly entertainment"[32] that depended for its effect on elaborate scenic machinery, is at the imaginative center of Shakespeare's *Tempest*: it is in presenting a masque that Prospero most flamboyantly shows off his magical powers.[33] In this context, the uneasy relationship between Shakespeare's text and Greenaway's spectacle can thus be seen to recapitulate, some four hundred years later, the bitter rivalry between playwright, poet, and writer of masques Ben Jonson and his collaborator, the architect and scenic genius Inigo Jones. Stephen Orgel has defined the nature of the conflict, citing Jonson's remark that the court masques "eyther have bene, or ought to be the mirrors of mans life." "But to his collaborator, the great architect and stage designer Inigo Jones," they were " 'nothing else but pictures with Light and Motion.' "[34] *The Tempest* itself is a kind of masque, and as such, it allows us to imagine that however much Prospero might be seen as a stand-in for Shakespeare, he is also a stand-in for Inigo Jones, an observation that momentarily shifts our attention from poetry to Ben Jonson's "shows, shows, mighty shows, . . . the mere perspective of an inch board."[35] *Prospero's Books* is an homage to both Shakespeare and Inigo Jones, or at least the spirit of Inigo Jones.[36] Greenaway reproduces something of the machinery of the masque throughout the film: his sets have the cutout effect that resembles what we know of seventeenth-century masque designs, with their movable, three-dimensional triangles known as periaktoi, along with flies, angles, and wings.

Greenaway's wedding of film and theater in *Prospero's Books* manifests itself in another textual referent: John Gielgud. Gielgud himself presents us with a series of dualities. Though he is primarily known as a stage actor, his long life was virtually coterminous with the first century of cinema, and he appeared in numerous films. On the stage, Gielgud spent the greater part of his career with the classics—most notably Shakespeare, but also Chekhov, Congreve, and Wilde. In his sixties and seventies he began a new career as a star of the contemporary British theater, appearing in new work by Harold Pinter, Edward Bond, and David Storey. Thus Gielgud is at once classic and modern, and his performing temperament reflects this. The qualities, apart from his vocal delivery, that made Gielgud a successful Shakespearean actor are hard to pin down precisely, but he is at his best in roles with a strong neurotic tinge to them: Richard II, Hamlet, Leontes in *A Winter's Tale*, Cassius in *Julius Caesar*, King Lear, Angelo in *Measure for Measure*, and, of course, Prospero, a role he played four times on the English stage. More straightforward characters—Othello, for example—have generally defeated him.

Gielgud's function in *Prospero's Books* is similarly fraught with ambiguities. He can be seen, on the one hand, as a guarantor of Shakespearean authenticity as well as a material testament to the authority of the word—in reputation, at least, he is unparalleled as a speaker of verse, and Greenaway has him recite virtually all of the play's lines. At the same time, however, Greenaway places Gielgud in a mise-en-scène that threatens to overwhelm

Lexis versus Opsis

Greenaway, who has testified to his fascination with the Inigo Jones/Ben Jonson relationship,[37] may have deliberately attempted in *Prospero's Books* to preserve the aspect of the court masque that Jonson thought—and no doubt hoped—would be impossible to preserve, which "cannot by imagination, much less description, be recovered to a part of that spirit it had in the gliding by."[38] Certainly, as Allardyce Nicoll claims, what Jones created must have been impressive: "Inigo Jones's magic was magic indeed, increased rather than dissipated for those privileged to move behind the scenes, there to view the arrays of grooves, capstans, ropes, and platforms necessary for calling into being the mysteries of cloud palaces and of enchanted seas."[39] In the end, however, Jonson clearly won: his masques—his words—have survived. The precise nature of Jones's machines can only be guessed at on the basis of drawings and the written evocations of, ironically enough, Ben Jonson and the other poet/playwrights who composed texts for masques. Jones, nevertheless, was highly praised in his own time as a magician whose effects were achieved with the aid of a superior, invisible technology. *Prospero's Books*, for its part, appears to both embrace and reject theater. Greenaway often treats space as theatrical in a specifically seventeenth-century fashion. Not the space of Shakespeare's Globe, certainly, and not precisely the kind of space available in the private theaters of the era either. Rather, he has constructed a space reminiscent of the *intermezzi* of the Italian theater, the type of spectacle that in fact influenced the Jacobean masque. Greenaway's frame, though mobile, is mobile in a lateral fashion, his camera moving inexorably right or left, reminding us of the theater of dioramas and treadmills. The space is only illusionistically three-dimensional. At other moments, the film frame constructs an impossible theatrical space, a space that incorporates and weds different orders of temporal and physical reality.[40]

his corporeality while opening up a world of non-Shakespearean allusions and distorts his voice by electronic manipulation or by layering of another voice over or under his so that we are robbed of much of its musicality and resonance. In effect, Gielgud both is and is not at the center of *Prospero's Books*: his presence is inescapable, but it is mediated and aestheticized to such an extent that it almost ceases to be a presence at all. "In Greenaway's film," Amy Lawrence writes, "Gielgud is treated with extravagant respect."[41] The very extravagance of that respect, however, suggests a certain anxiety—insofar as Gielgud is Prospero is Shakespeare (is Greenaway?), a critique

(even an autocritique) appears to be built into the manner in which Greenaway approaches the transformation of Shakespeare's play into his own highly
idiosyncratic film.

One way to think of *Prospero's Books* is as a hypertext, "an information
technology consisting of individual blocks of text, or lexias, and the electronic links that join them."[42] *Prospero's Books* is not literally a hypertext in
this sense, although Prospero's relationship to and manipulation of the world
around him is in some ways analogous to hypertextuality. In the words of
Mariacristina Cavecchi, "The visual and symbolic hyper-stratification and
the endless process of quotations lead to a disruption of the filmic unity so
that the film absorbs *The Tempest*'s imagery and text and turns into an ency-
clopedic container of images drawn from literature, painting, architecture,
music, etc."[43] Following the lead of Peter Donaldson, we can at least imagine
Prospero's Books existing in an interactive hypermedia environment where
the entire image surface would consist of links capable of taking us not only
to other frames/fields of the film itself but also to the whole range of allusive
material therein contained.[44] Click on a close-up of John Gielgud and we are
in another Shakespeare film—say one of the two *Julius Caesars* (1953, 1969)
or *Chimes at Midnight* (1966)—or we are presented still photos of Gielgud as
a stage Prospero in 1930, 1940, 1957, 1974, or we hear him speaking Prospero's lines from the audio recording of *The Ages of Man*, his tour de force
Shakespeare recital. My point is that *Prospero's Books*, in its allusiveness and
omnipresent referentiality, is always already a hypertext of this sort, demanding that we point our mental mouse on a multitude of links. Like a true
hypertext, those links take us to places far removed from and seemingly irrelevant to our originary text; much like the hypertextuality of the Internet, we
ultimately chart our own path, a path in no way predetermined for us by the
creator of the primary text.

Though it is useful to think of Greenaway's film as in some sense re-creating the court masque, we have very little sense of what a pre-Restoration
production of *The Tempest*, or of any play, would have looked like; we do not
even know for certain what theatrical venue Shakespeare might have had in
mind when he composed the play. The first recorded performance (November 1, 1611) was for King James I at Whitehall, but it was very likely presented both at the outdoor Globe and the indoor Blackfriars as well—three
very different physical spaces. I would suggest, nonetheless, that Greenaway,
perhaps without conscious intention, fashioned a production of *The Tempest*
much like what an audience in the early 1600s would have experienced.
Apart from the animated magic of his twenty-four books and his picture-in-

picture technology, Greenaway is careful to restrict his depiction of Prospero's magical arts to effects that, as far as we can tell, could have been presented on a seventeenth-century stage. Even the storm is presented symbolically and metonomically: a model ship, a bathtub, a pissing boy. Some of Greenaway's more spectacular effects may have been in the reach of Jacobean masque makers. The author of one recent study of *The Tempest* argues that by 1606, "Inigo Jones was gracefully and astonishingly levitating large numbers of masquers together with luminous fabric clouds and chariots above the stage area of the Banqueting House [at Whitehall] . . . and he was doing so by the methods of magical illusionists on modern stages without the use of visible ropes or wires or other, crude, visible means of support."[45]

Here a comparison with Derek Jarman's avant-garde cinematic deconstruction of *The Tempest* (1979) is instructive. Jarman's film strips away much of the rich mise-en-scène Shakespeare's poetry invokes, the language that, in *The Tempest* in particular, constructs a theatrical event that cannot be materialized on any actual stage. Greenaway, in contrast, provides a peculiarly overrich, formalized, and explicit material embodiment of the language of *The Tempest* that essentially freezes the imagery to such an extent that Shakespeare's text can no longer evoke at all—the chain of signification is stopped dead in its tracks, transferred, as it has been, to a virtual environment—from baroque painting to the nineteenth-century heroic work of Gericault and others—at once essentially alien to the possibilities of Shakespeare's imagination (which, however we wish to define it, was not essentially baroque)[46] and tied to an aesthetic vocabulary (Venetian easel painting and Greco-Roman architecture) whose familiarity and specificity are temporally bound. And yet, for all of the differences between their approaches to Shakespeare's text, both Jarman and Greenaway emphasize the essential theatricality of *The Tempest*, foregrounding mise-en-scène over more specifically cinematic tools like continuity editing, camera placement, and special photographic effects. As Vernon Gras notes, "More attention is given [in Greenaway's films] to how a particular scene is framed and shot than to fast cuts, changing camera positions, and the suspenseful development of a story line."[47] Jarman's own description of his intentions ("In *The Tempest* we paint pictures, frame each static shot and allow the play to unfold in them as within a proscenium arch")[48] could stand as well for the effect Greenaway achieves throughout much of *Prospero's Books*.

Anticipating Peter Greenaway, Derek Jarman once thought of having Prospero play all the parts, and he asked John Gielgud, who demurred, to play Prospero in old age (another actor would play a young Prospero).[49] For

Jarman's *Tempest*

Derek Jarman's *The Tempest* (1979), shot in 16 millimeter and filmed in the crumbling interior of an eighteenth-century "Great House" (Stoneleigh Abbey), features such oddities as an Ariel in a boiler suit, a youngish Prospero, a Miranda who seems a cross between a young lady to the manor born and a punk groupie, and a moving as well as funny finale in which Elizabeth Welch sings Cole Porter's "Stormy Weather" as sailors dance around her. Elements of mise-en-scène, including "magical" effects, are created with economy and simplicity: a few illuminated objects spotlighted in the midst of darkness, an arrangement of candles suggesting the aura of a magus, and an Ariel who materializes in a mirror when a light is turned on next to him. Scenes are often tinted in one color, having been shot through a filter. Costumes are eclectically undefinable. Miranda, who is barefooted throughout, wears what appears to be a tattered, petticoated party dress and her hair, in Afro style, looks as if it were braided with straw. Stephano is dressed like a chef, while the ship's crew are uniformed like nineteenth-century sailors. At once a challenge to conventional approaches to filming Shakespeare and an essentially straightforward adaptation of Shakespeare's play, Jarman's film weds amateurishness and professionalism—or erases the distinction altogether. Nearly everything in the film feels spontaneous and improvised, and yet a viewer/auditor cannot help but feel a precise and careful planning behind each shot, camera setup, performance, and "magical" effect. If Jarman's film is subversive of anything, it is the overreverent, "good taste" approach to culture that has traditionally governed English attitudes to Shakespeare; *The Tempest* is in no way subversive of Shakespeare himself.[50] The radical displacements signaled by mise-en-scène and the slicing up and reconstruction of the text are all in the service of the play. Jarman, as Russell Jackson observes, "tells the play's story forcefully and engagingly, moving with the text through illusion, threats, vengeance, and comedy to a joyous sense of release,"[51] though Jarman's Prospero, as played by Heathcote Williams, is perhaps more sinister and harsh than is customary: Jarman quite deliberately cuts the speech of Prospero renouncing his magic. This is a Prospero who has no intention of giving up his power.

his part, Greenaway was undeniably influenced by Jarman's film. His Caliban, for example, is a similarly bald, grotesquely obscene figure; he includes flashback images of the child Miranda and the witch Sycorax; almost all of the action takes place in interior locations. Both films feature "full frontal nudity." Visually, however, the films are very different. Greenaway packs his frames with baroque decor and rich color, whereas Jarman, whose influences appear to include the nocturnal paintings of Caspar David Friedrich, makes do with a few crucial items (Miranda's rocking horse, Prospero's magic wand) picked out from the darkness that envelops much of the film.

Like Jarman, Greenaway, even with all of the resources of cinema at his disposal (presumably on a relatively modest budget), chose to give us Prospero's magic without employing elaborate camera tricks or special effects. Critics who fault Greenaway for his excesses too often ignore or forget the remarkable results he achieves with minimal means. An artist and a student of art history, he is able to construct trompe l'oeil imagery of notable power: the shots of Ariel imprisoned in a tree, for instance, reinforce without simply duplicating the evocative language Shakespeare employs to describe Ariel's punishment:

> She did confine thee, . . .
> Into a cloven pine, within which rift
> Imprisoned thou didst painfully remain
> A dozen years; . . .
>   where thou didst vent thy groans
> As fast as mill-wheels strike. (1.2.274–81)

The effect is achieved simply enough, through barklike makeup, dreadful cries of pain, and editing that evokes Ovidian transformation without having to employ even minimal in-camera magic or postproduction manipulation.

In traveling the distance from Shakespeare's 1604 play to Greenaway's 1991 film, we find ourselves moving backward to the beginning of modern times, a moment when technology was taking art into a brave new world, a moment when the "money-get, mechanic age,"[52] in Ben Jonson's phrase, threatened poetry itself. But if words could survive what another playwright, Thomas Dekker, called the "hard-handed mercy of Mychanitiens,"[53] they may survive our technology as well. Shakespeare allowed Prospero to drown his magic book "deeper than did ever plummet sound" (5.1.56). Greenaway, on the other hand, has Caliban rescue two of Prospero's books from their watery grave. These are Shakespeare's own texts, "a thick volume called *Thirty-Six Plays*" and a much slimmer volume, *The Tempest*. Greenaway indulges in a peculiar irony here, given that the Caliban world is very specifically shown as one where books are defaced and desecrated, ripped, marred with tears, covered with raw eggs, pissed on, and vomited over. As is frequently true with Greenaway, bodily functions and excremental gestures lie on the very edges of orderly form. Caliban is a challenge to all that is tidy, neat, rational, and balanced. He is not Shakespeare's comic fish/man, but more like a man-sized turd, an in-your-face embodiment of obscenity and sacrilege. And yet, for all that, Greenaway allows him the grace of the artist by having his role essentially danced by Michael Clark. He is not in fact monstrous and sports no obvious horns or tail, as he does in Greenaway's script. He is all too human, his physical form in no way deformed with hair, gills, scales, or feathers, as are so many stage Calibans. Seen in close-up, his face has a fresh, almost sweet expression. He is associated in the film with the "Book of Minerals," as if to underline Prospero's epithet for him, "thou earth." His home is, illogically, both underground, in a kind of sewer ("like a hippopotamus pool in a Victorian zoo"),[54] and at the same time coterminous with and on the same level as Prospero's lodging; to walk out to the edge of Prospero's living quarters is to be in Caliban's world. The two are not truly separate but are interpenetrating spaces, the one melding into the other, aspects of one—books, for example—present in the other.

The film thus ends as it began, with Shakespeare's text, his words preserved in books. Greenaway, who asks to be identified with both Prospero and Shakespeare, ends up as a cross between Caliban and Inigo Jones. Like the Caliban of the film, as Douglas Lanier suggests, Greenaway is a desecrater of books who nevertheless saves them from oblivion.[55] Like Jones, Greenaway threatens to make words irrelevant, threatens to turn lexis into opsis, even "to make boards to speak." But if Jones had no need for words, as Ben Jonson lamented ("O shows, shows, mighty shows! / The eloquence of masques! What need of prose, / Or verse, or sense to express immortal you?"),[56] Greenaway cannot escape them. Words remain throughout *Prospero's Books* as material objects, as manuscript and print on the surface of his images. And so Greenaway's film, in its constant backward-and-forward movement through time, in its slide from the early modern to the postmodern and back, in its imaginative reconstruction of the original moment of authorship with the tools developed over four centuries of technological change, concludes with the kind of ambivalence that, according to Stephen Orgel, lies at the heart of Shakespeare's *Tempest*. As Orgel points out,[57] we never actually see

Shakespeare's Prospero break his staff or drown his book of magic: the promise is eternally deferred. So too Greenaway cannot give up on the word. His book of the film, attractively produced and illustrated with his own drawings, with photos of European painting, sculpture, and architecture, with Paintbox images and with stills from the film, and reproducing much of Shakespeare's play together with Greenaway's commentary on both the play and his film, becomes a testament to the magic that can emerge, bidden and unbidden, from between the covers of a book.

Coda: Why Shakespeare, Why Now?

Although the "boom" in Shakespeare films appears at this writing to be over, the proliferation of Shakespeareana in turn-of-the-millennium America is a phenomenon that invites special notice. It seems particularly ironic that at the same moment that conservatives push Shakespeare as the highbrow answer to the vulgarization of culture on the one hand and the obfuscations of the race/class/gender nexus on the other, Shakespeare himself becomes increasingly positioned in popular culture, becomes more and more the "Schlockspeare" Richard Burt has identified as the central role he occupies in contemporary media discourse,[58] even as he remains a key player in the poststructuralist, postmodern discourse conservatives abhor. The Shakespeare who is meant to be the cornerstone of Western culture is simultaneously the Shakespeare of comic books, the Internet, pornography, romance fiction, popular music, and so on.[59] The Shakespeare who stands as the white, Protestant, Anglo-Saxon guardian of "real" literary achievement is simultaneously the center of academic volumes with titles like *Post-Colonial Shakespeare*, *Homosexuality in Shakespeare's England*, *Shakespeare and Deconstruction*, *Shakespeare after Theory*, *Shakespeare and Social Class*, *Shakespeare against Apartheid*, to mention a few. As Gail Kern Paster writes in a recent flyer promoting *Shakespeare Quarterly*, "Shakespeare studies has been at the epicenter of every emerging critical area: feminism, postcolonialism, psychoanalysis, deconstruction, new historicism, Marxism, ethnic studies, gender and queer theory, and others." The conservatives not only have failed to get their facts straight but are missing the point.

What a true conservative should be concerned about is not the disappearance of Shakespeare from culture but rather his too easy and too prominent place in it. The true classics, Homer and Aeschylus, Tacitus and Thucydides, Apuleius and Plato, have indeed disappeared from the general college curriculum and have become the preserve of the "fit though few." Even George

Will, one suspects, doesn't read them. Yet Shakespeare, in part because of leftist academics, has become "popular" and everywhere available. And here we can find another explanation for the proliferation of Shakespeare in contemporary culture. Early in the much maligned 1960s Shakespeare began to be taught not as literature but as theater; he ceased to be a poet and became a playwright. For nearly half a century, students have been told that Shakespeare is theater and his plays essentially performance texts. The way to teach Shakespeare is to perform him. The method is reading aloud, acting out scenes, learning Elizabethan stage practice, and, not incidentally, looking at the movies (which, in the classroom, means video clips). Shakespeare is easy, not hard; he is a working playwright, not a precious "poet"; he is a craftsman, not an artist; and, most significantly, he is a capitalist, a shareholder in a business venture who retired at an early age on a comfortable pension, not some poor schlemiel living in a garret and practicing his "art" for its own sake. Shakespeare, it turns out, is really one of us.

Shakespeare on film has, in a wide variety of generic guises, made a significant contribution to the construction of Shakespeare as "one of us." From its origins in the late nineteenth century into the beginning of the twenty-first, the Shakespeare film has continually taken on new identities: literary adaptation, "heritage" film, canned theater, art cinema, epic, star vehicle, musical comedy, costume film, and many others. In the absence of a single identity, the Shakespeare film is a chameleon genre, able to change shape and form as changing styles and tastes require. Shakespeare has been adapted to film in part because his plays are so adaptable. As noted earlier, Shakespeare's success as a playwright can be associated with his generic flexibility. Ultimately, it may not be the characters, plots, and themes of Shakespeare that are universal, but rather the forms he employed in bringing these elements to life. As Susan Snyder notes, for Shakespeare "genre conventions provided shape rather than limitation, in musical terms a kind of ground on which—and sometimes against which—he played the individual descant of each play."[60] What the early-modern playwright borrowed and transformed from his genre models has been in turn borrowed and transformed for the modern media of cinema and television. With the often interactive art and technology of the new millennium, we can expect that Shakespeare and his works will continue to be transformed, albeit into shapes and guises that we cannot now foresee.

Notes

1. See Fredric Jameson, "Postmodernism, or the Cultural Logic of Late Capitalism," *New Left Review* 146 (July–August 1984): 53–92.

2. Michael Almereyda, *William Shakespeare's Hamlet*, introduction by Ethan Hawke (London: Faber & Faber, 2000), vii.

3. The film ends with a clear reference to Luhrmann's *Romeo + Juliet*, with Robert McNeil reading an editorial off a teleprompter (a passage taken, with a hint from Harold Bloom, from *The Murder of Gonzago*).

4. Anthony Dawson, *Shakespeare in Performance: Hamlet* (Manchester: Manchester University Press, 1995), 83.

5. Dawson, *Hamlet*, 84.

6. *Manchester Guardian*, August 26, 1925, cited in Dawson, *Hamlet*, 88.

7. *Manchester Guardian*, August 26, 1925, cited in Robert Hapgood, *Shakespeare in Production: Hamlet* (Cambridge: Cambridge University Press, 1999), 63.

8. Dawson, *Hamlet*, 88.

9. Almereyda, *Hamlet*, xiv.

10. See Mark Thonton Burnett, "'To Hear and See the Matter': Communicating Technology in Michael Almereyda's *Hamlet* (2000)," *Cinema Journal* 42 (Spring 2003): 48–69.

11. Almereyda, *Hamlet*, xii.

12. Stanley Wells, "Shakespeare Performances in London and Stratford-upon-Avon, 1986–87," *Shakespeare Survey* 41 (1989): 159–81; 179.

13. Kenneth Tynan, quoted in Alan Dessen, *Shakespeare in Performance: Titus Andronicus* (Manchester: Manchester University Press, 1989), 18.

14. *New Statesman*, October 20, 1972, cited in Dessen, *Titus Andronicus*, 37.

15. *New Statesman*, October 20, 1972, cited in Dessen, *Titus Andronicus*, 34.

16. *New Statesman*, October 20, 1972, cited in Dessen, *Titus Andronicus*, 45.

17. For a comparison of Taymor's stage and film versions, see David McCandless, "A Tale of Two *Tituses*: Julie Taymor's Vision on Stage and Screen," *Shakespeare Quarterly* 53 (2002): 487–511.

18. Jonathan Bate, ed., *Titus Andronicus*, The Arden Shakespeare, 3d ser. (London: Routledge, 1995), 63.

19. See Richard Burt, "Shakespeare and the Holocaust: Julie Taymor's *Titus* Is Beautiful, or Shakesploi Meets (the) Camp," in *Shakespeare after Mass Media*, ed. Richard Burt (New York: Palgrave, 2002), 295–329.

20. Charles Marowitz, *Recycling Shakespeare* (New York: Applause, 1991), 77.

21. *Titus*, directed by Julie Taymor (20th Century Fox DVD, 2000), commentary track.

22. Wells, "Shakespeare Performances," 181.

23. *New Statesman*, October 20, 1972, cited in Dessen, *Titus Andronicus*, 106.

24. Lisa Hotchkiss, "The Incorporation of Word as Image in *Prospero's Books*," *Post Script* 17, no. 2 (1998): 8–25.

25. For the connection between European art film and low culture, see Joan Hawkins, "Sleaze Mania, Euro-Trash, and High Art: The Place of European Art Films in American Low Culture," *Film Quarterly* 53, no. 2 (1999–2000): 14–29.

26. In addition to the books and essays cited throughout, useful studies of *Prospero's*

204   ∿   Chapter 7

Books in the context of Greenaway's career as a visual artist are Leon Steinmetz and Peter Greenaway, *The World of Peter Greenaway* (Boston: Journey Editions, 1995); David Pascoe, *Peter Greenaway: Museums and Moving Images* (London: Reaktion, 1997); Alan Wood, *Being Naked—Playing Dead: The Art of Peter Greenaway* (Manchester: Manchester University Press, 1996); Peggy Phelan, "Numbering Prospero's Books," *Performing Arts Journal* 41 (1992); James Tweedle, "Caliban's Books: The Hybrid Text in Peter Greenaway's *Prospero's Books*," *Cinema Journal* 40 (Fall 2000): 104–26; Maria Nadotti, "Exits and Entrances: On Two Tempests," *Art Forum* 30 (1991): 20–21; Suzanna Turman, "Peter Greenway" [sic], *Films in Review* 43, no. 3–4: 1992): 105–8.

27. Peter Greenaway, *Prospero's Books: A Film of Shakespeare's* The Tempest (New York: Four Walls Eight Windows, 1991), 9.

28. Stephen Orgel, ed., *The Tempest* (Oxford: Oxford University Press, 1987), 25.

29. The technology Greenaway employs is discussed in some detail in Howard Rodman, "Anatomy of a Wizard," *American Film* 16 (1991): 34–39.

30. "It [the dance choreography] is an attempt to make live performers on film look as much like computer animation as possible," Peter Donaldson, "Shakespeare in the Age of Post-Mechanical Reproduction: Sexual and Electronic Magic in *Prospero's Books*," in *Shakespeare, The Movie: Popularizing the Plays on Film, TV, and Video*, ed. Lynda E. Boose and Richard Burt (London: Routledge, 1997), 169–85; 171.

31. Erik Barnouw, *The Magician and the Cinema* (New York: Oxford University Press, 1981), 98.

32. Allardyce Nicoll, *Stuart Masques and the Renaissance Stage* (London: G. Harrap, 1938), 19.

33. "Prospero's Masque for His Daughter's Betrothal Constitutes the Prime Example We Are Shown of His Art," in Orgel, *The Tempest*, 43.

34. Stephen Orgel, *The Jonsonian Masque* (Cambridge: Harvard University Press, 1965), 3.

35. Ben Jonson, *An Expostulation with Inigo Jones*, in *Complete Poems*, ed. George Parfitt (Harmondsworth, U.K.: Penguin, 1975), 346.

36. Greenaway has voiced a long-held interest in the Ben Jonson–Inigo Jones relationship: "I suppose they [Jonson and Jones] made something like thirty masques in a period of fifteen years, but apparently all the time they were quarrelling," quoted in Marlene Rogers, "Prospero's Books—Word and Spectacle: An Interview with Peter Greenaway," *Film Quarterly* 45, no. 2 (1991–1992): 11–19; 11.

37. "I have written a screenplay called *Jonson and Jones* about their relationship in making masques for the Jacobean court. . . . I always felt that Ben Jonson needed Inigo Jones to enlighten the word, to put the rise in the bread, to flourish," quoted Christel Stalpaert, "An Interview with Peter Greenaway," in *Peter Greenaway's Prospero's Books: Critical Essays*, edited by Christel Stalpaert (Gent: Academia Press, 2000), 40.

38. Quoted in Enid Welsford, *The Court Masque* (Cambridge: Cambridge University Press, 1927), 272.

39. Nicoll, *Masques*, 126. Interestingly, Nicoll's phrasing—cloud palaces and enchanted seas—has itself been inspired by Shakespeare's poetry in *The Tempest*.

40. My discussion here is meant, in part, to modify Peter Donaldson's observation that "in so thoroughly a bookish and literary origin for not only the text but the performance of the play (Prospero reads all the lines of the play as the characters move), Greenaway's Shakespeare media elides the theater." See Peter Donaldson, "'All Which It Inherits': Shakespeare, Globes, and Global Media," *Shakespeare Surveys* 52 (1999): 183–200; 197.

41. Amy Lawrence, *The Films of Peter Greenaway* (Cambridge: Cambridge University Press, 1997), 149.

42. George Landow, ed., *Hyper/Text/Theory* (Baltimore: Johns Hopkins University Press, 1994), 1.

43. Mariacristina Cavecchi, "Peter Greenaway's *Prospero's Books*: A Tempest between Word and Image," *Literature/Film Quarterly* 25, no. 2 (1997): 83–89; 89.

44. Peter Donaldson has in fact made a start on precisely such a project: see "Digital Archives and Sibylline Fragments: *The Tempest* and the End of Books," published in the online journal *Postmodern Culture* 8, no. 2 (1998). http://jefferson.village.virginia.edu/pmc/issue.198/8.2miles.html.

45. John G. Demaray, *Shakespeare and the Spectacles of Strangeness: The Tempest and the Transformations of Renaissance Theatrical Forms* (Pittsburgh: Duquesne University Press, 1998), 84.

46. For a contrary argument, see Nicholas Brooke, ed., *The Tragedy of Macbeth* (Oxford: Oxford University Press, 1990), 22–34.

47. Vernon Gras, "Dramatizing the Failure to Jump the Culture/Nature Gap: The Films of Peter Greenaway," *New Literary History* 26 (1995): 123–43; 123.

48. John Collick, *Shakespeare, Cinema, and Society* (Manchester: Manchester University Press, 1989), 103.

49. Tony Peake, *Derek Jarman: A Biography* (Woodstock, N.Y.: Overlook, 2000), 231, 266.

50. Russell Jackson, "Shakespeare's Comedies on Film," in *Shakespeare and the Moving Image*, ed. Anthony Davies and Stanley Wells (Cambridge: Cambridge University Press, 1994), 99–120; 109.

51. "The film's radicalism largely stems from the fact that *The Tempest* was made at the height of Punk, a movement that seemed to reflect the radical critiques of the underground cinema in its attack on bourgeois conventionality." Collick, *Shakespeare, Cinema, and Society*, 106.

52. Ben Jonson, "An Expostulation with Inigo Jones," in *Complete Poems* ed. George Parfitt (Harmondsworth, U.K.: Penguin, 1975), 346.

53. Dekker, quoted in Nicoll, *Masques*, 23.

54. Greenaway, *Books*, 92.

55. Douglas Lanier, "Drowning the Book: *Prospero's Books* and the Textual Shakespeare," in *Shakespeare, Theory, and Performance*, ed. James Bulman (London: Routledge, 1996), 187–209, 202; see also Maurice Yacowar, "Negotiating Culture: Greenaway's *Tempest*," *Queen's Quarterly* 99, no. 3 (1992): 689–97. "For all his dedication to the literary tradition, Greenaway treats books with irreverence," 696.

56. Jonson, "Expostulation," 346.

57. Orgel, *The Tempest*, 53.

58. The concept is thoroughly examined in Richard Burt, *Unspeakable ShaXXXspeares: Queer Theory and American Kiddie Culture* (New York: St. Martin's, 1998).

59. See Douglas Lanier, *Shakespeare and Modern Popular Culture* (Oxford: Oxford University Press, 2002); and the collection edited by Richard Burt, *Shakespeare after Mass Media* (New York: Palgrave, 2002).

60. Susan Snyder, "The Genres of Shakespeare's Plays," in *The Cambridge Companion to Shakespeare*, ed. Margreta de Grazia and Stanley Wells (Cambridge: Cambridge University Press, 2001), 83–97; 95.

Bibliography

Affron, Charles, and Mirella Jona Affron. *Sets in Motion: Art Direction and Narrative Film*. New Brunswick, N.J.: Rutgers University Press, 1995.

Almereyda, Michael. *William Shakespeare's Hamlet*. Introduction by Ethan Hawke. London: Faber & Faber, 2000.

Anderegg, Michael. *Orson Welles, Shakespeare, and Popular Culture*. New York: Columbia University Press, 1999.

Andrew, Dudley. *Film in the Aura of Art*. Princeton: Princeton University Press, 1984.

Ball, Robert Hamilton. *Shakespeare on Silent Film*. London: George Allen & Unwin, 1968.

Banham, Martin. "BBC Television's Dull Shakespeares." *Critical Quarterly* 22, no. 1 (1980): 31–40.

Barnouw, Erik. *The Magician and the Cinema*. New York: Oxford University Press, 1981.

Bate, Jonathan, ed. *Titus Andronicus*. London: Routledge, 1995.

Bazin, André. *What Is Cinema?* Vol. 1., edited and translated by Hugh Gray. Berkeley: University of California Press, 1967.

Belsey, Catherine. "Shakespeare and Film: A Question of Perspective." *Literature/Film Quarterly* 11, no. 3 (1983): 152–58.

Boose, Lynda E., and Richard Burt, eds. *Shakespeare, The Movie: Popularizing the Plays on Film, TV, and Video*. London: Routledge, 1997.

Branagh, Kenneth. *Beginning*. New York: St. Martin's, 1989.

———. *Hamlet: Screenplay, Introduction, and Film Diary*. New York: Norton, 1996.

———. *Henry V: The Screenplay*. New York: Norton, 1997.

———. *Much Ado about Nothing: The Making of the Movie*. New York: Norton, 1993.

Braudy, Leo. *The World in a Frame: What We See in Films*. Garden City, N.Y.: Anchor, 1977.

Brecht, Bertolt. *The Messingkauf Dialogues*. Translated by John Willett. London: Methuen, 1965.

Breight, Curtis. "Branagh and the Prince, or a 'Royal Fellowship of Death.'" *Critical Quarterly* 33, no. 4 (1991): 95–111.

Brode, Douglas. *Shakespeare in the Movies*. New York: Oxford University Press, 2000.

Brooke, Nicholas, ed. *The Tragedy of Macbeth*. Oxford: Oxford University Press, 1990.

Brown, Constance A. "Olivier's *Richard III*: A Reevaluation." *Film Quarterly*, Summer 1967, 23–32.

Browne, Nick, ed. *Refiguring American Film Genres*. Berkeley: University of California Press, 1998.

Buchanan, Judith. "Virgin and Ape, Venetian and Infidel: Labellings of Otherness in Oliver Parker's *Othello*." In *Shakespeare, Film, Fin de Siècle*, edited by Mark Thornton Burnett and Ramona Wray, 179–202. New York: St. Martin's, 2000.

Buchman, Lorne M. *Still in Movement: Shakespeare on Screen*. New York: Oxford University Press, 1991.

Buhler, Stephen. *Shakespeare in the Cinema: Ocular Proof*. Albany: State University of New York Press, 2002.

Bulman, James C. "The BBC Shakespeare and the 'House Style.'" *Shakespeare Quarterly* 35 (1984): 571–81.

Bulman, James C., and H. R. Coursen, eds. *Shakespeare on Television*. Hanover, N.H.: University Press of New England, 1988.

Burnett, Mark Thornton, "'To Hear and See the Matter': Communicating Technology in Michael Almereyda's *Hamlet* (2000)." *Cinema Journal*, Spring 2003, 48–69.

Burnett, Mark Thornton, and Ramona Wray, eds. *Shakespeare, Film, Fin de Siècle*. New York: St. Martin's, 2000.

Burt, Richard. "Shakespeare and the Holocaust: Julie Taymor's *Titus* Is Beautiful, or Shakesploi Meets (the) Camp." In *Shakespeare after Mass Media*, edited by Richard Burt, 295–329. New York: Palgrave, 2002.

———. "*Shakespeare in Love* and the End of the Shakespearean: Academic and Mass Culture Constructions of Literary Authorship." In *Shakespeare, Film, Fin de Siècle*, edited by Mark Thornton Burnett and Ramona Wray, 203–31. New York: St. Martin's, 2000.

———. "To E- or Not to E-: Disposing of Schlockspeare in the Age of Digital Media." In *Shakespeare after Mass Media*, edited by Richard Burt, 1–32 . New York: Palgrave, 2002.

Burt, Richard, ed. *Shakespeare after Mass Media*. New York: Palgrave, 2002.

———. *Unspeakable ShaXXXspeares: Queer Theory and American Kiddie Culture*. New York: St. Martin's, 1998.

Cartmell, Deborah. *Interpreting Shakespeare on Screen*. New York: St. Martin's, 2000.

Cavecchi, Mariacristina. "Peter Greenaway's *Prospero's Books*: A Tempest between Word and Image." *Literature/Film Quarterly* 25, no. 2 (1997): 83–89.

Charney, Maurice, and Gordon Hichens. "On Mankiewicz's *Julius Caesar*." *Literary Review* 22 (1979): 433–59.

Colley, Scott. *Richard's Himself Again: A Stage History of Richard III*. New York: Greenwood, 1992.

Collick, John. *Shakespeare, Cinema, and Society*. Manchester: Manchester University Press, 1989.

Collier, Susanne. "Post-Falklands, Post-Colonial: Contextualizing Branagh as Henry V on Stage and on Film." *Essays in Theatre* 10, no. 2 (1992): 143–54.

Coursen, H. R. "Branagh's Two Hour *Hamlet*: A Review Essay." *Shakespeare Bulletin*, Summer 2000, 39–40.

Cox, John, ed. *Shakespeare in Production: Much Ado about Nothing.* Cambridge: Cambridge University Press, 1997.

Crowl, Samuel. "Changing Colors Like the Chameleon: Ian McKellen's *Richard III* from Stage to Screen." *Post Script*, Fall 1997, 53–63.

———. "The Marriage of Shakespeare and Hollywood: Kenneth Branagh's *Much Ado about Nothing.*" In *Spectacular Shakespeare: Critical Theory and Popular Cinema*, edited by Courtney Lehmann and Lisa S. Starks, 110–24. Madison, N.J.: Fairleigh Dickinson University Press, 2002.

———. "*A Midsummer Night's Dream.*" *Shakespeare Bulletin*, Summer 1999, 41–42.

———. "'Our Lofty Scene': Teaching Modern Film Versions of *Julius Caesar.*" In *Teaching Shakespeare into the Twenty-first Century*, edited by Ronald E. Salomone and James E. Davis, 222–31. Athens: Ohio University Press, 1997.

———. "A World Elsewhere: The Roman Plays on Film and Television." In *Shakespeare and the Moving Image: The Plays on Film and Television*, edited by Anthony Davies and Stanley Wells, 146–62. Cambridge: Cambridge University Press, 1994.

Cubitt, Sean. *Timeshift: On Video Culture.* London: Routledge, 1991.

Davies, Anthony. "The Film Versions of *Romeo and Juliet.*" *Shakespeare Survey* 49 (1996): 153–62.

———. *Filming Shakespeare's Plays.* Cambridge: Cambridge University Press, 1988.

Davies, Anthony, and Stanley Wells, eds. *Shakespeare and the Moving Image.* Cambridge: Cambridge University Press, 1994.

Dawson, Anthony. *Shakespeare in Performance: Hamlet.* Manchester: Manchester University Press, 1995.

Dawtrey, Adam, and Monica Roman. "'Love' Triangle Times 3." *Variety*, March 23, 1999. *Shakespeare in Love* clipping file, Margaret Herrick Library.

Deats, Sara Munson. "Rabbits and Ducks: Olivier, Branagh, and *Henry V.*" *Literature/Film Quarterly* 20 (1992): 284–93.

De Grazia, Margreta, and Stanley Wells, eds. *The Cambridge Companion to Shakespeare.* Cambridge: Cambridge University Press, 2001.

Demaray, John G. *Shakespeare and the Spectacles of Strangeness: The Tempest and the Transformations of Renaissance Theatrical Forms.* Pittsburgh: Duquesne University Press, 1998.

Dent, Alan. "Text-editing Shakespeare." In *Hamlet: The Film and the Play*, edited by Alan Dent. London: World Film Publications, 1948.

Dessen, Alan. *Shakespeare in Performance: Titus Andronicus.* Manchester: Manchester University Press, 1989.

Donaldson, Peter. "Digital Archives and Sibylline Fragments: *The Tempest* and the End of Books." *Postmodern Culture* 8, no. 2 (1998). http://jefferson.village.virginia.edu/pmc/issue.198/8.2miles.html.

————. *Shakespearean Films/Shakespearean Directors*. Boston: Unwin Hyman, 1990.

————. "Shakespeare in the Age of Post-Mechanical Reproduction: Sexual and Electronic Magic in *Prospero's Books*." In *Shakespeare, The Movie: Popularizing the Plays on Film, TV, and Video*, edited by Lynda E. Boose and Richard Burt, 169–85. London: Routledge, 1997.

————. "Taking on Shakespeare: Kenneth Branagh's *Henry V*." *Shakespeare Quarterly* 42, no. 1 (1991): 60–71.

Durgnat, Raymond. *A Mirror for England: British Movies from Austerity to Affluence*. New York: Praeger, 1971.

Dymkowski, Christine, ed. *Shakespeare in Production: The Tempest*. Cambridge: Cambridge University Press, 2000.

Eckert, Charles, ed. *Focus on Shakespearean Films*. Englewood Cliffs, N.J.: Prentice-Hall, 1972.

Evans, G. Blakemore, ed. *Romeo and Juliet*. Cambridge: Cambridge University Press, 1984.

Fitter, Chris. "A Tale of Two Branaghs: Henry V, Ideology, and the Mekong Agincourt." In *Shakespeare Left and Right*, edited by Ivo Kamps, 259–75. New York: Routledge, 1991.

Gardner, Helen. "The Noble Moor." *Proceedings of the British Academy* 41 (1955): 189–205.

Geduld, Harry M. *Filmguide to Henry V*. Bloomington: Indiana University Press, 1973.

Gras, Vernon. "Dramatizing the Failure to Jump the Culture/Nature Gap: The Films of Peter Greenaway." *New Literary History* 26 (1995): 123–43.

Greenaway, Peter. *Prospero's Books: A Film of Shakespeare's The Tempest*. New York: Four Walls Eight Windows, 1991.

Halpern, Richard. *Shakespeare among the Moderns*. Ithaca, N.Y.: Cornell University Press, 1997.

Hankey, Julie, ed. *Plays in Performance: Richard III*. London: Junction, 1981.

Hapgood, Robert. "Popularizing Shakespeare: The Artistry of Franco Zeffirelli." In *Shakespeare, The Movie: Popularizing the Plays on Film, TV, and Video*, edited by Lynda E. Boose and Richard Burt, 80–94. London: Routledge, 1997.

————. ed. *Shakespeare in Production: Hamlet*. Cambridge: Cambridge University Press, 1999.

Harris, Dana. "Much Ado about Nothing?" *Hollywood Reporter*, February 11, 1999. *Shakespeare in Love* clipping file, Margaret Herrick Library.

Hatchuel, Sarah. *A Companion to the Shakespearean Films of Kenneth Branagh*. Winnipeg: Blizzard, 2000.

Hawkins, Joan. "Sleaze Mania, Euro-Trash, and High Art: The Place of European Art Films in American Low Culture." *Film Quarterly* 53, no. 2 (1999–2000): 14–29.

Hedrick, Donald. "War Is Mud: Branagh's Dirty Harry V and the Types of Political Ambiguity." In *Shakespeare, the Movie: Popularizing the Plays on Film, TV, and Video*, edited by Lynda E. Boose and Richard Burt, 45–66. London: Routledge, 1997.

Hoffman, Michael. *William Shakespeare's A Midsummer Night's Dream*. New York: HarperCollins, 1999.

Hodgdon, Barbara. "*William Shakespeare's Romeo + Juliet*: Everything's Nice in America?" *Shakespeare Survey* 52 (1999): 88–98.

Holderness, Graham. "Radical Potentiality and Institutional Closure: Shakespeare in Film and Television." In *Political Shakespeare*, edited by Jonathan Dollimore and Alan Sinfield, 182–201. Ithaca, N.Y.: Cornell University Press, 1985.

———. "'What Ish My Nation?': Shakespeare and National Identities." *Textual Practice* 5, no. 1 (1991): 74–93.

Holmer, Joan Ozark. "The Poetics of Paradox: Shakespeare's versus Zeffirelli's Cultures of Violence." *Shakespeare Survey* 49 (1996): 163–79.

Hopkins, Lisa. "'How Very Like the Home Life of Our Own Dear Queen': Ian McKellen's *Richard III*." In *Spectacular Shakespeare: Critical Theory and Popular Cinema*, edited by Courtney Lehmann and Lisa S. Starks, 47–61. Madison, N.J.: Fairleigh Dickinson University Press, 2002.

Horowitz, Robert. "History Comes to Life and *You Are There*." In *American History/American Television*, edited by John E. O'Connor, 79–94. New York: Ungar, 1983.

Hotchkiss, Lisa. "The Incorporation of Word as Image in *Prospero's Books*." *Post Script* 17, no. 2 (1998): 8–25.

Houseman, John. *Entertainers and the Entertained*. New York: Simon & Schuster, 1986.

———. "This Our Lofty Scene." *Theatre Arts*, May 1953, 26–28.

Howlett, Kathy M. *Framing Shakespeare on Film*. Athens: Ohio University Press, 2000.

Hutton, Clayton. *Macbeth: The Making of the Film*. London: Max Parrish, 1960.

Iyengar, Sujata. "Shakespeare in Heterolove." *Literature/Film Quarterly* 29, no. 2 (2001): 122–27.

Jackson, Russell. "From Playscript to Screenplay." In *The Cambridge Companion to Shakespeare on Film*, ed. Russell Jackson, 15–34. Cambridge: Cambridge University Press, 2000.

———. "Kenneth Branagh's Film of *Hamlet*: The Textual Choices." *Shakespeare Bulletin*, Spring 1997, 37–38.

———. "Shakespeare and the Cinema." In *The Cambridge Companion to Shakespeare*, ed. Margreta de Grazia and Stanley Wells, 217–33. Cambridge: Cambridge University Press, 2001.

———. "Shakespeare's Comedies on Film." In *Shakespeare and the Moving Image*, edited by Anthony Davies and Stanley Wells, 99–120. Cambridge: Cambridge University Press, 1994.

———. ed. *The Cambridge Companion to Shakespeare on Film*. Cambridge: Cambridge University Press, 2000.

Jameson, Fredric. "Postmodernism, or the Cultural Logic of Late Capitalism." *New Left Review* 146 (July-August 1984): 53–92.

Jonson, Ben. *Complete Poems*. Edited by George Parfitt. Harmondsworth, U.K.: Penguin, 1975.

Jorgens, Jack J. *Shakespeare on Film*. Bloomington: Indiana University Press, 1977.

Jorgenson, Paul. "Castellani's *Romeo and Juliet*: Intention and Response." *Quarterly Review of Film, Radio, and Television*, Fall 1955, 1–10.

Kennedy, Dennis. *Looking at Shakespeare: A Visual History of Twentieth-Century Perform-ance*. Cambridge: Cambridge University Press, 1993.

Kennedy, Douglas. "Shakespeare and Cultural Tourism." *Theatre Journal* 50 (1998): 175–88.

Kliman, Bernice W. *Hamlet: Film, Television, and Audio Performance*. London: Associated University Presses, 1988.

———. "The Setting in Early Television: Maurice Evans' Shakespeare Productions." In *Shakespeare and the Arts*, edited by Cecile Williamson Cary and Henry S. Limouze, 135–53. Washington, D.C.: University Press of America, 1982.

———. *Shakespeare in Performance: Macbeth*. Manchester: Manchester University Press, 1992.

Kuney, Jack. "The Art of TV Directing: The Hallmark Hall of Fame and Other Drama." *Television Quarterly* 23 (1988): 21–32.

Landow, George, ed. *Hyper/Text/Theory*. Baltimore: Johns Hopkins University Press, 1994.

Lane, Robert. "'When Blood Is Their Argument': Class, Character, and Historymaking in Shakespeare's and Branagh's *Henry V*." *ELH* 61 (1994): 27–52.

Lanier, Douglas. "'Art Thou Base, Common, and Popular?': The Cultural Politics of Ken-neth Branagh's *Hamlet*." In *Spectacular Shakespeare: Critical Theory and Popular Cinema*, edited by Courtney Lehmann and Lisa S. Starks, 149–71. Madison, N.J.: Fairleigh Dickinson University Press, 2002.

———. "Drowning the Book: *Prospero's Books* and the Textual Shakespeare." In *Shake-speare, Theory, and Performance*, edited by James Bulman, 187–209. London: Routledge, 1996.

———. *Shakespeare and Modern Popular Culture*. Oxford: Oxford University Press, 2002.

Lawrence, Amy. *The Films of Peter Greenaway*. Cambridge: Cambridge University Press, 1997.

Leavis, F. R. "Diabolic Intellect and the Noble Hero: A Note on *Othello*." *Scrutiny* 6 (1937): 259–83.

Leff, Leonard J. "Instant Movies: The Short Unhappy Life of William Sargent's Electron-ovision." *Journal of Popular Film and Television* 8, no. 1 (1980): 19–29.

Lehmann, Courtney. "*Shakespeare in Love*: Romancing the Author, Mastering the Body." In *Spectacular Shakespeare: Critical Theory and Popular Cinema*, edited by Courtney Leh-mann and Lisa S. Starks, 125–45. Madison, N.J.: Fairleigh Dickinson University Press, 2002.

———. *Shakespeare Remains: Theater to Film, Early Modern to Postmodern*. Ithaca, N.Y.: Cornell University Press, 2002.

———. "Strictly Shakespeare? Dead Letters, Ghostly Fathers, and the Cultural Pathol-ogy of Authorship in Baz Luhrmann's *William Shakespeare's Romeo + Juliet*." *Shake-speare Quarterly* 52 (2001): 189–221.

Lehmann, Courtney, and Lisa S. Starks. "Making Mother Matter: Repression, Revision, and the Stakes of 'Reading Psychoanalysis Into' Kenneth Branagh's *Hamlet*." *Early Modern Literary Studies* 6, no. 1 (2000): 1–24.

Lehmann, Courtney, and Lisa S. Starks, eds. *Spectacular Shakespeare: Critical Theory and Popular Cinema*. Madison, N.J.: Fairleigh Dickinson University Press, 2002.

Lenihan, John H. "English Classics for Cold War America." *Journal of Popular Film and Television*, Fall 1992, 42–51.

Levenson, Jill. *Shakespeare in Performance: Romeo and Juliet*. Manchester: Manchester University Press, 1987.

———. "Stoppard's Shakespeare: Textual Revisions." In *The Cambridge Companion to Tom Stoppard*, edited by Katherine E. Kelly, 154–70. Cambridge: Cambridge University Press, 2001.

Levin, Harry. "Form and Formality in *Romeo and Juliet*." *Shakespeare Quarterly*, Winter 1960, 3–11.

Levine, Lawrence W. *Highbrow/Lowbrow: The Emergence of Cultural Hierarchy in America*. Cambridge: Harvard University Press, 1988.

Loehlin, James N. *Shakespeare in Performance: Henry V*. Manchester: Manchester University Press, 1996.

———. *Shakespeare in Production: Romeo and Juliet*. Cambridge: Cambridge University Press, 2002.

———. "'These Violent Delights Have Violent Ends': Baz Luhrmann's Millennial Shakespeare." In *Shakespeare, Film, Fin de Siècle*, edited by Mark Thornton Burnett and Ramona Wray, 121–36. New York: St. Martin's, 2000.

Loney, Glenn, ed. *Staging Shakespeare: Seminars in Production Problems*. New York: Garland, 1990.

Luhrmann, Baz. *William Shakespeare's Romeo + Juliet*. Fox Laser Disc, 1997.

Lull, Janis, ed. *Richard III*. Cambridge: Cambridge University Press, 1999.

Lyons, Bridget Gellert, ed. *Films in Print: Chimes at Midnight*. New Brunswick, N.J.: Rutgers University Press, 1988.

Madden, John. *Shakespeare in Love*. DVD, Miramax, 2000.

Manvell, Roger. *Shakespeare and the Film*. New York: Praeger, 1971.

Marowitz, Charles. *Recycling Shakespeare*. New York: Applause Theatre Book Publishers, 1991.

McBride, Joseph. *Orson Welles*. New York: Viking, 1972.

McCandless, David. "A Tale of Two *Tituses*: Julie Taymor's Vision on Stage and Screen." *Shakespeare Quarterly* 53 (2002): 487–511.

McClintic, Guthrie. *Me and Kit*. Boston: Little, Brown, 1955.

McKellen, Ian, and Richard Loncraine. *William Shakespeare's Richard III: A Screenplay*. Woodstock, N.Y.: Overlook, 1996.

Metz, Christian. *The Imaginary Signifier: Psychoanalysis and the Cinema*. Translated by Celia Britton, Annwyl Williams, Ben Brewster, and Alfred Guzzetti. Bloomington: Indiana University Press, 1982.

Miller, Anthony. "*Julius Caesar* in the Cold War: The Houseman-Mankiewicz Film." *Literature/Film Quarterly* 28, no. 2 (2000): 95–100.

Miller, Mark Crispin. "The Shakespeare Plays." *The Nation*, July 12, 1980.

Morrison, Michael A. *John Barrymore: Shakespearean Actor.* Cambridge: Cambridge University Press, 1997.

Mullin, Michael. "Orson Welles's *Macbeth*: Script and Screen." In *Focus on Orson Welles,* edited by Ronald Gottesman, 136–45. Englewood Cliffs, N.J.: Prentice-Hall, 1976.

Naremore, James. *The Magic World of Orson Welles.* Rev. ed. Dallas: Southern Methodist University Press, 1989.

———. *More Than Night: Film Noir in Its Contexts.* Berkeley: University of California Press, 1998.

Nathanson, Sam. Letter to Richard Wilson, March 7, 1950. Richard Wilson Papers, UCLA Special Collections.

Neale, Steve. *Genre and Hollywood.* London: Routledge, 2000.

Nicoll, Allardyce. *Stuart Masques and the Renaissance Stage.* London: G. Harrap, 1938.

Olivier, Laurence. *On Acting.* London: Weidenfeld & Nicolson, 1986.

Orgel, Stephen. *The Jonsonian Masque.* Cambridge: Harvard University Press, 1965.

———. ed. *The Tempest.* Oxford: Oxford University Press, 1987.

Pascoe, David. *Peter Greenaway: Museums and Moving Images.* London: Reaktion, 1997.

Peake, Tony. *Derek Jarman: A Biography.* Woodstock, N.Y.: Overlook, 2000.

Pearce, Craig, and Baz Luhrmann. *William Shakespeare's Romeo & Juliet: The Contemporary Film, The Classic Play.* New York: Bantam Doubleday Dell, 1996.

Pennington, Michael. *Hamlet: A User's Guide.* New York: Limelight, 1996.

Pilkington, Ace. "Zeffirelli's Shakespeare." In *Shakespeare and the Moving Image,* edited by Anthony Davies and Stanley Wells, 163–79. Cambridge: Cambridge University Press, 1994.

Potter, Lois. *Shakespeare in Performance: Othello.* Manchester: Manchester University Press, 2002.

Rabkin, Norman. "Rabbits, Ducks, and Henry V." *Shakespeare Quarterly,* Summer 1977, 279–96.

Richmond, Hugh M. *Shakespeare in Performance: Richard III.* Manchester: Manchester University Press, 1989.

Ripley, John. *Julius Caesar on Stage in England and America.* Cambridge: Cambridge University Press, 1980.

Rodman, Howard. "Anatomy of a Wizard." *American Film* 16 (1991): 34–39.

Rogers, Marlene. "Prospero's Books—Word and Spectacle: An Interview with Peter Greenaway." *Film Quarterly* 45, no. 2 (1991–1992): 11–19.

Romeo and Juliet by William Shakespeare: A Motion Picture Edition. London: Arthur Barker, 1936.

Rosenthal, Daniel. *Shakespeare on Screen.* London: Hamlyn, 2000.

Rothwell, Kenneth S. *A History of Shakespeare on Screen.* Oxford: Oxford University Press, 1999.

Rothwell, Kenneth S., and Annabelle Henkin Melzer. *Shakespeare on Screen: An International Filmography and Videography.* New York: Neal-Schuman, 1990.

Rutter, Carol Chillington. "Looking at Shakespeare's Women on Film." In *The Cambridge*

Companion to Shakespeare on Film, edited by Russell Jackson, 241–60. Cambridge: Cambridge University Press, 2000.

Salinger, J. D. *Catcher in the Rye*. Boston: Little, Brown, 1991.

Shakespeare in Love Pressbook, Margaret Herrick Library. N. p., n. d.

Sinfield, Alan. "*Macbeth*: History, Ideology, and Intellectuals." *Critical Quarterly* 28, no. 1–2 (1986): 63–77.

Snyder, Susan. "The Genres of Shakespeare's Plays." In *The Cambridge Companion to Shakespeare*, ed. Margreta de Grazia and Stanley Wells, 83–97. Cambridge: Cambridge University Press, 2001.

Sobchack, Vivian. "Lounge Time: Postwar Crises and the Chronotope of Film Noir." In *Refiguring American Film Genres*, edited by Nick Browne, 129–70. Berkeley: University of California Press, 1998.

Steinmetz, Leon, and Peter Greenaway. *The World of Peter Greenaway*. Boston: Journey, 1995.

Tatspaugh, Patricia. "The Tragedies of Love on Film." In *The Cambridge Companion to Shakespeare on Film*, edited by Russell Jackson, 135–59. Cambridge: Cambridge University Press, 2000.

Taymor, Julie. *Titus*. 20th Century Fox DVD, 2000.

Tweedle, James. "Caliban's Books: The Hybrid Text in Peter Greenaway's *Prospero's Books*." *Cinema Journal*, Fall 2000, 104–26.

Tynan, Kenneth. *Tynan Right and Left*. New York: Atheneum, 1967.

Uricchio, William, and Roberta E. Pearson. *Reframing Culture: The Case of the Vitagraph Quality Films*. Princeton: Princeton University Press, 1993.

Vahimagi, Tise. " 'When You Care Enough to Send the Best': Televised Shakespeare and the Hallmark Hall of Fame." In *Walking Shadows: Shakespeare in the National Film and Television Archives*, edited by Luke McKernan and Olwen Terris, 207–18. London: British Film Institute, 1994.

Walker, Roy. "In Fair Verona." *Twentieth Century*, November 1954, 464–71.

———. "Look upon Caesar." *Twentieth Century*, December 1953, 469–74.

Welles, Orson. Interview. *New York Post*, November 24, 1937. Mercury *Julius Caesar* clipping file, New York Public Library for the Performing Arts, Lincoln Center.

Wells, Stanley. "The Challenges of *Romeo and Juliet*." *Shakespeare Survey* 49 (1996): 1–14.

———. "Shakespeare Performances in London and Stratford-upon-Avon 1986–87." *Shakespeare Survey* 41 (1989): 159–81.

Welsh, James M., et al. *Shakespeare into Film*. Preface by Kenneth Rothwell. New York: Checkmark, 2002.

Willis, Susan. *The BBC Shakespeare Plays: Making the Televised Canon*. Chapel Hill: University of North Carolina Press, 1991.

Willson, Robert F., Jr. *Shakespeare in Hollywood: 1929–1956*. Madison, N.J.: Fairleigh Dickinson University Press, 2000.

Wilson, Edwin, ed. *Shaw on Shakespeare*. New York: Dutton, 1961.

Wilson, Richard. Letter to Orson Welles, May 7, 1949. Richard Wilson Papers, UCLA Special Collections.

Wood, Alan. *Being Naked—Playing Dead: The Art of Peter Greenaway*. Manchester: Manchester University Press, 1996.

Woudhuysen, H. R. *Love's Labour's Lost*. The Arden Shakespeare, 3d ser. Walton-on-Thames, U.K.: Thomas Nelson, 1998.

Yacowar, Maurice. "Negotiating Culture: Greenaway's *Tempest*." *Queen's Quarterly* 99, no. 3 (1992): 689–97.

Zeffirelli, Franco. *Zeffirelli: The Autobiography of Franco Zeffirelli*. New York: Weidenfeld & Nicolson, 1986.

Index

Numbers followed by *b* or *p* refer to boxed text and photographs respectively

About the Author

Michael Anderegg is professor of English and film studies at the University of North Dakota. He is the editor of *Inventing Vietnam* (1991) and author of *William Wyler* (1979), *David Lean* (1982), and, most recently, *Orson Welles, Shakespeare, and Popular Culture* (1999).